INFLECTED LANGUAGE:
TOWARD A HERMENEUTICS OF NEARNESS

D0732630

SUNY Series in
Contemporary Continental Philosophy

Dennis J. Schmidt, Editor

INFLECTED LANGUAGE: TOWARD A HERMENEUTICS OF NEARNESS

Heidegger, Levinas, Stevens, Celan

Krzysztof Ziarek

STATE UNIVERSITY OF NEW YORK PRESS

Production by Ruth Fisher
Marketing by Bernadette LaManna

Published by
State University of New York Press, Albany

For information, address State University of New York Press,
State University Plaza, Albany, NY 12246

Library of Congress Cataloging-in-Publication Data

Ziarek, Krzysztof, 1961–
    Inflected language : toward a hermeneutics of nearness:
Heidegger, Levinas, Stevens, Celan / Krzysztof Ziarek.
        p.   cm. — (SUNY series in contemporary continental
philosophy)
    Includes bibliographical references and index.
    ISBN 0–7914–2059–0 (alk. paper). — ISBN 0–7914–2060–4 (pbk. :
alk. paper)
    1. Hermeneutics.   2. Language and languages—Philosophy.
3. Literature—Philosophy.   4. Heidegger, Martin, 1889–1976.
I. Title. II. Series.
BD241.Z53   1994
121'.68—dc20   93–23644
                                                          CIP

10 9 8 7 6 5 4 3 2 1

To my mother,
Maria Ziarek (1933–1992)

∽ CONTENTS ∾

Acknowledgments   ix

Abbreviations   xiii

Introduction: Inflecting Difference   1

1. Rethinking the Parameters of the Heideggerian
   Hermeneutics: Heidegger on Poetry and Thinking   21

   Dichten-Denken: Beyond a Philosophy of Poetry   23
   Heidegger's Language: From Difference to the Infold   33

2. Refiguring Otherness: A Heideggerian Bypass of Ethics?   43

   Aside from Metaphysics: Heidegger on Nearness   46
   Beyond Ontology and Ethics: The Two Sides of
   Gelassenheit   55

3. Semantics of Proximity: Levinas on Non-Indifference   65

   The Abrahamic Departure from Totality   66
   The Non-Indifferent Face   78
   Semantics of Proximity   84
   The Trace   93

4. The Other Notation:
   Stevens and the Supreme Fiction of Poetry   103

   Poet on the Dump: Stevens's Reckoning with the
   Romantic Legacy   105
   Notes toward Otherness: A Supreme Fiction?   113
   Perhaps Other: Stevensian Notes on Difference   125

5. Chiasmus of Otherness:
   Reading Celan and His Interpreters   133

   The Unwritten Text and the Name of the Other   137
   "Two Kinds of Strangeness": Celan on the
   Possibility of Signifying the Ethical in Poetry   150

6. Celan's Poetic Meridians   161

Coda: Semiosis of Listening or an Other Meeting between
   Heidegger and Celan   181

Notes   207

Index   235

❧ ACKNOWLEDGMENTS ❧

It is a pleasure to acknowledge here many friends and colleagues who read and commented on this work or its sections. I am especially indebted to Rodolphe Gasché, Jill Robbins, Henry Sussman, and Robert Creeley, who guided this project in its earliest stages. My work has benefitted greatly from their advice and comments. I would like to thank Gerald Bruns, Joseph Buttigieg, Fred Dallmayr, Stephen Fredman, Chris Fynsk, Carol Jacobs, Jacquelyn Vaught Brogan, Stephen Watson, and Ziba Rashidian for their perceptive reading, advice, and encouragement. I also want to thank John Llewelyn for his insightful comments about Levinas's relationship to Celan's works. I am grateful to Robert Bernasconi and Véronique Fóti, who advised me on the completed manuscript.

I am especially grateful to Ewa Ziarek for her encouragement, understanding, advice, and, above all, for her most exacting criticism of my work. Her comments and suggestions have made this a better book.

Sections of this work appeared in various forms in other publications. An earlier version of chapter III appeared in *Research in Phenomenology*, volume 19 (1989). I thank the editors of Humanities Press International, Inc., for permission to reprint. A much condensed version of chapter IV, "Poetics of Disclosure in Stevens' Late Poetry," was published in *Arizona Quarterly* 46, no. 1 (1990). The editor's permission to reprint is gratefully acknowledged. The original version of the Coda, "Semiosis of Listening," appeared in *Research of Phenomenology*, 24 (1994), published by Humanities Press International, Inc. I am grateful to the editor of *Research in Phenomenology* for permission to reprint.

I would also like to thank my colleagues at the University of Notre Dame for the criticism and suggestions which they offered during the sessions of the Humanities Colloquium and the English Department Colloquium, where I had the opportunity to present abridged versions of chapters III and VII. Finally, I want to express my gratitude to the Graduate School at the University of Notre Dame for its generous help in defraying the cost of obtaining permissions to reprint poetry in my book.

Greatful acknowledgment is made to the publishers who have generously given permission to use quotations from the following works:

From *Mohn und Gedächtnis* by Paul Celan, copyright 1952 by Deutsche Verlags-Anstalt GmbH, Stuttgart, by permission of the publisher.

From *Vom Schwelle zu Schwelle* by Paul Celan, copyright 1955 by Deutsche Verlags-Anstalt GmbH, Stuttgart, by permission of the publisher.

Paul Celan, "Mit Brief und Uhr," "Niedrigwasser," "Sprachgitter," "Schliere," and "Engführung," taken from *Sprachgitter*, © S. Fischer Verlag, Frankfurt am Main 1959, reprinted by permission of the publisher.

Paul Celan, "Kolon," "An Niemand Geschmiegt," "Es war Erde in Ihnen" and "Tübingen, Jänner," taken from *Die Niemandsrose*, © S. Fischer Verlag, Frankfurt am Main 1963, reprinted by permission of the publisher.

From *Atemwende* by Paul Celan, © Suhrkamp Verlag Frankfurt am Main 1967, by permission of the publisher, Suhrkamp Verlag.

From *Fadensonnen* by Paul Celan, © Suhrkamp Verlag Frankfurt am Main 1968, by permission of the publisher, Suhrkamp Verlag.

From *Lichtzwang* by Paul Celan, © Suhrkamp Verlag Frankfurt am main 1970, by permission of the publisher, Suhrkamp Verlag.

From *Schneepart* by Paul Celan, © Suhrkamp Verlag Frankfurt am Main 1971, by permission of the publisher, Suhrkamp Verlag.

"Komm" by Paul Celan, taken from *Zeitgehöft* by Paul Celan, © Suhrkamp Verlag Frankfurt am Main 1976, by permission of the publisher, Suhrkamp Verlag.

From prose pieces included in *Gesammelte Werke*, Bd. III, by Paul Celan, © Suhrkamp Verlag Frankfurt am Main 1983, reprinted by permission of the publisher, Suhrkamp Verlag.

From *"Speech-Grille" and Other Poems* by Paul Celan, trans. Joachim Neugroschel, copyright © 1971 by Joachim Neugroschel, by permission of the translator.

Poems of Paul Celan by Paul Celan, translated by Michael Hamburger. Introduction and translation copyright © 1972, 1980, 1988 by Michael Hamburger. Reprinted by permission of Persea Books and by permission of Anvil Press Poetry.

From *Last Poems* by Paul Celan (San Francisco: North Point Press, 1986), translated by Katharine Washburn and Margret Guillemin, copyright © 1986 by Katharine Washburn and Margret Guillemin, by permission of the translators.

Excerpts from Rosmarie Waldrop's translation of Paul Celan's *Collected Prose* © 1986 The Sheep Meadow Press, Riverdale-on-Hudson, New York. Reprinted by permission.

From *Collected Poems* by Wallace Stevens, copyright 1954 by Wallace Stevens, reprinted by permission of Alfred A. Knopf, Inc. (for United States, Canada and elsewhere except the British Commonwealth) and by permission of Faber & Faber (for the British Commonwealth excluding Canada).

✍ ABBREVIATIONS ❧

AEAE Emmanuel Levinas, *Autrement qu'être ou au-delà de l'essence* (The Hague: Martinus Nijhoff, 1974).

BW Martin Heidegger, *Basic Writings*, intro. and ed. David Farrell Krell (New York: Harper and Row, 1977).

BT Martin Heidegger, *Being and Time*, trans. John Macquarrie and Edward Robinson (New York: Harper and Row, 1962).

CP Wallace Stevens, *The Collected Poems of Wallace Stevens* (New York: Alfred A. Knopf, 1954).

CPP Emmanuel Levinas, *Collected Philosophical Papers*, trans. Alphonso Lingis (The Hague: Martinus Nijhoff, 1987).

DC *Deconstruction in Context*, ed. Mark C. Taylor (Chicago: University of Chicago Press, 1986).

DEHH Emmanuel Levinas, *En découvrant l'existence avec Husserl et Heidegger* (Paris: Vrin, 1967).

DVI Emmanuel Levinas, *Dieu qui vient a l'idée* (Paris: Vrin, 1982).

ÉD Jacques Derrida, *L'écriture et la différence* (Paris: Éditions du Seuil, 1967).

EGT Martin Heidegger, *Early Greek Thinking*, trans. David Farrell Krell and Frank A. Capuzzi (New York: Harper and Row, 1975).

EM Jacques Derrida, "En ce moment même dans cette ouvrage me voici," in *Textes pour Emmanuel Levinas*, ed. François Laruelle (Paris: Jean-Michel Place, 1980).

GW Paul Celan, *Gesammelte Werke*, 5 vol. (Frankfurt am Main: Suhrkamp, 1975).

H Martin Heidegger, *Holzwege* (Frankfurt am Main: Vittorio Klostermann, 1980, 6th ed).

HAH Emmanuel Levinas, *L'humanisme de l'autre homme* (Montpellier: Fata Morgana, 1972).

HS Emmanuel Levinas, *Hors sujet* (Montpellier: Fata Morgana, 1987).

IM   Martin Heidegger, *An Introduction to Metaphysics*, trans. Ralph Manheim (New Haven: Yale University Press, 1959).

LP   Paul Celan, *Last Poems*, trans. Katharine Washburn and Margret Guillemin (San Francisco: North Point Press, 1986).

MF   Winfried Menninghaus: *Paul Celan: Magie der Form* (Frankfurt am Main: Suhrkamp, 1980).

NP   Emmanuel Levinas, *Noms propres* (Montpellier: Fata Morgana, 1976).

OBBE   Emmanuel Levinas, *Otherwise than Being or Beyond Essence*, trans. Alphonso Lingis (The Hague: Martinus Nijhoff, 1981).

OWL   Martin Heidegger, *On the Way to Language*, trans. Peter D. Hertz (New York: Harper and Row, 1971).

P   Paul Celan, *Collected Prose*, trans. Rosmarie Waldrop (Riverdale-on-Hudson, New York: Sheep Meadow Press, 1990).

PE   Philippe Lacoue-Labarthe, *La poésie comme expérience* (Paris: Christian Bourgois Editeur, 1986).

PLT   Martin Heidegger, *Poetry, Language, Thought*, trans. Albert Hofstadter (New York: Harper and Row, 1971).

PPC   Paul Celan, *Poems of Paul Celan*, trans. Michael Hamburger (New York: Persea, 1988).

RL   *Re-reading Levinas*, ed. Robert Bernasconi and Simon Critchley (Bloomington: Indiana University Press, 1991).

SG   Paul Celan, *Speech Grille and Other Poems*, trans. Joachim Neugroschel (New York: E.P. Dutton, 1971).

SI   Werner Hamacher, "The Second of Inversion: The Movement of a Figure through Celan's Poetry," in *The Lesson of Paul de Man, Yale French Studies* 69 (1985): 276–311.

SZ   Martin Heidegger, *Sein und Zeit* (Tübingen: Niemeyer, 1986).

TB   Martin Heidegger, *On Time and Being*, trans. Joan Stambaugh (New York: Harper and Row, 1972).

TeI   Emmanuel Levinas, *Totalité et Infini: Essai sur l'extériorité* (The Hague: Martinus Nijhoff, 1961).

TI   Emmanuel Levinas, *Totality and Infinity: An Essay on Exteriority*, trans. Alphonso Lingis (Pittsburgh: Duquesne University Press, 1969).

UZS   Martin Heidegger, *Unterwegs zur Sprache* (Pfullingen: Neske, 1959).

VA   Martin Heidegger, *Vorträge und Aufsätze* (Pfullingen: Neske, 1954).

W   Martin Heidegger, *Wegmarken* (Frankfurt am Main: Vittorio Klostermann, 1978, 2d ed).

WD   Jacques Derrida, *Writing and Difference*, trans. Alan Bass (Chicago: Chicago University Press, 1978).

ZSD   Martin Heidegger, *Zur Sache des Denkens* (Tübingen: Niemeyer, 1976).

↩ INTRODUCTION ↪
Inflecting Difference

This difference in proximity between the one and the other, between me and a neighbor, turns into non-indifference, precisely into my responsibility. Non-indifference, humanity, the-one-for-the-other is the very signifyingness of signification, the intelligibility of the intelligible, and thus reason . . . the pre-original reason of difference, non-indifference, responsibility, a fine risk . . .

       —Levinas, *Otherwise than Being or Beyond Essence*

In the aftermath of poststructuralist debates, *Inflected Language* proposes to rethink the ontological and ethical dimensions of language by rereading Heidegger's work, more specifically his reflection on poetry, and by engaging Levinas's ethics and contemporary poetics. The need for a rearticulation of the role of the ethical, that is, the relation to the other, and the ontological, namely, the relation between language and the world, in the discussions of language gains urgency in the context of hasty dismissals of postmodern critiques of the humanist legacy of modernity. This rejection of poststructuralist critiques is often prompted by the alleged disconnection of these language-oriented theories from the world and their downplaying of responsibilities to those who inhabit this world. Hence the rebuttals of postmodernism claim that the emphasis the post-Heideggerian critique places on language, textuality, and discourse means in effect separation from the world, and, in particular, from its socio-political and ethical dimensions. It is therefore crucial to reappraise how the ontological and ethical thematics function in those philosophical and poetic discourses that specifically take issue with the metaphysical concept of the subject. Building on the readings of Heidegger, Levinas, Stevens, and Celan, *Inflected Language* contends, against common misinterpretations, that their approach to language in fact forces us to reexamine the very basis of relations to alterity, whether that of the world, things, or persons. It demon-

1

strates that the emphasis their works place on language not only does not forget the world and others but, conversely, mandates a rethinking of these relations apart from the metaphysical paradigm of subjectivity and its corollary models of language. In this context, I argue for a change of focus in the philosophico-literary debate about language by showing how the apparently neutral differential play of signification is already, and unavoidably, invested with ethical and worldly signification. In order to avoid obliterating this elusive signification in theorizing language, I propose to follow a new mode of reading—a post-Heideggerian and post-Levinasian "hermeneutics of nearness," which foregrounds the poetic element in language and its ways of figuring the other.

It is important to recognize that the privileging of the linguistic problematic characteristic of postmodern thought in general does not amount to locking oneself in the prisonhouse of language and signification but instead changes the very optics within which relations to alterity are conceived. The most radical part of Heidegger's project involves not only articulating the ontological thematic (the relation to the world in its otherness and difference from language and thought) and the ethical (the inscription in language of its own relation to and figuration of the other) but specifically refiguring the very connection between them. As a result of this inquiry, the boundary between the cognitive and descriptive aspects of the ontological relation to the world and the prescriptive character of ethical responsibility becomes increasingly fluid and problematic. What necessitates this revision of the relation between the cognitive and the ethical in Heidegger is the implication of thought in the erasure of alterity associated with technological culture and its dominant forms of objectification. The critique of metaphysical modes of thought, with the erasure of alterity intrinsic to them, calls for a different practice of thinking that acknowledges and preserves the alterity of what it examines. For in this view, thought's job is not, first and foremost, cognition, in the sense of understanding, calculation, and definition, but instead bringing what is other for language and thought into the "openness" of its alterity and maintaining this alterity against the power of cognitive assimilation. Such thinking is less concerned with the logic of its propositions than with preserving, with a rigor that Heidegger would more readily call poetic than philosophical, the fragile inscriptions of otherness. Hence the presence of poetry in my project is not a matter of exemplification of a philosophical paradigm but an integral, perhaps the most important, moment in refiguring language's relation to the other.

That this project should engage Heidegger before proceeding to Levinas and poetry is, of course, hardly surprising, since Heidegger's work has served as a battleground on which many crucial polemics in contemporary philosophy and theory have been launched and settled: between Derrida and Gadamer, between Heidegger and Levinas, Levinas and Derrida, not to mention the internal polemics between early and late Heidegger. This book enters those debates, however, with a new focus. It addresses the question of the poetic and its relation to the philosophical in an effort to develop a post-Heideggerian "hermeneutics" of otherness that would be different from both Gadamer's and Derrida's elaborations of Heidegger. What is most important and momentous in this return to Heidegger is the very correlation and even overlapping of the ontological and the ethical thematic characteristic of his later writings, something that is often lost or less clearly articulated in the postmodern thinking he influenced. *Inflected Language* follows and underscores this conjunction in order to articulate the possibility of what one might call, after Heidegger, an other thinking (*das andere Denken*), an avenue opened by taking into account how Heidegger's encounter with poetry figures critically in his late thought. I argue that overlooking the extent and the implications of this confrontation with the poetic (*Dichtung*)[1]—or the way in which it influences precisely the late Heideggerian model of thinking—results in an often disproportionate emphasis on the dependence of the Heideggerian idiom on metaphysical conceptuality, identifying it with a deeply rooted nostalgia for origin, primordiality, or a unique, even if indeterminate, word for Being.

One can get a sense of the effects that an absence of interest in the possibility of "the other thinking" has on the perception of Heidegger by taking a look at two very different readings, by Habermas and by Derrida. In a Habermasian reading this nostalgia "amounts in the end to 'a temporalized superfoundationalism,'" which devalues forms of argumentative and discursive thought and leaves nothing but the "empty, formulaic avowal of some indeterminate authority."[2] Habermas in fact appears to object most strongly to what may be called the poetic in the thought of Heidegger, not only disavowing any importance it might have for philosophical concerns or the critique of modernity at large but seeing in it a ruse to avoid accountability or paradoxes of critique from which "Heidegger flees . . . to the luminous heights of an esoteric, special discourse, which absolves itself of the restrictions of discursive speech generally and is immunized by vagueness against any specific objections" (185). Derrida, on the other hand, though clearly much more

sympathetic toward and deeply involved with the Heideggerian
project, underscores and dissociates himself in his reading, at least
in the early "Différance," from what he recognizes as a nostalgic
expectation of an unheard-of name, a desire for quasi-transcendental fulfillment in Heidegger's work: "[t]here will be no unique name,
even if it were the name of Being. And we must think this without
nostalgia. . . . From the vantage of this [Nietzschean] laughter and
this dance, from the vantage of this affirmation foreign to all dialectics, the other side of nostalgia, what I will call Heideggerian *hope*,
comes into question."[3] Yet the poetic in Heidegger cannot be
reduced to an "esoteric, special discourse" for the initiated or identified squarely with the need for a final, essential word, because,
above all, Heidegger's encounter with the poets helps him diagnose
language's uneasy proximity to otherness and its effects on the
processes of conceptualization and metaphorization.

Without the wish or the need to absolve Heidegger's work of
its problematic sides, I propose here another way of looking at
what he refers to, in the context of the poetic-thinking language of
the Pre-Socratics, as "another beginning." Specifically, I examine
this issue with a view to how the encounter with poetry radicalizes
the meaning of such a beginning not only beyond the question of
a retrieval or a cultural anamnesis of the past covered by philosophical reason but even beyond the postulates of a destruction
and an overcoming of metaphysics.[4] Heidegger's trips to the pre-
Socratic Greek do not indicate reclaiming something lost or forgotten, nor, on the other hand, simply a purification of the discourse
of philosophy in search for the "one and only" word, but rather an
attempt at thinking otherwise. Heidegger briefly suggests the parameters for such thinking in "Letter on Humanism": "[s]uch thinking has no result. It has no effect. It satisfies its essence in that it is.
But it is by saying its matter. . . . Its material relevance is essentially
higher than the validity of sciences, because it is freer. For it lets
Being—be."[5] As Heidegger explains, this thinking does not articulate itself positively, as a body of arguments or propositions, or
negatively, as a project of dismantling or a critique, but rather
investigates how the proximity to alterity can "empower" or inflect
language so that it takes place as *Seinlassen*, as letting be.[6] Without
operating in terms of stakes or arguments, such thinking nevertheless affects, by its specifically "poetic" rigor, the very conceptuality
of stakes and arguments, their paradigmatic application to thought
and the systems of valorization inherent in them.

Detecting a residue of hierarchization even in the current discussions of the problematic of "philosophy and literature,"

Inflected Language explores the parameters of such thinking through a series of readings of the ontological and ethical "commitments" of language. Although my book can be seen as belonging to the Nietzschean critique of rationality, which draws upon resources of rhetoric and poetics, what it seeks is not a reading of rhetorical, figurative, or metaphorical dimensions of philosophical discourse or their impact upon its conceptual and argumentative articulations but a clarification of the "ontological" and ethical ramifications of these scenarios. To put it differently, it identifies Heidegger not only with the enterprise of the overcoming and destruction of metaphysics, on the one hand, or a desire for the essential word or essentializing cohesiveness of Being, on the other, but instead points toward an overstepping of the boundaries of philosophy and opening toward a poetics, a poetic thinking (of otherness). Rather than formulating these insights into a theory, whose premises the very nature of these findings questions, my book follows closely the crossings between philosophical and poetic language not only to advance arguments but also to render language more attentive to its own proximity to (ontologico-ethical) otherness and its figurations in terms of difference.

Such a rereading of Heidegger is enabled, on the one hand, by the poets, in particular Celan, and, on the other, by Levinas's notion of ethical alterity. Levinas's critique of Heidegger, extending from his engagement with Nazism, and especially "his silence about the Final Solution, the Holocaust, the Shoah," to the priority of ontology over ethics in his work, foregrounds the issues of otherness and responsibility with particular urgency.[7] Levinas's criticisms of Heidegger are by now well known: for Levinas, Heidegger's thought comes short of giving its due to the other, affirms the priority of ontology over ethics, and, in the end, extends the dominion of the Same in thinking. In "Ethics as First Philosophy," Levinas counters Heidegger's argument by claiming ethics as *prima philosophia* and showing how the ethical extends beyond and signifies otherwise than "the meaning of Being": "Fear for the other man's death does not turn back into anguish for my death. It extends beyond the ontology of the Heideggerian *Dasein* and the *bonne conscience* of being in the sight of that being itself."[8] In Levinas's view, the insufficient attention given to the other by Heidegger may lie behind the scandal associated with his rectorship and involvement with the Nazi regime. Levinas's critique of Heidegger is of crucial importance at least for two reasons. First, by directly confronting contemporary philosophy (as well as art and literature) with the ethical demand and the problem of alterity, made

momentous by the Second World War, Levinas keeps reminding us
not only of the alliance with National Socialism of Heidegger's
thought in the 1930s but also of the inevitability and critical
importance of posing the question of the other in the context of
Heidegger's break with traditional philosophy. Second, though taking issue with Heidegger's mode of questioning and its gesture of
granting priority over the other to Being, Levinas's critique nevertheless does not purport to legitimize a return to conservative
humanism. On the contrary, it radicalizes the critique of violence
and domination inherent in the humanist paradigm and its philosophical symptoms visible in the notions of the same, consciousness, subject, or even intersubjective dialogue. In other words, the
Levinasian oeuvre allows us to differentiate between, on the one
hand, a critical engagement with Heidegger that revises, extends,
and modifies Heidegger's own critique of humanism in view of the
ethical alterity of the other and, on the other, the polemics and
attacks that use the denunciation of Heidegger's thought to legitimize a retreat from the insights of the postmodern thought of difference back to the humanist paradigm of subjectivity.[9]
Approached in this way, Levinas's polemics with Heidegger not
only opens the possibility but in fact makes unavoidable a reading
of Heidegger from the point of view of "ethical alterity."

All the more so since Heidegger's work from the 1940s on,
after the self-professed "turn" and critique of the entanglements of
his work with National Socialism, increasingly focuses on the problem of domination in metaphysical thought and its culmination in
the technological paradigm: "Humanism is opposed because it
does not set the *humanitas* of man high enough. Of course the
essential worth of man does not consist in his being the substance
of beings, as the 'Subject' among them, so that as the tyrant of
Being he may deign to release the beingness of beings into an all
too loudly bruited 'objectivity'" (*BW*, 210). Heidegger's still highly
inflated rhetoric and excessive pathos aside, the tyranny and domination of beings, which he detects even in the "highest" manifestations of the humanist doctrine, are here rejected in the name of a
thinking that "guards" beings in their Being, that is, in the specificity of their otherness. Although my book does not follow the
implications for politics of Heidegger's critique of domination and
violence in the humanist paradigm of the subject, the discussion of
the ethico-ontological aspects of *Gelassenheit* clears the way for further deliberations. In particular my notion of the "hermeneutics of
nearness" brings to the front the close link between Heidegger's critique of the subject, with its diagnosis of the need for thinking oth-

erwise, and the problem of domination, violence, and the forgetting of alterity characteristic of what Heidegger, but also Adorno,
describes as the technological worldview.[10]

Bearing in mind the brunt of Levinas's critique, his insistence
on the "otherwise" of the ethical signification irreducible to the
paths of thinking, I propose an engagement between Levinas and
Heidegger that takes us into the often unexplored aspects of Heidegger's work: the ontologico-ethical dimensions of his work on
poetry and the place of otherness in it. Amplifying these issues
through a critical perspective of Levinas and Celan, *Inflected Language* offers a new reading of Heidegger, responsive to Levinas's critique and its demand for thinking that respects the alterity of the
other. Differently put, my book restages this encounter not in
terms of overcoming but according to a scenario proposed by Levinas himself, although addressed to a different philosophical ear:
"[i]ndeed, the ridiculous ambition of 'improving' a true philosopher is not our intention. To meet him on his way is already very
commendable and is probably the very modality of the philosophical encounter."[11] With a decisive influence of Levinas and Celan's
poetry, this book highlights, then, the ethical possibilities in Heidegger's thought—the possibilities often downplayed not only by
his interpreters but even by Heidegger himself. Needless to say, the
most obvious instance when such possibilities are compromised is
Heidegger's involvement with National Socialism and his silence
on the Holocaust in his post-war writings. In contrast to Heidegger's silence, the continual reinscription of the memory of the
Holocaust in Celan's poetry foregrounds emphatically the importance of the ethical signification in contemporary preoccupations
with language, history, and memory.

This is why the role of the third party who mediates between
Levinas's conception of alterity and Heidegger's thought of Being is
played in my study by Celan. The focus of Celan's work on the
problem of otherness, its ethical, political, and linguistic dimensions in the aftermath of the Holocaust, as well as his engagement
with Heidegger's insights into language and poetry, provides a
unique opportunity for confronting the issue of the role of others
in Heidegger's thinking. In particular Celan's address "The Meridian," with both its proximity to and inflections of the Heideggerian terminology, reminiscent of Levinas's strategy of inverting and
deforming Heidegger's terms from trace, through proximity, to saying, opens the possibility of rearticulating the play of otherness in
Heidegger's work. Indeed, Celan's attentiveness to the problem of
writing, to the involuted breath/subject of his poems, emblema-

tized in his term *Atemwende*, is what has prompted my rereading of the remarks on listening and friendship that Heidegger makes in the context of poetry and pre-Socratic thinking. In this way also, the implications of the encounter between Celan and Heidegger figure prominently in recasting the problem of otherness in Heidegger vis-à-vis the Levinasian critique. The prominence given in my study to Celan and, in particular, his interest in Heidegger shows how important it is to stage these encounters between Heidegger and, respectively, Levinas, Stevens, and Celan in the context of Heidegger's articulation of the poetic, that is, his notion of *Dichtung*, or its radical impact on his understanding of language and otherness. For previous readings, if they at all broached the problem of poetry, usually cast the poetic in an ancillary role rather than see in it the primary source of Heidegger's ideas about language.[12]

By rearticulating the relation between Heidegger and Levinas in the context of Stevens's and Celan's poetry, *Inflected Language* ties this post-Heideggerian "hermeneutics" of otherness to a rethinking of the role and importance of the poetic to current critical and theoretical projects. It argues that the question of what Heidegger calls the "neighborhood of poetry and thinking" is indispensable in reading Heidegger, not only because its absence leads inevitably to underrating the importance of proto-ethical concerns for otherness in Heidegger's work but also because a careful consideration of what late, "poetic" Heidegger offers affords us a new and unexplored perspective on the questions of otherness and difference.

It is important at this point to make clear what this book, acknowledging Heidegger's increasing reluctance to even use the word in his later work, understands under the name "hermeneutics." Heidegger's most interesting remarks on this topic come in "A Dialogue on Language," in an exchange with a Japanese interlocutor that makes explicit Heidegger's discomfort with traditional categorizations his own thought borrowed with ease in *Being and Time*: "J: I am all the more puzzled that you have meanwhile dropped both words (that is, hermeneutics and phenomenology) / I: That was done, not—as is often thought—in order to deny the significance of phenomenology, but in order to abandon my own path of thinking to namelessness. / J: An effort with which you will be hardly successful. . . . / I: . . . since one cannot get by in public without rubrics."[13]

Hoping similarly to open room for discussion, my project explores how the initial problematic, terms, and intentions outlined in *Being and Time* are modified and inflected through Heidegger's texts on language and poetry. If in *Being and Time* hermeneutics could still be taken to mean interpretation itself, the later texts shift the emphasis from the task of elaborating and illuminating to delivering and letting be. Hermeneutics no longer denotes *Auslegung*, a laying out or open that would lay bare the meaning of what is under interpretation, but rather *Entsprechung*, a response, a listening that takes place in the manner of saying after (*nachsagen*) of the saying (*Sage*). As Heidegger explains in "A Dialogue on Language": "The expression 'hermeneutic' derives from the Greek verb *hermeneuein*. That verb is related to the noun *hermeneus*, which is referable to the name of the god Hermes by a playful thinking that is more compelling than the rigor of science. Hermes is the divine messenger. He brings the message of destiny; *hermeneuein* is that exposition which brings tidings because it can listen to a message" (*OWL*, 29). As Heidegger recounts a moment later, "[a]ll this makes clear that hermeneutics means not just the interpretation (*das Auslegen*) but, even before it, the bearing of message and tidings (*das Bringen von Botschaft und Kunde*)." No longer interpretation, "hermeneutics" refers to the particularity of the mode of being of *Dasein*, which predisposes humans to bring the saying of manifestation into words. It is thus language which defines the hermeneutic relation, for what Heidegger understands as bringing the message into words is tantamount to his description of the event of language in terms of the way of the saying of manifestation into words.

The role of *Dasein*, and thus, implicitly, the subject, is specified no longer along the lines of reading and interpreting a text that is already there but rather as a delivering that turns what is being "said phenomenally" into a text, that translates such *Sage* into words. For *Dasein* indeed describes the mode of being of a hermeneutist who, "by corresponding to the call of the two-fold [the ontico-ontological difference], . . . bears witness to it in its message" (*OWL*, 30) ("*insofern er dem Zuspruch der Zwiefalt entspricht und sie so in ihrer Botschaft bekundet*" [*UZS*, 122]). This peculiar hermeneutics does not therefore present an interpretive task; it does not "read" the meaning or truth of Being but instead draws attention to the proximity, the nearness, inscribed in what Heidegger calls *Entsprechung*—a fold into the way language occurs and "speaks" (*sprechen* at work in *Zuspruch* or *Anspruch*). Exploring specifically this model of resaying, response, *Entsprechung* at work in Heidegger, the way it unfolds, underlies, and continuously inflects language, this book proposes to read Heidegger in terms of a "hermeneutics of nearness." Such a reading is, I believe, mandated not only by the overriding significance of the notion of nearness (*Nähe*) for Heidegger's work but by the fact that Heidegger's understanding and refiguration of otherness are carried out precisely in terms of proximity and nearing. In other words, the exploration of nearness allows for an elaboration of Heidegger's reading of otherness, his "hermeneutics" of the other, critical to understanding the ethical or political stakes of his thought. As will become evident in my reading of Heidegger, such hermeneutics does not intend to interpret, understand, or extract meaning but induces language to "pay attention" to the inscriptions of otherness, of the unsaid, in what it brings to words. In the end, at stake is not a hermeneutics of knowing or understanding but one of listening, of *Seinlassen*, of letting come into one's own—efforts summed up by the enigmatic sense of nearing. It is a hermeneutics that, rather than simply reading and interpreting, attempts to deliver a message, to let it say itself, without covering or explaining away what remains baffling and other in it.

Far from postulating passive receptiveness, it invites, in Heidegger's view, a poetically rigorous attentiveness to language, a reading of words against themselves, as Celan would put it (*Gegenwort*), turning signification against its own laws, its hereditary economics of difference. It is in this precise sense that the project of the "hermeneutics of nearness" could be said to be poetic, concerned with working language against itself and "delivering" its silence, a task traditionally more readily undertaken by poets than philosophers. Since this hermeneutics concerns itself with what is other, its strategies will consist primarily in bringing language close to this otherness, as near as words will allow it, so that the otherness at play can show not its meaning, a content that could be rendered into an image, but rather its foreignness and strangeness. If such hermeneutics tropes anything it is only the effects or inscriptions that such coming near leaves in language; it "reads" the inflections that interpretation, understanding, and their "trafficking" in meaning sustain as a result of encountering the other. My book, therefore, refrains from providing a schema within which to read otherness or terms for interpreting it and, instead, shows why and how language, notwithstanding the pressure of thematization and the inevitable erasure of alterity that the process of signification and representation entails, can perhaps retain ethical and ontological significance. In other words, if language is bound to violence, not only as a result of specific cultural and discursive settings but, as Levinas puts it, by virtue of a "natural" allergy to otherness, which can perhaps account in part for the production of these different contexts, then what allows for the dislodging and inflection of discursive constructs are these moments of proximity that let alterity be. Again, this happens not passively or even diagnostically, but by an exertion, estrangement, and extraversion of language.

This reading of otherness in Heidegger in terms of nearness and proximity prepares the ground for taking into consideration the figurations of alterity in Levinas, Stevens, and Celan in an attempt to formulate a "hermeneutics" of otherness apart from the metaphysically invested notions of difference and interpretation. *Inflected Language* inquires into why it has been necessary both for Levinas and later Heidegger to abandon the notion of difference and replace it with almost, "nearly," synonymous terms of proximity and nearness. For them, difference can all too readily be identified with the distance between the subject and the object, and enclosed within their dialectical exchanges. Hence difference can easily remain complicitous with the dialectical sublation of otherness, with what Levinas and Heidegger diagnose variously as the violence or tyranny of thinking. By contrast, nearness (*Nähe*, *proximité*) underscores the rejection of domination and erasure of alterity intrinsic to difference and the attempt to circumvent the logic of objectification. In this context, it becomes obvious how my study is indebted in its general scope to Derrida's ongoing project of investigating and critiquing the workings of difference in thought and language.[14] For even Derrida's early coining of the non-concept *différance* already reflects the tensions and insufficiency associated with the term *difference* and the role it plays in conceptualizations, problems that his writings continue to diagnose and investigate on various planes and in multiple contexts: textual, historial, philosophical, literary, institutional, political. *Inflected Language* shows how the emphasis on nearness, by avoiding the pitfalls of formalist abstraction, prohibits common misreadings of the differential character of language in terms of its separation from world and others. Looking at it from another side, underscoring the commitments and obligations signified by nearness—language's proximity and indebtedness to others—disclaims the theoretical neutrality to which the concept of difference can be easily relegated. For example, by locating Levinas's notion of proximity between Heideggerian nearness and Celan's *Atemwende*, *Inflected Language* gives prominence to its intention of non-indifference, not only irreducible in its significance to the meaning of the other's alterity, its *difference*, but in fact signifying the effraction, dislocation, or, in Levinas's words, derailment of the differential procedures of signification. The blueprint for this new reading of otherness is provided by a close analysis of the crucial notions in Heidegger's and Levinas's thought and further elaborated by diagnosing the workings of otherness in Stevens's and Celan's poetry. Especially illuminating in this respect are Celan's language innovations, dislocating and deforming German syntax and vocabulary into a poetic construct that transpires "in the name of the other."

Though *Inflected Language* articulates otherness as an already familiar chiasm of ontological otherness and ethical alterity,[15] it argues for the necessity of reading it not according to difference but instead through the notions of Heideggerian nearness and Levinasian proximity. In effect, my book departs from the view that all meaning is the product of difference. It contends that the ontological and ethical dimensions of language cannot be regarded as the effects of difference, or, more correctly, of the differential play itself, which (dis)grounds language and disseminates meaning. For, on a Heideggerian or a Levinasian reading, differentiation finds the condition of its operation in proximity, to the extent that it is the extreme nearness to the other that allows difference to unfold, to become perceptible and meaningful. More specifically, my book explains the ontological otherness at work in Heidegger's and Steven's conceptualization of language in terms of the nearness of thought to the phenomenal, a proximity that allows for the differential character of manifestation in the first place. In a parallel way, it also argues that Celan's and Levinas's concern for language's ethical acknowledgment of the other's alterity imposes the necessity of seeing the ethical not as measured by the other's difference or the trace of that difference in language but primarily by the sense of language's ex-position, its non-indifference to the other, which underwrites all signification.

Inflected Language expounds, then, a non-foundationalist conception of language, which, as a follow-up to poststructuralist theories, "inflects" difference from its position as the regulative notion in order to disclose the prior ontological and ethical commitments of language. This change, however, does not result in replacing difference with its opposite(s)—identity, oneness, unity, which, as the differends of difference, are already inscribed in its differential mechanics. Instead, *Inflected Language* maintains that difference works and "makes sense," which means both produces meaning and becomes discernible as difference, in relation to ethico-ontological nearness. The way I read Heidegger's or Levinas's pursuit of the theme of difference makes clear, especially in the context of Derrida's questions regarding the metaphysical involvements of difference,[16] that the inflections of difference are predicated and contingent on the exploration of difference itself. For example, the possibility and the need to "inflect" difference arise in Heidegger only after a long inquiry into the nature of the ontico-ontological difference and difference as such. In this context, my book amplifies and explores precisely those moments when the texts I discuss come against the "limit" of difference and need, in order to communicate their ethico-ontological significance, to inflect difference, that is, to mark the limit of signification produced by/in difference.

I use here the term *ontologico-ethical* (or *ethico-ontological*) not as a binding category but instead as an indication of the direction(s) in which this critique of language moves. For Heidegger clearly displaces both terms, not in the least because their connotations bring up the heritage of metaphysical conceptuality, orienting discourse toward the dominant notions of subject, action, individuality, substantiality. Thus Heidegger claims that his thought is neither ontology nor ethics in the accepted senses of these words but that it is a new, other thinking (*das andere Denken*), which, by virtue of letting otherness be, is "ethical" or rather "proto-ethical" as such. Therefore, without subscribing to either category, it has nonetheless important implications for both ontology and ethics, as it examines the condition of their possibility, the horizon, the "open" within which the ontological and the ethical problematics "make sense" and become thinkable. Ethical here means, then, specifically thinking as letting-be, letting the other be other. It therefore indicates an ethical inflection of thinking and language in Heidegger. A similar level of analysis is appropriate for Levinas's ethics, which, as Derrida has shown, is always only the ethics of ethics, that is, ethics without specific content, rules, or laws. In other words, it is ethics as a linguistic prescription, with the prefix intimating, to use Levinas's own idiom, an an-archic or inoriginal character of the alterity that has already pre-scribed and pre-disposed language toward the other.

I use, therefore, both terms, *ontological* and *ethical,* all the time inflecting their established meaning, to indicate the stakes of my questioning, namely, language in its proximity to the phenomenal and its exposition to the other. To put it differently, at issue here are linguistic inflections, not rudiments of ethics or ontology. My reading shows how the semiotic processes bear with them the traces of these inflections, inflections without which, as Heidegger and Levinas show, one could not think either the question of ethics or the question of ontology. For Heidegger, in fact, there is virtually no distinction between the two, which does not signify an erasure of ethics but, on the contrary and against some prevalent interpretations, almost an unqualified importance of the ethical problematic, obviously in the revised and amended scope that Heidegger gives to this issue. For in order to understand the stakes of the Heideggerian questioning, one has to underscore the fact that here the ethical is not only no longer separated but in fact coextensive with the "ontological" thought of letting-be. In other words, the ethical and the ontological are the two sides of *Gelassenheit*, with a thin and fragile boundary that readily blurs itself, forcing, as Heidegger would say, an unexpected, perhaps even unprecedented, "poetic" rigor upon thinking.

Questioning the concept of difference itself, my book examines the implications of the priority granted to difference by Western tradition, as it is first foregrounded and, as I argue, inflected by Heidegger's and Levinas's exploration of the issue of nearness. One could claim in this Heideggerian-Levinasian context that the notion of difference is not neutral or, even in its most abstract articulations, purely structural but that it already contains a residue, an inflection. However, difference cannot quite notice or note its own inflection without inscribing and describing it as produced or unfolded through the heterological economy that, itself unwritten, regulates thought and signifying procedures. This is precisely the tension that the texts discussed here bring to our attention, forcing a recognition that any meaning that can be ascribed to this remainder, any discussion of it in the terms prescribed by the differential nature of language, is already inflected by a debt that difference bears with it, a debt its idiom, as Levinas would put it, cannot quite acknowledge except as an interruption of its discourse, a series of dislocations always rewoven back into its fabric. As I show, asking the ontological question together with the ethical in this particular context further radicalizes the question of difference, raising the issue of the extent to which the master trope of difference can, in addition to its both critical and generative force, encounter also a certain non-signifiable and non-traceable limit.

If, as the Levinasian term *non-indifference* suggests, the differential economy of meaning cannot quite accommodate the proximity at stake here, how then are the "ethical" and the "ontological" to be understood if we want to pay attention to Heidegger's, Levinas's, and the poets' notation of otherness otherwise than through difference? Can Levinasian phrases like "wholly otherwise," "absolutely other," or "otherwise than Being" have any meaning if they are not accommodable according to difference? What sense do these texts spring upon us if it cannot be transcribed semiotically, and yet cannot be simply designated as transcendental either? Without answering these questions hastily, I would like to point here to the complexity of Celan's poetic language, especially to the way in which otherness inflects this language without allowing itself to become defined or imaged. I want to suggest, then, that perhaps one can see the ethical and ontological inflections of Celan's texts as both refracting and complicating the already heteronomous "logic" of signification by virtue of questioning and problematizing the apparent "semiological neutrality" of the underside of language. In other words, emphasizing nearness in this context foregrounds and clarifies the prior commitments and obligations of difference; it accentuates the impossibility of its being, in Levinas's words, disinterested or indifferent, or yet purely structural.

I wish to underscore here the "perhaps," the only modality of discourse in which the figurations of otherness proposed by Heidegger, Levinas, Stevens, and Celan could be, as their own rhetoric suggests, maintained.[17] This peculiar modality in which otherness is noted here explains why *Inflected Language* refrains for the most part from turning its findings into a theory of text, language, or signification and prefers instead to take notice of this unstable sense of "perhaps" by intersecting close readings of its poetic and philosophical intimations. Theoretical or assertive mode, though it allows us to grasp the importance and contextualize the effects of this revision of otherness, also empties the "ethical" and the "ontological" of their sense of proximity and its pre-scriptive function for language and signification, not recuperable or signifiable even under the rubric of critique. For the mode of "perhaps" (Stevensian "fiction," Levinasian *"peut-être,"* Celanian *"vielleicht"*) does not indicate here something that can occur, that can become an actuality as a result of implementing a choice between various potentialities. In other words, the modality of perhaps that this study detects in the texts by Heidegger, Levinas, Stevens, and Celan escapes the framework delineated and sustained by the opposition of potentiality and actuality. To that effect, what is understood here under the rubric of perhaps is possible only as a may-be; it is, to put it differently, not readable according to the logic of propositions or assertions but instead as their "poetic" disruption. For such a perhaps to become actually possible would mean assuming the logic of signification, becoming spelled according to difference, and thus losing, to quote Stevens, its "separate sense" and its inflecting power with respect to the production of meaning. If one can at all propose a simultaneous dependence (nearness can signify only in language) and independence of this "otherwise" from the theoretical discourse in which it is presented, it is only through its modality of perhaps, a may-be, an inflection not exactly different from language and yet not quite consonant with it either. One can then formulate the stakes of my argument in this way: read in terms of difference, the alterity at work in proximity becomes undermined and erased within the paradigms of theoretical discourse; seen as an inflection of the economy of difference, it can retain its otherwise by exposing the very compromise that accommodates it in language and allows it to be theorized or imaged. The precarious status of this distinction in reading, and the demand that texts by Heidegger or Celan place on us to take it into account, constitute perhaps the very sign of proximity. Its "hermeneutics" means keeping language in view of this difficulty.

Why I want to keep these proximities distinct, to see them not simply as traces or inscriptions but inflections, whose markings can be approached at best only as a "failure" of tracing, may be illustrated by the dependence of any critique of conceptuality or language upon the notion of difference and, especially, the need that the analyzed texts exhibit to circumvent this terminology, to spell it otherwise. To put it simply, my book asks the question that has to be posed after Heidegger and Levinas, Derrida and other poststructuralist ventures: can the differential understanding of language account or take note of the ethico-ontological commitments of language, without reading them as differences, thus muting and making these inflections part, if not exactly of the economy of signification, then of its "other" economy of ruptures and reinscriptions, of its heterological "underwriting"? As Irigaray points out in another context, proximity brings difference to a halt and undercuts it by derailing the logic of separation and identity: "[n]earness so pronounced that it makes all discrimination of identity, and thus all forms of property, impossible. . . . This puts into question all prevailing economies."[18]

My book solicits this question by showing how in the analyzed texts difference is seen as operating in the wake of ethico-ontological nearness and/or proximity. Specifically, *Inflected Language* illustrates how in Heidegger's and Stevens's work the differential manifestation of things occurs always already in the nearness of thought to Being, which unfolds and translates itself, concealing itself in the process, into language. Difference "works" owing to nearness, whose valency, in contrast, is ontological rather than semiological. In Levinas or Celan, on the other hand, what describes the ethical alterity is not the other's difference but rather the impossibility of my non-indifference. In other words, the other's difference "makes sense" and can be recognized as difference only because of its non-indifference.

Reading the ethico-ontological chiasmus of otherness in terms of nearness and proximity, *Inflected Language* invests otherness with the valency of letting be, listening, giving. Detecting a certain self-imposed "limit" of difference, the notion of inflected language gives priority to the ontologico-ethical inflection that allows for and modulates the differential work of signification. This shift signals a new approach to the ethico-ontological significance of language, an approach that defines, after Levinas, the inquiry into the ethical character of language in terms of exposition rather than difference. In a similar manner, it also deemphasizes the preeminence of the ontological difference in the majority of poststructuralist discussions/critiques of Heidegger's notion of Being and focuses its argument on his often overlooked conception of language as the way of "phenomenal" saying into words. In this manner, my argument attempts to further radicalize the critique of Western rationality initiated by Nietzsche and Heidegger, to problematize even what makes possible and sustains the framework for their critique of modernity—the notion of difference—and to foreground how phenomenologically and ethically invested it is. The revision of the stakes to admit the ontological and ethical significance underwriting language also points to the importance of the poetic problematic and its relevance to ethical issues in Heidegger's work, which poststructuralism for the most part bypasses. This strategy allows me to use the unexplored aspects of Heidegger's work, in particular the understanding of language in its nearness to Being and the departure from the notion of difference, to open another perspective in which one can precisely critique the last vestige of metaphysics in poststructuralism—difference itself. Such an approach opens the door to an ethico-ontological reading of language in Stevens, Celan, and Levinas.

This new "hermeneutics" of otherness unfolds between poetry and philosophy, in their proximity, which also allows them to spell out their difference. In fact, the new direction in which *Inflected Language* proposes to take otherness is made possible by the intervention of the poetic into predominantly philosophical and theoretical debates. In Heidegger's account, poetry is perhaps uniquely predisposed for such intercession (Celan's works clearly show an awareness of this disposition of poetic language). For, despite its historically metaphysical substructure, poetic language is less dependent, less "addicted" to metaphysical terminology, to thinking through and in difference, than philosophy. As Heidegger implies in his readings in *On the Way to Language*, it is easier for poetry to transgress metaphysical limits, including that which makes the limits and their beyond possible—difference. In other words, it is easier for poetry to be *denkendes Dichten*, a thinking poetry, than for philosophy to become *dichtendes Denken*, a poetic thinking. Indeed, the enterprise of the "hermeneutics" of proximity appears to be basically poetic, and, for Heidegger at least, it spells "the end of philosophy" and the beginning of *das andere Denken*, another, poetic thinking. One reason is probably the modality in which such "hermeneutics" operates, its "perhaps," which inflects the essentially propositional and assertive modes of philosophical discourse, or, in broader terms, the tendency of language to figure, to represent, to render meaningful and intelligible. Reconsidering the relationship between poetry and thinking, literature and philosophy, *Inflected Language* claims that what questions the discursive line that separates them, what brings poetry and philosophy together, into a neighborhood, is precisely the vicinity of alterity and the figurations of their own proximity to it. To reconstitute this neighborhood and thus to revise our understanding of language—this is what may become possible, even desirable, in the wake of the hermeneutics of nearness.

Following these (post)Heideggerian leads, the coda of the book reads together Heidegger and Celan, intimating how the poetic intervention affords us a view of the relationship between the Levinasian and Heideggerian hermeneutics of otherness, perhaps the focal intersection for Continental thought, not in traditional terms of overcoming or critique, but rather according to the "ideal" of an ethical encounter prescribed by Levinas himself. The poetic milieu in which their meeting takes place, in particular Celan's remarks about twofold otherness, invites us to evaluate to what extent the chiasm of otherness possibly traced in Heidegger's remarks on friendship is similar to the distinction in otherness that Levinas proposes between the radical alterity of the Other and the otherness manifest in "living from . . . ," even if, in his reading, this latter eventually falls prey to consciousness. Are those conceptions as radically different as Levinas's critique of Heidegger implies, or can their inflections of the conceptuality of difference be seen as "neighbors"? Celan's poetry can play a unique mediating role in foregrounding this relation, as it bridges the central concerns of both Heidegger's thought and its Levinasian critique.

Complicating these encounters, the poetic intervention in my book helps trace the outline of a "hermeneutics" of nearness and proximity that can perhaps begin to attend to inflected language otherwise than (in)difference. Since *Inflected Language* elaborates aspects of the interrelation between poetry and philosophy, it cannot limit itself to one kind of audience; instead, it hopes to foster dialogue and exchange between those interested in philosophy, those engaged with poetry, and those preoccupied with the ongoing critique of modernity.

～ 1 ～

RETHINKING THE PARAMETERS OF THE HEIDEGGERIAN HERMENEUTICS
Heidegger on Poetry and Thinking

It is no great secret that Heidegger's engagement with poetry and, especially, the effect of this encounter on the configuration and bearings of his thought remain largely unexplored. Even though there have been books and essays on Heidegger's conception of language and his reading of poetry, notably Hölderlin's, they have, for the most part, elaborated the question of Heidegger's influence on literary study rather then exact the stakes and the implications of this concern with poetry for Heidegger's own work. Recent studies by Véronique Fóti and by John Llewelyn begin to remedy this situation,[1] insisting on the importance of Heidegger's reading of the poets for understanding, in particular, the direction and the possible ethical import of his questioning of otherness. The opening of such a new perspective on what I have provisionally called the Heideggerian "hermeneutics" of otherness, of letting the other be, is obviously contingent upon a shift in the way we read Heidegger. To put it differently, this change of optics requires asking the question about the importance of reading both Heidegger's proximity to poetry and Heidegger *in* proximity to poetry. In other words, what does it mean to read Heidegger not through *Being and Time*, or through his war lectures on Nietzsche and Parmenides, or even, more recently, through *Beiträge zur Philosophie*, but rather through his late essays on poetry and language? Such inquiry has no intention of discovering a third or a fourth Heidegger through an arbitrary periodization of his work but, on the contrary, examines the consequences of Heidegger's continuous requestioning of Being and difference for his late thought. To that effect, it contends, through a circumspect reading of the "poetic" Heidegger, that his thought offers us a novel, radical, or, to refer to the title of this book, an *inflected* perspective on otherness and difference.

Refocusing the Heidegger debate through the prism of his encounter with the poets underscores, above all, the indispensability of poetry in recognizing the radicality of his questioning. This claim is not simply a matter of taking into account the thematic variety of his texts but instead of clarifying how a lack of understanding about the way in which Heidegger's preoccupation with poetry weighs upon his thought impedes the recognition of the problematic of nearness and its ethico-ontological import. Foregrounding the poetic in Heidegger's work also manifests the extent to which his conception of language is absolutely central to recognizing the stakes and the claims of his thought. Though language plays an important role in Heidegger already in *Being and Time*, the most significant observations about language come in the texts on the pre-Socratic thinkers and on poetry,[2] elaborated in the context of what he calls the neighborhood of poetry and thinking. As I will argue, the specificity of Heidegger's understanding of language as a translation or a way of the saying (*Sage*) of manifestation into words can in fact be articulated only through the relation, the neighboring, of poetry and thinking.

It is precisely in the essays expounding the idea of the neighborhood of poetry and thinking that Heidegger develops his understanding of language as always shaped by the "relation" or, to be more exact, the nearing between thinking and Being. To that extent, reading the proximity of poetry and thinking becomes indispensable to discerning the distinctiveness of this non-relational bind (*entbindende Band*)[3] between thinking and the retreat of Being, an insight pivotal, as this book maintains, to any claims about understanding Heidegger's ideas on otherness and difference. This chapter explains this characteristic proximity of thinking to Being in Heidegger as the "infold," where thinking, itself a mode of being-human, gets underway by folding into Being. The infold works in a way that lets Being envelop language and at the same time withdraw itself from words and remain other. This sense of otherness becomes critical for Heidegger's notion of language, as it "grounds" it without ever providing a basis and makes room for the signifying matrix that lets meaning emerge.

The term *infold* is used here precisely to foreground the fact that this otherness should not be described in terms of difference. In other words, it diagnoses and explores a certain hesitation or resistance on the part of Heidegger in explaining the proximity of thinking and Being through difference. Basing my remarks on the pivotal essays from *On the Way to Language*, I detect in Heidegger's questioning of difference and identity a certain "limitation" of difference with respect to articulating ontological and proto-ethical stakes of language. The infold not only marks this limit but also inflects difference in order to communicate the ethico-ontological significance of language beyond, or rather otherwise than, the signification produced in and by difference. To that effect, it is the notion of the infold, as it comes to the fore in the interchange between poetry and thinking in Heidegger's work, that directs and guides the inquiry into Heidegger's inflection of difference.

Exploring this mechanics of infolding, I will show how the poetic leads Heidegger to a conception of thinking and language based on nearness rather than difference. For it is the poetic "influence" in Heidegger that steers his thinking from the ontological difference to the interplay of difference and identity and then difference as such and, finally, to the notion of nearness. In *On the Way to Language*, among other late texts, it becomes clear that, in spite of Heidegger's incessant return to the problematic of difference, the differential or unitary terms of his discussion fail to account for the notion of *Zusammengehören*, of belonging together of thinking and Being. Instead, thinking and Being trace a figure of proximity, a nearness, which not only does not explain itself as the very difference of identity and difference but, in fact, inflects it with an "always already" phenomenal and ethical significance. As a result, this inflection, revealed here as the operation of the infold, troubles and dislocates Heidegger's own inquiry into difference; it ultimately angles and rewrites his rhetoric of identity and difference. I propose to explain the "logic" of this flection, and to amplify it beyond the degree of discernment afforded by Heidegger's texts, by examining the neighborhood of poetry and thinking, with a view specifically to how Heidegger means the poetic and, by extension, thinking in this context.

Dichten-Denken: *Beyond a Philosophy of Poetry*

The German words introducing this section are used here to emphasize from the start Heidegger's idiosyncratic use of both terms, which, much too often, have been taken at their face value in the Heidegger scholarship. To put it briefly and simply, what Heidegger designates as *Dichtung* is not poetry in its usual sense, just as *Denken* is not thinking, and certainly not metaphysical thought. These claims can be substantiated by following Heidegger's use of the word *dichten* and the way in which his texts on art and poetry precipitate the revision of the initial project of fundamental ontology and the thought of Being into poetic thinking. I will examine, therefore, Heidegger's statements about *Dichtung* and poetic language in order to outline the view of the poetic that regulates his texts, even when it is not expressly acknowledged or extensively described there. The understanding of the poetic will in turn provide an insight into how the proximity of thinking to poetry modifies the parameters in which thinking has come to think of itself and define its own specificity—both itself as the thought of difference and its difference from other discourses.

Heidegger's singular interest in poetic language manifests itself already in *Sein und Zeit*, in particular in the chapters dealing with language, understanding (*Verstehen*), and interpretation (*Auslegung*).[4] Although in *Being and Time* language is discussed within the analytic of *Dasein* and its essence referred to as *Rede* (discourse), Heidegger already specifies *"dichtende" Rede* as one of the modes of *Dasein*'s Being-in. The quotation marks in which *dichtende* appears in Heidegger's text prefigure the special status poetry will attain in later writings. In particular, they seem to suggest that poetry (*Dichtung*) is already demarcated from the usual meaning it carries in philosophy or literary criticism. In the context of the procedure Heidegger adapts with respect to other metaphysical concepts, for example, language, interpretation, mood, etc., one can assume that poetry as well must be reinterpreted within the perspective of Being, and that *dichtende* will mark the "esse-ntial" dimension of language.

In subsequent writings, poetry and the poetic (*Dichtung, dichterisch*) become increasingly significant, to the point that the essence of language, in the active sense with which Heidegger invests *Wesen*, can be disclosed only through and as the poetic. Although this position is explained in the essays from *On the Way to Language*, it already informs "The Origin of the Work of Art," where Heidegger defines art in terms of the poetic: *"All art*, as the letting happen of the advent of the truth of what is, is, as such, *essentially poetry"* (*"'Alle Kunst' ist als Geschehenlassen der Ankunft der Wahrheit des Seienden als eines solchen 'im Wesen Dichtung'"*).[5] This remark makes clear that Heidegger intends poetry (*Dichtung*) in a broad sense, as a kind of "poeticity" or "poetizing" that lies at the bottom of art.[6] To translate *Dichtung* as "poetry" in this context is therefore both correct and misleading, as the "field" of *Dichtung*, though at certain points overlapping with that of poetry, is fundamentally different. All the more so since Heidegger raises some doubts as to "whether art, in all its modes from architecture to poesy [poetry in the narrow sense, German *Poesie*], exhausts the nature of poetry" as *Dichtung* (*H*, 60/*OWL*, 74). Heidegger claims that poetry, understood in the narrow sense, only at certain moments—for example, ancient Greek literature, Hölderlin's late poetry—participates in *Dichtung*. As the same is true of other arts, it is obvious that for Heidegger only a small portion of artistic production finds its place within the scope of *Dichtung*, and even then, at best, only as pointers or traces of what *Dichtung* is essentially (*im Wesen*).

It is rather surprising that this distinction, upon which "The Origin of the Work of Art" pivots and which informs and structures Heidegger's subsequent texts on poetry, has not gained much currency in Heidegger scholarship, especially since the difference between *Dichtung* and *Poesie* underlies Heidegger's conception of language and the articulation of the tenets of the new or the other thinking (*das andere Denken*). Most important, this division comes to indicate, without erasing their differences, a degree of proximity between the poetic and the philosophical that, of their own accord, perhaps neither philosophy nor poetry would willingly admit. Within this specific context, it becomes clear that, to understand both what *Dichtung* originarily means and how it shows itself through, and showing differs itself from, *Poesie*, it is necessary to think of *Dichtung* as always belonging together with thinking (*Denken*). This view is confirmed by another work from the same period as "The Origin of the Work of Art," namely, *Introduction to Metaphysics*, where Heidegger traces the intimacy between poetry and thinking back to the Pre-Socratics, in particular to the fragments of Heraclitus and Parmenides. *Introduction to Metaphysics* describes the Heraclitean and Parmenidean sayings precisely as *denkerisch-dichterisch*, because, to Heidegger, they are both poetry and thinking,[7] or, to be more exact, because the philosophical and the poetic have not as yet been sharply demarcated in them. Heidegger claims, therefore, that the discourse of Parmenides and Heraclitus moves in the plane of the originary bonding of poetic and philosophical thinking.

To see the critical impact of this relation between poetry and philosophy on Heidegger's understanding of language and, subsequently, of difference and otherness, it is necessary to maintain distinctions between the two modes of *Dichtung*: the originary *Dichtung*, which happens always in the interrelation with *Denken*, and *Dichtung* that is revealed or traced through poetry—the essential poeticity of art. For the sake of the clarity of this presentation, the German term will be used to indicate the first mode; *poetry* will be reserved for that art, in particular poetry in the narrow sense, to which Heidegger sometimes refers as *Dichtung*, in order to indicate that *Dichtung* happens through it. A similar distinction has to be introduced with respect to the notion of thinking. Consequently, the German term, *Denken*, will refer to the originary mode of thinking in its proximity to *Dichtung*, while the English *thinking* will indicate these philosophical writings in which *Denken* in its originary sense can be traced.

Yet how is it possible to claim that *Dichten-Denken* is more primordial than poetry and thinking as the happening of truth? Is there in Heidegger's thought something "prior" to language *as poetry and/or thinking*? One can begin answering this question in the context of "The Origin of the Work of Art," and, more specifically, by looking at how *Dichtung* traces the peculiarly dislocated temporality of its "origin" (*Ur-sprung*) in the work of art. Describing the relation between work and truth, Heidegger maintains that art gathers its value from the intimacy between the most universal and the most particular, from truth happening always in a unique, thus also temporal, manner. For the universal truth to happen in a particular way, truth must come to stand in an image, a figure (*Gestalt*) (*H*, 50/*PLT*, 64). Thus art owes its particularity to its *Gestalt*, while its universality comes from truth, which in its originary way happens as poetizing, *Dichtung*. Yet *Dichtung* precedes art; it poetizes prior to the casting into the figure, since, as Heidegger remarks, *Dichtung* indicates an "illuminating projection (*lichtender Entwurf*), [which] unfolds of unconcealedness and projects ahead into the design of the figure" (*H*, 58/*PLT*, 72). *Dichtung*, therefore, is a saying, "a projecting of the clearing," a de-signing projection into art. The abstract terminology that Heidegger uses here serves the purpose of indicating what may be very inexactly called the "structuring" prior to the emergence of art.

In this particular context, *Dichtung* names that which, concealing itself in art, makes "place" for art: it "projects" and "outlines" (*entwerfen*) in such a way that it keeps itself from emerging and, in this peculiar withdrawal, opens art. In other words, *Dichtung* marks the *Ur-sprung*, the "origin" that remains unnamed, unexpressed, since, as the originary leap, it is never present (in the sense in which artistic creations are), that is, it has always already, namely, beyond any traceable past, taken place. It is a leap that does not span or bridge, whose "from where" can be indicated only as absenting itself from the work of art, though not as mere absence. The hyphen in *Ur-sprung*, besides tracing the etymology of the word, separates otherwise than the temporal distance between the past and the present. What remains in the work of art is the sign, the trace of this interrupted, severing leap. It seems, therefore, legitimate to claim that *Dichtung* is "more" primordial than art, for, as it describes the leap (*Ur-sprung*) into *Gestalt*, *Dichtung* becomes the design of the opening for art. This opening can never be outlined and projected "totally" into the *Gestalt* but instead withdraws itself and remains as a trace in what has been projected into the art work.

It is clear that the relation between what I have termed *Denken* and thinking shares a similar dynamics. When, for example, in *What Is Called Thinking?*, Heidegger describes the workings of language as a "grid" of junctures, it is apparent that this grid-like structure is *Denken* in its originary mode, in which *Denken* says the twofold: Being/beings—*Eon*. Characterizing the way the twofold calls for *Denken*, Heidegger says:

> *Eon* speaks of what speaks in every word of the language, and not just in every word, but before all else in every conjunction of words, and thus particularly in those junctures of the language which are not specifically put in words.[8]

Thus *Denken* is not so much words themselves as the "junctures" of language, which most often do not come to words. It is the opening "between," that which by differing holds words together and makes intelligibility and language possible. The primordiality of this linguistic opening characterizes *Denken* in a manner similar to that in which *Entwurf* brings to light the nature of *Dichtung*, and as such it draws our attention to the originary binding between poetry and thinking and to the specifics of the Heideggerian reading of it. The term *junctures of language* also provides a hint about the direction in which *Dichten-Denken* should be thought if it is to reveal its primordiality. From Heidegger's remarks about the conjunctions of words, it becomes evident that *Dichten-Denken* comes into actual words very rarely, and that always in a sense as a repetition, an after-saying: it retreats from speech and writing, from thinking and poetry. Readers of Heidegger are quite familiar with the mechanics of such retreat, which traces by means of erasing and retracting and which works, in Derrida's term, as a re-trait. However, in the context of poetry and thinking, the significance of this figure of withdrawal lies not so much in its structure as in the fact that the self-veiling and "othering" character of *Dichten-Denken* leads Heidegger to an idiosyncratic conception of language. To illustrate this connection, one has to examine the way in which Heidegger's understanding of the proximity between *Dichten* and *Denken* informs his notion of the saying and its defining influence in the elaboration of otherness and difference in *Ereignis*.

In order to work our way toward understanding how the specificity of the poetic determines the place of otherness in Heidegger's view of language, it is important to note that the withdrawal of *Dichten-Denken* from words is the result not of some deficiency or inadequacy of the human cognitive powers but rather of the very elusiveness and otherness of the poetic. In the Hölderlin essays, Heidegger often claims, echoing Nietzsche's statement about the origin of poetry from *The Birth of Tragedy*, that the essence of language is shrouded in mystery, that, making humans its speakers, it refuses itself to them.[9] This paradigm of refusal, withdrawal, and othering, far from harboring mystic tendencies, in fact continues and inflects Heidegger's initial elaboration of otherness in terms of the ontico-ontological difference. Already in the introduction to *Being and Time*, Heidegger states that the difference between Being and beings is so radical that it is no longer perceptible as difference (*SZ*, 9/*BT*, 29). As *Introduction to Metaphysics* repeatedly suggests, difference can open itself only upon a plane of belonging-together: two differends can be differentiated only with respect to that which bonds them, which makes the opposition possible in the first place and does not let the opposites flow in chaotic indifference (*IM*, 144). Yet, because of the otherness of Being, the "difference" between Being and beings is so abysmal that there is no common plane that would structure and hold the opposition, since it is Being itself that is the opening of the plane upon which differing can happen. Therefore, the "difference" immediately becomes "undifference": Being covers itself with beings, and in its retreat it becomes indistinguishable from beings, almost a being itself. This retreat is visible in the "language of Being," which continually missays and unsays Being, unable to escape describing it in the same syntactical and grammatical terms as entities. In the end, this mutation of Being corroborates the refusal of the ontological "undifference" to language or at least to words.

It is evident from Heidegger's work on poetry that a similar paradigm of otherness as denial and withdrawal is at work in the neighborhood of poetry and thinking, with that difference, though, that the complex *Dichten-Denken* has to be thought directly within the notion of language (*Sprache*) as it arises in and as a response to Being. The implication of this parallel is that *Dichten-Denken* differs from words in such an abysmal way as to make that difference in the end no difference at all but instead something other or otherwise than difference. If *Dichten-Denken* is indeed this "other" opening for words, for language as speech and writing, how are we then to conceive the relation between Being,

Dichten-Denken, and language as speech/writing? Can they be maintained as the different elements of the "same" differential relation, or is there a new paradigm emerging here, one no longer thinkable as either relation or difference? To answer these questions and to see how their effects implicitly inform and disturb Heidegger's investigations of the "way to language," I propose to examine how this inquiry into language leads Heidegger to the fundamental difference, if one can use this "ontic" term with respect to Being, that marks itself within Being: the difference, or rather the fold, between modes of Being that appears with the irruption of *Dasein* into Being. As Christopher Fynsk convincingly argues, though the term *Dasein* appears very rarely in Heidegger's late writings, the conception of language presented in them is always implicitly correlated with *Dasein*'s characteristic mode of Being.[10] In fact, it is because of the difference in Being, of the "apartness" of *Dasein*, that the thematization of Being can take place, that Being can be led into its self-refusing saying through the response of thinking to Being's call.

What has remained unexplored, however, is the effect that this questioning of the relation of thinking to Being against the backdrop of poetry has on Heidegger's view of difference itself, an effect so radical that one is tempted to call it, punning on Heidegger's own idiom, *nearly* untraced or untraceable. In order to reclaim the claim this inflection of difference has on Heidegger's texts, we have to think the inscription of otherness in the relation between thinking and Being according to the graphic of *Dichten-Denken*. In other words, we need to examine how the fold of thinking into Being "originates," in the sense of *Ur-sprung*, or initiates language in Heidegger's most important texts on language: "The Nature of Language" and "The Way to Language."[11] These essays make clear that the complexity of the irruption in Being of the thinking of Being can be discussed only in the context of what Heidegger calls the "neighborhood of poetry and thinking," the originary closeness of the poetic and the philosophical.

Defining "neighborhood" as "dwelling in nearness" (*UZS*, 199/*OWL*, 93), Heidegger remarks that poetry and thinking dwell in nearness because they are both modes of the saying, that is, of presencing as the showing saying. It has to be stressed from the outset that for Heidegger the saying does not mean speech or simply linguistic expression: "Saying is in no way the linguistic expression added to the phenomena after they have appeared—rather, all radiant appearance and all fading away is grounded in the showing Saying (*in der zeigenden Sage*)" (*UZS*, 257/*OWL*, 126). Thus Heidegger understands saying as the very process of appearing (in an eminently verbal sense), in which beings, as they come to be, are also "said." To put it differently, the saying refers to the placing or positioning of a being in a nexus of "relations" (*Bezüge*) to other beings, which lets that being be; it describes an interlacing (*Geflecht*) that underwrites signification and itself interlaces, nears, brings into proximity the linguistic and the phenomenal. There is no doubt in this context that for Heidegger *Ereignis*, the event of manifestation, the phenomenon par excellence, must be of a proto-linguistic nature—it is itself a form, or better, a design (*Riss*) of the saying.

Such understanding of the saying becomes possible only in the aftermath of Heidegger's consideration of the double meaning of poetry and thinking, that is, of their specific function of letting beings be. In fact, Heidegger's repeated engagement with poetry and its resultant articulation of language in *On the Way to Language* in terms of a mistranslation or an interrupted translation of the saying into words must be seen as an attempt to clarify the distance between, respectively, poetry and *Dichtung*, and thinking and *Denken*. To put it briefly, trying to understand how art is "essentially," *im Wesen*, *Dichtung*, Heidegger is faced with the problem of conceiving the relation of thinking to Being in a way that could account for the inscription and erasure of the saying of manifestation in words. Rephrasing the question in terms proposed by this study, can one still think here the tie between thinking and Being in terms of difference as such and maintain the specificity of Heidegger's view of language, especially its ontological stakes? It is precisely for that reason that, in "The Way to Language," Heidegger devotes considerable space to the discussion of the human mode of Being and its "appropriateness" for the saying (of Being). Explicating the tracing of the saying in words, he claims that humans, by virtue of their specific mode of Being, are always already made "appropriate" for the task of the "speakers" of Being: they are listeners made "appropriate," that is, responsive to and responsible for the saying (*UZS*, 260/*OWL*, 129). Since the way they encounter the saying constitutes also their answer, their role as speakers lies in answering, saying after, "countersaying," or "listening saying"— *nachsagen* or *entsprechen*. Because Heidegger understands the showing saying as "soundless word," humans are the ones who endow language with voice, who "voice" the saying in the sense that what is "said" through phenomenal self-showing is resaid in actual words through thinking or poetry.

What needs to be explained in the context of Heidegger's engagement with difference is precisely this "after" (*nach-*) or "counter" (*ent-*), which implies an inner distance, an interval between the showing saying and the human "saying after." Analyzing briefly this interval and its implications for the beginning of Heidegger's enterprise as the "question" (of Being), Derrida, in a footnote to *De l'esprit: Heidegger et la question*,[12] explains that, in the context of this pause at the essence of language, it would appear that every act of language, even that of questioning itself, is already inscribed in this essential distance. Derrida underscores in this context the structure of *zusprechen* (to address, to impart by way of mouth) and the fact that before human beings question, language has already been addressed to them. *Zuspruch* then has a double meaning: the very address is also that which addresses itself. It is because of the twofoldness of the address that human beings are addressed and claimed by language in such a way that their every linguistic act reflects this address, without ever bringing it into the open. In this perspective, even the very possibility of questioning (*Fragen*) would seem to presuppose human acquiescence, the welcoming of Being and language.[13] Although Derrida does not explore the possibility that such an articulation of the mechanics of language could in the end spell a shift, an inflection, in Heidegger's treatment of otherness, I would argue that it is precisely the understanding of this interval that harbors the possibility of a Heideggerian "hermeneutics" of nearness.

In order to pursue such a project, one needs to explicate carefully the link between the "re-trait" of the saying in words and the fold of thinking into Being. It is important, therefore, to note that for Heidegger the interval of the address constitutes the "essential" way-making movement of language: "*Die Be-wëgung bringt die Sprache (das Sprachwesen) als die Sprache (die Sage) zur Sprache (zum verlautenden Wort)*"/"This way-making puts language (the essence of language) as language (Saying) into language (into the sounded word)" (*UZS*, 261/*OWL*, 130).[14] The quotation articulates the workings of language in terms of a tripartite "structuring movement" of language: the saying, the between, and the sounded word. Human beings come into this play, so to speak, "at the end" of the way, bringing with them the possibility of voice. Yet it does not mean that they come into the process of language as an addition, as merely its last step, for Heidegger leaves no doubt that without the incision that they make in Being, language would never get "under way."

Nevertheless, it would be a mistake to take the response (of thinking) to the saying as the "essence" (*Wesen*) of language. Even though language cannot be otherwise than through its speakers, human beings are not the agency behind language. Since language is called forth by Being, with the presencing of beings regarded as its first saying, the most essential (*wesentlich*) in language is the unfolding of the link in the tripartite structuring of language—the interval, the way that language has always already made into words. The "way" has to be understood here in the active, verbal sense of the way-making of language, which does not refer simply to the fact that the saying has to reach the sounded word. Instead, as Heidegger remarks in *Introduction to Metaphysics*, the saying happens only to the extent that it has always already been apprehended (*IM*, 140–141). The most important aspect of this relating, however, is that the saying and the apprehending are not "coupled" once and for good. This belonging-together, in order to be a genuine passage from the saying to the apprehending, has to happen "anew" every moment. In other words, *der Weg* indicates not a way that is simply opened but rather a way-making that continuously opens itself as the path(s) of language.

As soon as we realize that this apprehension, or, as Heidegger later calls it, the (cor)responding (*Entsprechung*) to the saying, is never simple but instead enacts the difference between poetry and thinking, the statement about *Dichtung* from "The Origin of the Work of Art" becomes fraught with decisive implications for Heidegger's entire thought. For it becomes evident that what allows Heidegger to articulate the specificity of the phenomenal saying and its self-veiling way into words, into the human language, is expressly the idea of the withdrawal of *Dichten-Denken* from poetry and thought. As John Llewelyn explains, Heidegger's use of *Sagen* to describe the proto-linguistic nature of manifestation, the showing saying in Heidegger's idiom, derives from his elaboration of the proximity of thinking to poetry: "*Sagan* (or *Sagen* in this sense) is the common root of *Dichten* and *Denken*, the previously mentioned *dictare*."[15] It is precisely in the intersection of the phrases *Denken heisst Dichten* and *Dichten heisst Denken* that the conception of a phenomenal proto-language has its ancestry. For, considered in the context of the neighborhood of poetry and thinking, the way-making of language as the positioning or interlacing of beings in the nexus of relations is what we have called here *Dichten-Denken*. Although one could perhaps claim that language as such should be thought more broadly, in most of Heidegger's writings *Dichten-Denken* implicitly becomes the *Wesen* of language, and the other modes of "saying Being," for example, statesmanship, drop out of the picture.[16] *Denken* and *Dichten* function thus as the primal differends of language, which clear the space for different modes of actual saying—poetry and thinking. The interval of language, even though at this point it is only on the verge of coming through human beings into words, is already marked by a rift, which prepares the way for the two distinct modes of discourse.

To return to our initial question, the view of language as the way of language (the saying) into words from *On the Way to Language* can be seen as Heidegger's rearticulation and broadening of the idea of the twofold nature of poetry and thought. Enacting this rifted proximity in his texts on language, Heidegger eventually reinscribes this entire problematic into the question of how to think the re-traiting and dislocating bind between thinking and Being. To the extent, then, that Heidegger consistently makes his project pivot on this relation, we have to understand language, and, consequently, its troping of otherness, expressly within this tear or fold of thinking. Can, however, what Heidegger more often than not refers to as the "same" (*das Selbe*) of thinking and Being be figured as the play of difference, or, inversely, has that play already and always been inflected by thought's nearness to the event of manifestation?

Heidegger's Language: From Difference to the Infold

Although there is plenty of evidence, especially in early Heidegger and his concern for the ontological difference, to support the former reading, an argument in favor of the latter can be made from the intersection of Heidegger's rewriting of Heraclitus and Parmenides. Bringing together Heidegger's reading of the Heraclitean *logos* and the Parmenidean proximity between *noein* and *einai* will illustrate the manner in which Heidegger's version of this closeness deflects and dislocates its own attempts to read itself as difference. It will show that this repeated engagement with the Pre-Socratics and, in particular, with their explanations of thought's position with respect to *phusis*, variously understood as *logos* by Heraclitus and as *einai* by Parmenides, prepares the way for the most precise articulation of the problematic of difference in Heidegger's late writings on poetry, as well as in *On the Way to Language* and "Time and Being." To that extent, there is a very close link not only between Heidegger's reading of *homologein* in Heraclitus and the Parmenidean *noein* but, most important, between the recasting of the Greek thought, and thus the tradition of Western philosophy, in pre-Socratic terms and the conception of language from "The Nature of Language" and "The Way of Language." In other words, Heidegger's attempt to redefine the nature of thinking in his texts on the Pre-Socratics works together with his encounter with the poets and its resulting conception of language. Both reading tracks produce, at their intersection, a revision of the way in which thought's relations to otherness has been conceived.

We need to turn our attention first to the implicit stakes of Heidegger's "recommencement" of thinking in the vicinity of the Pre-Socratics, of what he calls "an other beginning" (*der andere Anfang*),[17] unrepeatable and displaced beyond any sense of recuperation afforded by the notions of origin, cause, ground, memory, consciousness, or interiorization. More specifically, this course involves reading *legein* in proximity to *noein* in order to open a new perspective on Heidegger's definition of *sprechen*, of the "speaking" of language, in *On the Way to Language*.

In "Logos," Heidegger makes clear that the incision of thinking into Being, called forth by Being itself, and the saying resulting from it are arranged by and according to the *logos*. To avoid collapsing this claim into one more pronouncement of logo- or phono-centrism, *logos* must be thought in conformity with the way Heidegger continuously redefines and retranslates it, keeping it clearly apart from the reading of *logos* that forms the basis of the logocentric tradition.[18] He begins this project already in *Being and Time*, where *logos* no longer designates "reason," "judgment," "definition," "concept," "ground," or "relationship," but "discourse" (*Rede*), which Heidegger understands as the determination of the "essence" of language. This notion of discourse cannot be here misunderstood as empirical discourse, as either speech or writing. Since the *logos* lets something be seen "phenomenally," that is, as it shows itself in itself and from itself, it means therefore "letting-see" (*Sehenlassen*), and as such it is always on the way to "vocal proclamation in words" (*SZ*, 32/*BT*, 57). In German, *stimmliche Verlautbarung* brings in another important connotation: this voicing is also a tuning (*stimmen*).[19] It is in this twofold connotation of *stimmliche* that the *logos* displays its characteristic function in Heidegger's texts: since the human response to the address of language results in the "voicing" of this address into speech and writing, it is the *logos* that regulates, tunes, and "appropriates" the voicing for the address. This understanding of *logos* makes clear why Heidegger associates the saying with showing, why the saying (*Sage*) is always a showing saying. When beings show themselves and let themselves be seen (that is, thought, in the sense of *Denken* and *Dichten*) by human beings, they also "say" themselves: *Sehenlassen* indicates thought's response to the primordial *sagen*. Becoming aware of Being means thinking it as the originary saying, where thought turns into a response, a resaying and voicing of the saying. In "Logos," Heidegger stresses the fact that *logos* refers to both saying and speaking but only when it is understood in the context of the interval of the address taken as the "essencing" of language: "The saying and talking of mortals comes to pass from early on as *legein*, laying."[20]

Heidegger understands *legein* in its originary sense of the overall gathering—the gathering manner in which beings are laid open and let be seen (*sehenlassen*). Defining *legein* as the gathering laying, Heidegger remarks that the most significant moment of this laying is the between of hearing and speaking. He shows that Heraclitus speaks in his fragments not about empirical hearing but hearing in the fundamental sense (*EGT*, 67), where proper hearing means the hearing that goes towards the *logos*, the hearing that happens within *legein* as *legein* itself. It is because the human response, its *Denken* and *Dichtung*, despite its difference from *legein*, or rather despite the fact that it happens against *legein*, occurs still essentially *as legein* that language in its essence can be the self-withdrawing, unwordable, "other" saying of Being: "[p]roper hearing occurs essentially in *legein* as *homologein*" (*EGT*, 66) "*Im 'legein' als dem 'homologein' west das eigentliche Hören*";[21] and "[t]he *original* [emphasis mine] *legein*, laying, unfolds itself early and in a manner ruling everything unconcealed as saying and talking" (*EGT*, 63) ("*Das ursprüngliche 'legein', das Legen, entfaltet sich früh und in einer alles Unverborgene durchwaltenden Weise als das Sagen und Reden*" [*VA*, 212]).

It is, then, in *legein* that the "essence" of language displays its verbality, its characteristic "on-the-way." Moreover, the saying and speaking that Heidegger writes about have to be sharply differentiated from vocalized (or written) language. *Legein* is not only not determined by vocalization and/or the play of signification but instead understood as itself opening the way for signification, vocalization, and writing. This is why *legein* is described through terms such as *gathering* and *laying*, which suggest that *legein* pre-structures (in a verbal sense) the interval of the address and, as the very principle of gathering, lays open the "invisible" mesh (*Geflecht*) of relations (*Bezüge*), differences, oppositions, etc. The word "mesh" is insufficient here and may be used only when one realizes that at stake is the meshing that makes possible relations and differences, the interlacing that "underprints" itself, and thus is neither present nor absent in the empirical manifestations of language. What is particularly important in these quotations is the primordiality with which Heidegger understands *legein*, which points simultaneously to the primordial meaning inherent in poetry and thinking, the *logos* regulating unconcealment as the saying, and the fact that hearing happens *as*, though also *against*, *legein*. One cannot overemphasize the significance of this proximity at work in Heidegger's conception of language, for it is because *Dasein*, the human mode of Being, though as listening speaking it demarcates itself in a radical manner from all other modes of Being, is still in all its singularity a mode of Being that Being can be "said."

To that effect, language, understood as the self-erasing saying of Being, is possible, for Heidegger, precisely because of the fold inscribed in the "sameness" of the differential unfolding of *legein*: *noein*, thinking and poetry, happens in a gathering manner (cor)responding to *legein*. In his reading in *Identity and Difference* of the Parmenidean saying "for thinking and Being are the same," Heidegger explicates the character of this corresponding in terms of belonging, and the title of this text leads one to expect that what transpires between thought and Being, and as such describes the dictate of *Ereignis*, should be explained in differential terms. Yet, when Heidegger reads Parmenides' saying about the nature of the relation between thinking (*noein*) and Being (*einai*) through *Zusammengehörigkeit* (etymologically, "belonging-together"), he implies the need to trace the notion of *Ereignis* back to what still remains hidden in the Parmenidean saying. In the context of how Heidegger's texts register a certain hesitation about the sufficiency of the notion of difference as such, I am inclined to read that which remains covered in the Parmenidean fragment as antedating—or better, in order to avoid the trappings of causality and origin, as inflecting—the unfolding of difference.

According to Heidegger's translation, the maxim reads: "*Das Selbe nämlich ist Vernehmen (Denken) sowohl als auch Sein*" (For the Same are thinking as well as Being).[22] For Heidegger, the pivotal word in this saying is the *same*, the term that names the way in which thinking belongs to Being, and in which thinking, in the sense of primordial *Denken*, and Being belong "to each other" prior to any representational thinking, reflection, consciousness, or knowledge. Heidegger refers to this belonging as *Übereignung*, which Gianni Vattimo aptly translates as "transpropriation."[23] Such transpropriation names the process of nearing of thought and Being, the nearing that constitutes also the opening of language. The "trans-" marks in this case the mutuality of this propriation, in which human beings are already determined by their mode of Being: they always "are," and Being "is," that is, it "is said," only to the extent that human beings respond to it and resay it. Finally, and most important, there is no doubt that this propriation is determined by the "in" indicative of the fact that thinking is always already "immersed" and dwells in Being.

It is perhaps this immersion in the phenomenality of *Ereignis*, the "in" or "to" of thought's proximity to what the Pre-Socratics rendered as *einai*, that registers that which remains hidden in the Parmenidean maxim. This "between" of *legein* and *noein*, taken here as the "essencing" of language, is obviously not a dialectical movement of the sublation of difference under sameness; but is it, on the other hand, sufficient to say that the hidden, the unsaid, is difference as such, the very occurrence of differing that unfolds (into) differences? In other words, can what transpires in *Ereignis* be measured by difference, and can such an appraisal give its due to the residue of the saying of manifestation, which characterizes language for Heidegger? Or does this residue mark, perhaps, a hardly acknowledged inflection of difference?

To trope the possibility of this inflection I will read the "relation" between *legein* and *noein* as an "infolding." In other words, *noein* will be seen here as the apprehending thinking, which infolds into *legein* in such a way that, happening still according to *legein*, it can respond and resay *legein*. On this reading, language, in its very "essence," is an infold, an opening that happens as infolding. Heidegger needs to articulate this moment as an infold in order to show how language almost "touches" Being, since the infold describes the way human presencing infolds into presencing qua presencing, into Being. Reading here Heidegger's various figures for the proximity of Being and thought as the infold allows us to see how this event makes room, an abode or a dwelling, for human beings to think the nexus of references between beings, its linguistic interlace (*Geflecht*)—the world.

This rather lengthy and detailed explanation of the positioning of *noein* against *legein* allows us to forestall charges of Heidegger's complicity with logocentrism, prompted by his reference to *logos* as regulating the unfolding of language. Though in Heidegger's reading of Heraclitus *logos* indeed "arranges" language so that it can produce meaning, its regulative propensity does not have a unitary structure but instead occurs as an infold. It not only does not guarantee unity but, conversely, and to the extent that *logos* gathers and holds in a relation, it makes all differences, relations, otherness, and their meaning possible. This characteristic, non-logocentric reading of the *logos* prompts us to speak therefore about an inflection of the origin of meaning imprinting itself on

Heidegger's work. When in *Being and Time* Heidegger defines *logos* as discourse—"[d]iscourse is the Articulation of intelligibility" (*SZ*, 161/*BT*, 203–204)—he indicates that *legein* is precisely the way Being comes to mean *as* Being, that is, as its withdrawal from words and signification, as the dissignification of its never proper sense. This formula suggests, then, that it is in the infold of *legein* (as the apprehending gathering of thinking) into *legein* (as the overall gathering and positioning of beings) that Being *means*. Since in the same section of *Being and Time* Heidegger declares that meaning is articulated primordially in *Rede*, the occurring of presencing is also the primordiality of meaning: to mean in the fundamental way is "to be," that is, to be let into and positioned in the nexus of *Bezüge*. As Jean-Luc Marion observes in "L'étant et le phénomène," when Heidegger discusses the "meaning of Being" (*der Sinn des Seins*), it is not simply the meaning of the word "Being" that is at stake. Instead, the double genitive marks the "essence" of language—*der Sinn des Seins* describes "Being as meaning, meaning as Being."[24] Hence Being can be very cautiously called the interrupted and erased "origin" of meaning, the origin in quotation marks since as such it always conceals itself, for it itself cannot be interpreted "meaningfully."

It has become clear by now that the Heideggerian notion of "origin," *Ur-sprung*, must also be read as a version of the infold, its hyphen inescapably recalling the hyphenation of *dichten* and *denken* and the mark of the fold, its non-internal "in." This approach is evidenced especially in Heidegger's analysis of the manner in which language occurs—of its "speaking." Heidegger's essay "Language" will serve as an example here, illustrating the working of the infold in the way-making of language. In this essay, Heidegger defines his conception of language through the polysemic play of the derivations of the verb *sprechen*—*ansprechen* and *entsprechen*, to claim and to (cor)respond, to answer, to "countersay." In this way, the German word for language, *Sprache*, like *logos*, far from reasserting the old dominion of logocentric speech, describes the field within which all the claims, calls, and responses with which Heidegger describes language, both its writing and its speaking, find their originary place.

What strikes one in this conception is the fact that all the circuits of calling and claiming that Being directs toward *Dasein* are already built of linguistic materials. If Being can claim thought's attentiveness (*Achtsamkeit*), it is because its claim occurs in a linguistic fashion; it comes to pass as *ansprechen*, a "speaking" that by nature of being a saying, a language, finds itself in proximity to thought and its language. To put it differently, the language of Being, the manner in which Being shows itself, happens (*er-eignen*) in such a way that it (ap)propriates (*an-eignen*) human beings for language. "Appropriation" here does not mean an erasure of difference and an impending univocity of speaking but rather delineates an extreme proximity in which difference as such becomes discernible. As the mark of this proximity, *an-eignen*, sounding the *an* of *Anspruch*, indicates that the initial human attitude is that of listening: "Mortals speak insofar as they listen. . . . Their listening draws from the command of the dif-ference what it brings out as sounding word. This speaking that listens and accepts is responding (*Entsprechung*)" (*PLT,* 209). This response belongs and listens (*gehören*) to dif-ference, already rewritten and hyphenated by Heidegger, the *Unter-Schied*, which evades not only the Greco-Latin cognates in which the English and French translations slip but also displaces the old writing of difference, its insufficient articulation as the anti-, the opposition, the limit, the (same's) other, etc. Notwithstanding the references to Derrida's reading of Heidegger, I am less interested in tracing here perhaps an antecedent to Derrida's *différance* or in measuring the change in stakes and procedures between the Heideggerian hyphen and the Derridean silent rewriting of *e* into *a* than in discerning how and by what procedures the call of dif-ference can matter at all, how it can have any meaning and thus produce meaning itself, how, in other words, it can be heard and brought into words.

Heidegger makes clear that the thought's response draws from difference, that whatever it can bring into words comes from the spatio-temporal play of dif-ference. However, the very drawing from difference, the writing or sounding into words, occurs because of the nature of the response, of the *Ent-sprechung*. To the extent that this word encodes the Heideggerian "hermeneutics" of otherness, not as interpretation but rather as letting-be, a listening response escaping the polarity of the passive and the active into the modality of the middle voice, it also indicates an inflection of difference. Even though Heidegger's text puts the stress expressly on the play of difference, elaborating on its work in the scission between world and things, what allows for such distribution of emphases and, at the same time, inclines, tilts, or inflects them is the infold of thought into Being—*Dasein*'s listening response figured here as the *Entsprechung*.

The modality of this inflection is barely discernible as the play of the prefix *ent-*, its oscillation between the meaning of "un," on the one hand, and "opposite," "toward," "in the face of," on the other. *Ent-* indicates that the attentive response of thinking, which takes the form of language, unfolds out of the speaking or, better, of the saying, of language as such, in other words, from the saying of the differential event of manifestation. Such unfolding, however, folds in a way that gathers itself toward that from which it has been unfolding, and does so in a manner of a response, a resaying or after-saying (Heidegger employs in this context the verb *nachsagen*). This linguistic response can bring words only to the extent that it already infolds into the claim of the saying. This infolding of *entsprechen* into *ansprechen* outlines the way that language has already traversed, in the manner of an *Ur-sprung*, into words. From the correlation of the words that Heidegger uses to define language, it becomes clear that humans belong to language (*gehören*) in a way that makes this belonging equivalent to hearing (*hören*) the saying that addresses itself to them and claims their attention. The inscription of hearing into the human response, which belongs to language by virtue of its function as an after-saying, cannot be treated in terms of an inside-outside opposition, for it itself makes this paradigm possible. To put it briefly, *ge-hören*, another way in which the infold underwrites Heidegger's thought, defines the way something can belong (inside) or not belong (outside). To that extent, the folding analyzed here retraces and redresses Heidegger's earlier description of the bearing of *noein* toward the *legein* of the *logos*.

In this perspective, Heidegger's most controversial and best known formula for language: "*Das Wesen der Sprache: Die Sprache des Wesems*" (The being of language: the language of being), provides another instance of the infold's operation in his work.[25] Here the inflection, which deregularizes and deflects Heidegger's writing on difference, marks itself in the reversal of positions between *Sprache* and *Wesen* "prescribed" by the colon. The colon erases and displaces the word *is* and thus the metaphysical connotations lingering in the term *Being*. Heidegger's work intimates, then, that what lets language onto its way to words can be "sensed," though only according to a semiosis discrete from the play of signification, as an inflection, an incline, never positively or negatively registered by the laws regulating the production of meaning.

Even if the infold does not displace the center of gravity of the Heideggerian text from the hyphen opening dif-ference, it nevertheless inflects its mechanics, the way in which difference produces meaning. This inflection, the bearing that it has on the differential operations themselves, can be perhaps explained in terms of giving sense and discernibility. In other words, what I am suggesting is that in Heidegger's thought what allows for the fact that there is differ-ence, and that as such it becomes discernible as difference and thus matters for thinking, is the infold. This is why any reading of differ-ence in Heidegger should take into account the effects of this inflec-tion of language, which reflects its proximity to the phenomenal, to the event of manifestation, regarded by Heidegger as the wordless saying of language. All the more so because this inflection is also at work in Heidegger's most celebrated piece on the question of difference, "Identity and Difference." For what in fact underlies this complex discussion of the suitability of two key philosophemes—difference and identity—for describing the singularity of the belonging-together (*Zusammengehörigkeit*) of thought and Being indicated in the Parmenidean maxim is Heidegger's implicit restate-ment of the infold: "*Der Mensch 'ist' eigentlich dieser Bezug der Entsprechung*" (*ID*, 94). Difference and its differend, identity, appear therefore to be underwritten, prescribed, by the undescribable and unwordable closeness of thinking to the phenomenal. The fact that difference has been inflected does not necessarily indicate an alter-ation in its mode of operation and signifying functions. Rather the work of difference, in the active sense of opening the time-space between what differs, the opening marked by the hyphen in *Unter-Schied*, must be seen as always carrying with it an additional sense, the sense of the already accomplished or given proximity of thought to the phenomenal, which, not explainable within the perimeter traced and regulated by difference, infolds each produc-tion of difference and thus reproduces itself as its inflection.

To see the radicality of this inflection of meaning in Heideg-ger, the infold as a semi-structure has to be strictly demarcated from circularity and bipolarity. Though Heidegger himself often refers to his enterprise as a hermeneutical circle, it is in fact regu-lated by the infold, a figure less prone to misinterpretations of vicious circularity or logical tautology. To put it differently, what Heidegger describes at first, still within the analytic of *Dasein*, as the pre-ontological (*vorontologisch*) understanding of Being, and later as the resaying or after-saying of the saying of language, is not a circle but an infold. Furthermore, the infold also marks the moment when the Heideggerian text evinces a certain resistance to difference and thus begins to evade its own rhetoric. In other words, the thought of difference, in spite of its regulatory function in many of Heidegger's texts, appears to lose its applicability to this particular inflection, an inflection that marks the route by which Heidegger's philosophy moves beyond the initial problematic of the ontological difference.

The infold, then, reveals a peculiar twist of the Heideggerian inquiry, which, in order to recover the opening of language, begins to unfold a novel mode of thought—"poetic" thinking. Characteristically, this modality relies constantly in its refigurations or inflections of otherness on the proximity, the neighborhood with poetry. This familiarity is evidenced most often by Heidegger's "poetic" treatment of language, where his insights are disclosed not so much by the mode of presentation itself or its argumentative rigor but instead by the exactitude of his verbal exploits and their accomplishments. I have in mind here especially the ingenious folds that Heidegger induces between *Sprache, sprechen, ansprechen, zusprechen,* and *entsprechen,* or *sagen, entsagen,* and *nachsagen,* in order to circumvent, or at least inflect, the masterhold of the economy of difference. Those are not only turns *of* language but also *about* language, as all the words quoted above expressly describe the event of *Sprache.* What communicates itself in those "language acts"—the inflection of difference—comes into relief in the "poetic" interchange between words, which, almost erasing their boundaries, maintains them folded into one another. It is perhaps in this aspect of Heidegger's writing that the encounter with the poets continues to exercise its influence beyond the texts expressly devoted to poetry, reminding us constantly of the role that the poetic, *Dichtung,* claims in inflecting the initial parameters of the Heideggerian enterprise and moving it perhaps beyond the question (of [ontological] difference).

ᘓ 2 ᕬ

REFIGURING OTHERNESS
A Heideggerian Bypass of Ethics?

For many years the guiding question in the Heideggerian studies has been the problem of the ontico-ontological difference and its corollaries: the question of overcoming metaphysics, the reappraisal of difference and, contingent upon it, the critique of presence. This perspective, while it has gained momentum in continental thought and played a crucial role in energizing the deconstructive or, more broadly, poststructuralist debates, has also often deemphasized to some extent the thought of late Heidegger, its intimate engagement with poetry and poetic language, as well as its effect on the continuing reevaluation of the problematic of difference and its metaphysical provenance. Though many of Heidegger's texts are obviously organized around the question of Being and the ontological difference, his later writings increasingly modify and inflect the initial parameters (the famous rewriting of *Sein* as *Seyn*, crossing it out, and, eventually, inscribing it in *Ereignis* and in the structure of *Es gibt*) or straightforwardly abdicate them. This shift should not really come as a great surprise, since the very formulation of the problematic of the ontological difference already carries with it the potential for its own displacement. To put it briefly, the way Heidegger characterizes the ontological difference implies that, because of its "abysmal" nature (in the sense of *Abgrund*), it in fact functions as an "undifference" or "non-difference," which not only simply resists difference but also inaugurates its possibility. Later displacements within Heidegger's thought, from the analytic of *Dasein*, through the ontological difference, the history or place of Being, to, finally, poetic thinking, *Ereignis*, nearness, and giving, continue and amplify these initial implications.

Even if for many years Heidegger indeed thinks the disclosive event of appropriation (*Ereignis*) side by side with the ontological difference, the undercurrent of his texts that inflects the differential problematic through the prism of the infold eventually brings about not only an already implicit modification but in fact nothing short of the departure or abandonment of the original concerns. It is in the perspective of this shift in Heidegger's thought that one can begin to appreciate the significance of the infold and also to describe and elaborate the singularity of its inflection. Such a possibility signals itself in "Time and Being," where the reversal of the problematic of *Being and Time* implied in the title brings with it an explicit reconfiguration of the relation between *Ereignis* and the ontico-ontological difference:

> We want to say something about the attempt to think Being without regard to its being grounded in terms of beings. The attempt to think Being without beings becomes necessary because otherwise, it seems to me, there is no longer any possibility of explicitly bringing into view the Being of what *is* today all over the globe, let alone of adequately determining the relation of man to what has been called "Being" up to now.[1]

This is certainly one of the most important passages in Heidegger's oeuvre, one that forcefully announces the revision of his project, and yet one that has not been given enough emphasis by Heidegger's interpreters. The passage quite evidently attempts to reconceive the very beginning of Heidegger's thinking, the question of the undifference between *Seiende* and *Sein*, which opens the enterprise of *Being and Time*. I see this reconceptualization as Heidegger's most explicit and open admission of the changed status of the ontological difference, the status already implicitly questioned with the appearance of *Ereignis* in *Beiträge zur Philosophie* and further inflected by the traces of Heidegger's departure from the thought of difference in the Hölderlin essays and especially in the texts from *Poetry, Language, Thought* and *On the Way to Language*.

This acknowledgment of change is marked by the emphatic tone of the passage and, in particular, by the repeated *without*, the adjective *necessary*, and the decisive phrase *no longer any possibility*. It is the repeated *without* that carries most weight, indicating the need for a revision of Heidegger's enterprise, an amendment amounting to thinking Being no longer in the perspective of the ontological difference but rather without it, that is, without beings: *Sein ohne das Seiende zu denken*. This recognition brings into focus the already remarked tensions that arise in some of Heidegger's texts when it comes to thinking difference. They underscore the fact that, even though the purpose of the ontological difference is to think beyond *Seiendheit*, in other words beyond the Being of a being, the dividing line between Being and beings, even if no longer conceived in terms of traditional difference, still contains a necessary reference to beings. Heidegger concedes here that his care in stressing that Being occurs as not-a-being, and also in describing it—as is the case, for instance, in "What Is Metaphysics?"—in terms of Nothing (*Nicht*) and Nihilation (*Nichten*), is not enough. The ontological difference, in spite of its insistence on thinking Being apart from beings, inevitably intertwines it with beings and continuously involves Heidegger's thought in metaphysics, as Derrida has repeatedly pointed out.[2] The assessment of the implications of Heidegger's distanciation from and rewriting of the question is, therefore, of paramount importance not only for understanding the historical development of his thought but especially for elucidating his engagement with the notions of difference and otherness. It would obviously be a mistake to take the statement about the necessity of thinking Being without beings as a call to forgetting beings, entities, or others. Questioning the unstable demarcation between Being and beings does not amount to a neglect of beings but instead aims at revising and remedying the difficulties in relating to otherness inherent in the concept of difference. In other words, the articulation of the fault between Being and beings is too precarious, too fraught with the danger of assimilation, to allow for thinking as letting be, as *Gelassenheit*. In order to let the otherness of other beings be, it is necessary to approach the question of Being otherwise, not through difference but by disengaging the problematic of language and *Ereignis* from beings and the ontological difference. Only then can "what has been called 'Being'" be at all addressed, and, furthermore, only in this perspective can the otherness of other beings be acknowledged. When Heidegger proposes, then, to dislocate the ontological difference, it is not to neglect beings but rather to allow for engaging them "thinkingly" in the perspective of "Being without beings." In effect, this move amounts to acknowledging that in order to think beings we have to engage Being as *Ereignis* and *giving*, without beings and their difference, and thus possibly revises the very parameters for thinking. Such displacement of beings, therefore, does not move them aside but in fact opens the possibility of working out a new approach to them, no longer mediated exclusively by the horizon of the ontological difference.

This inflection of the initial priority of the ontico-ontological difference is underscored by Heidegger's disavowal of the task of overcoming metaphysics:

Sein ohne das Seiende denken, heisst: Sein ohne Rücksicht auf die Metaphysik denken. Eine solche Rücksicht herrscht nun aber auch noch in der Absicht, die Metaphysik zu überwinden. Darum gilt es, vom Überwinden abzulassen und die Metaphysik sich selbst zu überlassen (*ZSD*, 25).

To think Being without beings means: to think Being without regard to metaphysics. Yet a regard for metaphysics still prevails even in the intention to overcome metaphysics. Therefore, our task is to cease all overcoming, and leave metaphysics to itself (*TB*, 24).

In order to think Being, it becomes indispensable not to overcome metaphysics but to abandon it. For leaving aside metaphysics and thus the ontological difference is the only way in which thought can approach what used to be called "Being." In other words, Heidegger sees his work as no longer proceeding to overcome metaphysics through the thinking of ontological difference and thus difference/differing as such but, characteristically for him, as striking off on a new path that abandons the metaphysical horizon and its "destruction." To that extent, "Time and Being" gathers the insights of Heidegger's texts on poetry and language and radicalizes his enterprise not by advancing or deepening it but rather by inflecting it.

Aside from Metaphysics: Heidegger on Nearness

Heidegger's late, poetic, thought ends, then, with a radical opening, which charts a possibility of thinking otherness otherwise—non-metaphysically and perhaps even non-differentially. This final "disclosure" can be read as a proposition of another "hermeneutics" of otherness, which outlines its concerns and develops its terminology not from the ontological difference but rather from *Ereignis*. The clues that would facilitate the understanding of this late reconfiguration of otherness are interspersed throughout Heidegger's work, but, as is implicit in "Time and Being," they can be gathered under the heading of "nearness" (*Nähe*). Emil Kettering has claimed as much in his book *Nähe: Das Denken Martin Heideggers*, maintaining that the thought of nearness, though not always couched in these terms, underlies and spans Heidegger's thought from *Being and Time* to "Time and Being."[3] Following the general drift of Kettering's argument, I propose to look at the problematic of nearness as Heidegger's attempt to figure otherness in the wake of metaphysics, that is, to attend to it otherwise than through difference. In this context, to attend to otherwise than through difference does not mean to erase the other's difference but, on the contrary, to underscore the radicality of this otherness and let it be. Since thought, as it operates according to difference, is always in danger of thematizing the other and thus turning it, to use Levinas's terms, into the other of the same, then Heidegger's move can be read as a proposition of "thinking otherwise."

It is in this perspective that one would have to explore the stakes and ramifications of Heidegger's *das andere Denken*, that is, to approach it as a thinking of nearness rather than difference. In other words, it would be seen not as a thinking advancing positive statements or making cognitive claims but rather as a thinking of inflections, dislocating and simultaneously withdrawing itself from the paradigms of thought. The effects of such inflections would pertain specifically to the modes of conceiving otherness, evidencing Heidegger's continued dissatisfaction with the way language "(mis)handles" the other. They mark Heidegger's repeated return, through the critique of technology and the *Gestell*-structuring, to a possibility of an other "logic," an other reading of *logos*, that would issue in the thinking *from Ereignis* and its linguistic character. As Heidegger's continuing preoccupation with the concerns from *Being and Time* demonstrates, this reconfiguration of otherness in terms of nearness requires a rethinking of our ideas about not only "what has been called 'Being'" but also history, time, space, and, most of all, language. The brief analysis offered here will demonstrate that Heidegger eventually comes to write about the notions organizing his thought in terms of proximity or nearness, developed from his repeated consideration of the closeness of poetry and thinking to the saying of manifestation, that is, of what I have called here the infold.

The abandoning of metaphysics and the inscription of both Being and time into *Ereignis* suggests that Heidegger no longer ascribes priority to Being but rather approaches it as one of the dual givens of the disclosive (ap)propriation, the other being time. Attempting in "Time and Being" to approach this relation in a "postmetaphysical" manner, Heidegger underscores precisely this twofoldness of *Ereignis*, its unfolding and giving of both time and Being: *es gibt Sein*, there is Being, or literally, it gives Being, and *es gibt Zeit*, there is (it gives) time. The fact that Heidegger describes *Ereignis* as a "structuring" of *es gibt*—there is/it gives—shows clearly the impossibility of finding or writing the one, the correct, word that could name "what has been called 'Being' up to now" and locates Heidegger's thought instead in the relation, the proximity of time and Being. The text does not use, as is the case with the term *Being*, one word but a structure, which with its "impersonality" and empty subject implies the refusal of naming. As in the grammatical structure "there is," what "means" is what comes after the verb, and the "there" (*es*) effaces itself and disappears behind the meaning, the word, the writing.

It seems that, with the structure of *es gibt*, Heidegger renders the particularity of the infold, which, breaking open and disseminating meaning, not only conceals itself in this opening but also inflects whatever comes to be in it. In other words, while the empty subject of "there is" effectively conceals itself, what remains and signifies are its given (*Gabe*): Being and time. Their "meaning," however, bears with it the inflection, the mark of the "ontological" nearness between the human (poetry and thinking) and the event of manifestation with its proto-linguistic saying. In other words, they make sense (become meaningful) and can in turn be articulated and thought in and because of this proximity. The nature of this proximity also prescribes the character of the relation between time and Being and disposes it in the manner of nearness. In order to underscore the regulatory influence of nearness, Heidegger explicitly ties the rethinking of the "giving" of time and Being to an articulation of the historical, especially to the manner in which *Ereignis* disposes and sends (into) history, implicit in the word *Schicken*: "A giving which gives only its gift, but in the giving holds itself back and withdraws, such a giving we call sending" (*TB*, 8).[4] It is as *Schicken*, as sending and disposing, that the history of Being unfolds. Heidegger expressly affirms that the history of Being (*die Geschichte des Seins*) cannot be understood to be a mere occurrence, happening, or presencing as implied in the word *Geschehen* but that it has to be instead approached from history (*Geschichte*) understood as unfolding in the manner of *Schicken* (*ZSD*, 9/*TB*, 9).

What is important about this Heideggerian emphasis is that it draws our attention precisely to the way in which the historial occurrence of time and Being is disposed and regulated by nearness rather than difference. This is why Beda Alleman is correct to remark in *Hölderlin und Heidegger* that it is the phrase *die Geschichte des Seins* that encodes the complexity of Heidegger's thinking of Being, the complexity not exhausted by treating Being as presencing.[5] This phrase, functioning in a manner parallel to Heidegger's earlier locution *der Sinn des Seins*, indicates that although Being can be interpreted narrowly as presencing, the way in which it is "sent" or disposed into history (*geschickt*) has to be thought beyond the determination of presence or absence. To that effect, Heidegger is always careful to remark that Being is given in such a way that it is in fact withdrawn and kept back (*einbehalten*) (*ZSD*, 6/*TB*, 6) and that the nature of this withdrawal, the refusal to come into the open and instead remain only as the opening, circumscribes the giving that characterizes *Ereignis*. Even though "Time and Being" states that "There is, It gives Being as the unconcealing of presencing" (*ZSD*, 6/*TB*, 6), Being cannot be simply described through *Anwesen* since presencing immediately implies absenting (*Abwesen*). One should not then mistake Being for presence or presencing, since Heidegger expressly treats it here as the setting of the stage for the interplay between presence and absence. As has already been pointed out,[6] Heidegger's discussion of *Sage* makes clear that the word-event of manifestation "says" beyond the opposition of presence and absence: "*Sie befreit Anwesendes in sein jeweiliges Anwesen, entfreit Abwesendes in sein jeweiliges Abwesen*" (*UZS*, 257)/"It liberates what presences into its specific presencing, de-liberates what absences into its specific absenting" (*OWL*, 126, trans. modified). *Ereignis*, then, demonstrates that "what has been called 'Being'" is thought by Heidegger beyond the difference of presence and absence. Most important for our discussion here, this non-metaphysical thinking of "Being" is both implicated and made possible by the notion of nearness. To put it differently, the non-metaphysical "face" of what Heidegger used to call "Being" can be recognized only through the inflecting effect of the infold, that is, in the nearness of thought to the saying, in the character of (human) language as *Entsprechung*.

One has to agree, therefore, with Alleman's comment that the most radical temporality of Being conceals itself precisely in the phrase *die Geschichte des Seins*: "*Im Titel 'Geschichte des Seins' verbirgt sich vielmehr die radikalste Temporalität des Seins selbst.*"[7] More important, however, this radical temporality and tied to it, the non-metaphysical thought of "Being" make sense only in light of Heidegger's questioning of difference and its eventual inflection through the problematic of nearness. As much lies implicit in the care with which "Time and Being" ties the historical disposition (*Schicken*) of *Ereignis* to the notions of reaching and nearing. The effect is that time in "Time and Being" cannot be approached within the perimeter of temporality understood as present, past, and future; rather, it must be seen precisely as *Reichen*, that is, as both reaching and giving. *Reichen* describes the radical temporality beyond the division into present, past, and future, and therefore time understood as reaching must be discerned from the three-dimensional time that makes it possible for presence and absence to be "reached" (*gereicht*) (*ZSD*, 14/*TB*, 13). It is the reaching nature of time that gives (here the double meaning of *reichen* is continuously at play) presence or absence into time understood as present, past, and future. Only in the context of this originary reaching and giving does time disclose its four-dimensional character: "*Die eigentliche Zeit ist vierdimensional*" ("True time is four-dimensional") (*ZSD*, 16/*TB*, 15). The rendering of *eigentlich* as "true" in English obscures the fact that the German *eigen* makes clear that Heidegger not only does not mean here something like the "authentic" time but instead refers to time as unfolded specifically from *Ereignis*, that is, from the polysemy of *eigen* and *eignen*.

Foregrounding Heidegger's discussion of time serves here the purpose of establishing that the displacement of the ontico-ontological difference suggested by the "priority" given to time in the essay's title and underscored by the early remarks about leaving metaphysics to itself takes place indubitably with a view to inaugurating the thinking of nearness. In other words, when Heidegger characterizes *Reichen* as *die nähernde Nähe* and *Nachheit*—the nearing nearness and nearhood (*ZSD*, 16/*TB*, 15)—he is not only proposing a revision of the understanding of time and its relation to space[8] but, in fact, recasting the enterprise of thinking apart from metaphysics into the terms of nearness, nearing, and proximity. The tensions and difficulties underlying such a transition mark Heidegger's own language in "Time and Being," culminating in three virtually untranslatable sentences: "*[Ereignis] ereignet Sein und Zeit*" (20) (*Ereignis* "appropriates, disposes, unfolds Being and time into their own" [19, modified]); "*Zeit und Sein ereignet im Ereignis*" (23) ("Time and Being appropriated in Appropriation" [22]); and "*Das Ereignis ereignet*" (24) ("Appropriation appropriates" [24]). Far from being just a language play, the proximity between the noun *Ereignis* and the verb *ereignen*, which each of the sentences underscores, reflects the strain put on Heidegger's idiom by the inflection of difference. This polysemic proximity in fact questions and destabilizes the grammatical and syntactical categorizations into nouns and verbs or subjects and predicates, effectively inflecting, if not exactly escaping, the differential economy of signification. To that extent, it also discloses *Ereignis* as an empty subject, too close to what it gives to be determined as different from it. Heidegger's deliberate erasure of difference and impending, though never as such possible, conflation of *Ereignis* and *ereignen* enacts, then, as far as this is possible in the Heideggerian text, the "logic" of nearness. In other words, it is no longer a matter of the self-erasing difference between Being and beings but rather of the resistance to difference of the fold between *Ereignis* and *ereignet*. What Heidegger is after, the nearing that underwrites his texts on poetry and language, is discernible and should be thought neither as *Ereignis* nor as *ereignen* but instead as this fold, the fold which unfolds difference. This fold is at the same time also a language fault (*"Das Wesen der Sprache: Die Sprache des Wesems"*) and a fault of language, which has no other recourse but to write this nearing as difference. These convolutions of Heidegger's language make clear, then, that the disposing (*schicklich*) and historial (*geschichtlich*) character of *Ereignis* and its unfoldment into language produces itself according to the infold: the nearness of thinking, itself a mode of *ereignen*, to the event of disclosive (ap)propriation.

The way Heidegger folds words into one another intimates the absence of any discernible "logical" hierarchy in the disclosive (ap)propriation between *Ereignis* itself, time, Being, and thinking. *"Das Ereignis ereignet"* in such a way that Being unfolds itself as sending (*Schicken*) and time as reaching (*Reichen*), with the two movements occurring in a parallel fashion, in the sense that reaching points beyond the paradigm of present/past/future while sending/disposing operates beyond the opposition of presence and absence. In other words, the event of disclosive appropriation unfolds (in) nearness; its constitutive elements are arranged in a relation that transpires as nearing, as coming too close for difference yet short of identification, unity, oneness. In this context, nearness functions somewhat like the condition of reaching difference. It indicates that "turn," understood apart from any change, through which giving reaches and holds itself back, so that when giving has always already reached, there is only what has been reached, with giving itself concealed, withdrawn, erased. In a way, nearness describes the tension, the stringing which, due to the proximity it arranges, maintains difference. It is therefore a tension reminiscent of the Heraclitean figure of *hen panta*, a tautness which holds and lays out difference. Heidegger's late texts intimate that this is perhaps as close as thought can get to understanding its own proximity to what it thinks, a nearness traced in the "failed" figure of Being.

In the same vein, Heidegger's thought can be seen as diagnosing the ontologico-linguistic mechanism according to which nearness has to, and yet cannot, be rendered as and by difference. In other words, the differential structuring of thought and language conceives of nearness as a difference between the human and the event of disclosive (ap)propriation. To the extent that language operates according to difference, it always transcribes the proximity of thinking to Being as another difference, even *the* difference, instead of seeing it as what makes difference possible, and thus envelops and inflects its course. This is why the radicalization of thinking that Heidegger proposes in the work on language and *Ereignis* effectively attempts to distance him from the ontological difference and from difference as such. In the wake of this thought, even if one can approach present/past/future and presence/absence in terms of difference, it no longer seems appropriate to describe *Ereignis* this way. For what characterizes the event of (ap)propriation is not difference but nearness, which explains why the moment in which giving reaches what it gives and veils itself is not described by Heidegger through difference. In other words, the moment when giving gives (reaches) its gift transpires as the nearness of giving and its gift, making the relation between giving (*Geben*) and the gift (*Gabe*) it reaches non-thinkable in terms of difference. This is why, in his analysis of "Time and Being," Jean-Luc Marion can disengage *Ereignis* from difference and approach the structure of "there is" in terms of a new dimension,[9] a dimension one could risk saying is both "near" difference and yet not exactly different from it.

My contention is that it is precisely this dimension of nearing that Heidegger repeatedly tries to describe through various terms, beginning with the meaning of Being in *Being and Time* and continuing through the history or place (*Ort* or *Ortschaft*) of Being into *Ereignis* and the way of language. This gesture is perhaps most pronounced in Heidegger's essays on language and poetry, which consistently describe the occurrence of the fourfold and the way of language in terms of nearness. Probably the most well-known passage about the nature of nearness in the context of language comes toward the end of "The Nature of Language," as an attempt to assemble into a figure the constitutive elements of the exchange called by Heidegger the neighborhood of poetry and thinking: "Saying, as the way-making movement of the world's fourfold, gathers all things up into the nearness of face-to-face encounter, and does so soundlessly, as quietly as time times, space spaces, as quietly as the play of time-space is enacted" (*OWL*, 108). What "The Nature of Language" establishes through the notion of nearness is a correlation, a link, or, in Heidegger's idiom, the "same" of the unfolding of the world, its fourfold, and the translative way of the saying of manifestation into words. For at the same time that the essay expressly defines nearness as "the movement paving the way for the face-to-face of the regions of the world's fourfold (*"die*

Be-wëgung des Gegen-einander-über der Gegenden des Weltgeviertes")
(*OWL*, 105/*UZS*, 211), it also claims the way-making, *die Be-wëgung*,
as the movement of language into words, which constitutes the
very "essence," the way, of language. In the end, it becomes possible for Heidegger to maintain that nearness as *Be-wëgung* rests in
the saying (*OWL*, 108/*UZS*, 215) or, even more strongly, that nearness and the saying are the same (*"Nähe und die Sage als das
Wesende der Sprache das Selbe sind"*/"nearness and Saying as the
essencing of language are the Same" [*UZS*, 214/*OWL*, 107, translation modified]).

What completes this brief picture of the function of nearness
in Heidegger's conception of language is the emphasis his texts
place on the proximity between the saying and *Ereignis*, proximity
that demands that the saying be determined from *Ereignis*: "Showing as appropriating thus transpires and Appropriation is the way-
making for Saying to come into language" (*"Also das Zeigen als das
Eignen ereignend, ist das Ereignis die Be-wëgung der Sage zur Sprache"*)
(*OWL*, 130/*UZS*, 261). From here there is only one step to saying
that *"der Weg ist ereignend."* Here the English translation, "the way
is appropriating" (*OWL*, 129), necessarily loses the polysemous
character of the German *ereignend*. The German text clearly indicates that the way to language is not simply appropriating, that is,
that the human manner of saying becomes appropriate for the saying of Being, but that the "essence" of language happens as
ereignen, and therefore has the same characteristics as the structure
of *es gibt*, which gives time and Being.

One could multiply here similar examples from any and all of
Heidegger's texts on language and poetry, but it will suffice to note
the dependency of Heidegger's notion of language on the infold of
the (human) after-saying into the saying, that is, on a nearness
that articulates how the linguistic character of manifestation, the
"world-moving Saying" (*OWL*, 107), enables the way of language
into words. As "The Way to Language" makes clear, the way of language transpires because saying is the most proper, most own, way
of *ereignen*: "As Showing, Saying, which consists in Appropriation,
is the most proper mode of Appropriating. Appropriation is by way
of saying [rather: Appropriation, *Ereignis* is sayingly]"/"*Die im Ereignis beruhende Sage ist als das Zeigen die eigenste Weise des Ereignens.
Das Ereignis ist sagend"* (*OWL*, 131/*UZS*, 262–263). The correlation
between Saying and Appropriation evidences that the reaching
and giving characteristic of *Ereignis* (*Reichen, Schicken, Geben*) is the
"same" reaching that moves the essence of language toward words,
that marks the infold underlying the Heideggerian conception of

language. Indeed, Heidegger's late thought pivots upon what I have called the infold of thinking into Being (*Ereignis*); and one realizes to what extent this is so only when the infold is seen to occur as nearness, for the nearness that Heidegger discerns between disclosive (ap)propriation and the saying is always motivated by the nearness of thinking to what both gives thinking and gives itself, though always as veiled, to thinking.

Heidegger's writings on language are, then, the best illustration of the complication that the infold introduces into the thought of difference. Heidegger in fact goes to great lengths to emphasize this quandary in his own language, as is evident especially in "The Nature of Language" and "The Way to Language," which employ the rhetoric of nearness and consistently avoid differential terminology, associated in this context with technological and calculative thought.[10] It is precisely this strategy that produces the "strangest" linguistic moments in Heidegger's works, moments too often relegated to the "poetic" side of Heidegger and dismissed as not having much direct philosophical relevance. I have in mind here the semi-tautological statements with which the texts on poetry and language proliferate, the phrases like "world worlds," "thing things," "time times," "space spaces," and, most important, *die Sprache spricht*, not "language speaks" but rather "language languages" to indicate the complexity of the Heideggerian way of language. Those locutions are indeed, as I indicated at the end of the first chapter, the unsettling results of Heidegger's encounter with the poets, which need to be taken not as obfuscations of his terminology but rather as the bearers of the most provoking insights. I see this maneuver of presenting the verbalization of nouns as a quasi-duplication of the noun into the verb not simply as undermining the syntactical distinction between the subject and the predicate but as writing the nearness, the proximity through which Heidegger describes language. In an attempt to sidestep tautology and circularity, on the one hand, and difference, on the other, Heidegger elaborates the idiom of nearness, which carries the message of the "hermeneutics" of otherness perhaps even more persuasively than the argumentative statements expressly devoted to it.

The nearness indicated by phrases like "world worlds," "language languages," or, most explicitly, "nearness nears," and marked as the whiteness that inflects the grammatical and syntactical differences and their signifying functions, is what, to paraphrase Heidegger, "way-makes" language, what, in other words, carries and underwrites the way of the saying of manifestation (*Ereignis*) into words. To that extent, the idiomatic phrases that arrange the discourse of late Heidegger spell the inflection his enterprise undergoes through its engagement with the language of poetry. This is obviously also the language inflection indicated in the title of this book, an inflection of the play of signification perpetrated and perpetuated by the nearness that earmarks the infold: the listening response in/to the saying of manifestation, which echoes in the sentence "*Das Ereignis ist sagend.*" It keeps re-marking itself in Heidegger's work through various figures of the infold, from the preontological understanding to *Entsprechung*, underscoring the extent and the meanders of his rethinking of difference. It also keeps our focus on the phenomenal and the transport of its saying into words, highlighting the revisions this entire problematic undergoes in the discussions of *Ereignis*. Above all, it is precisely in the perspective of how nearness inflects and affects Heidegger's thought that his conception of language can be appreciated for its "poetic" character, and its bearing on the debates about difference, otherness, and ethics recognized.

Beyond Ontology and Ethics: The Two Sides of Gelassenheit

Even though such language inflection is minimal, erased and forgotten by the mechanics of signification, its effects are of singular significance not only for the conceptualization of thought, poetry, or language itself but, first and foremost, for refiguring otherness. The significance of this rewriting, which motivates the Heideggerian enterprise, manifests itself above all in the reconceptualization of language in the neighborhood of poetry and thinking in a way that would be mindful of the otherness of other beings. A dense yet remarkably lucid passage that appears toward the end of "The Nature of Language" will serve as the illustration of the complexity of the scenario Heidegger proposes:

> Where this [that is, the nearness as the face-to-face of the fourfold] prevails, all things [beings, including humans] are open to one another in their self-concealment; thus one extends [reaches] itself to the other [forgoes itself to/for the other], and thus all remain themselves; one is over the other as its guardian watching over the other, over it as its veil (*OWL*, 104, modifications mine).

> Im waltenden Gegen-einander-über ist jegliches, eines für das andere, offen, offen in seinem Sichverbergen; so reicht sich eines dem anderen hinüber, eines überlässt sich dem anderen,

und jegliches bleibt so es selber; eines ist dem anderen über als das darüber Wachende, Hütende, darüber als das Verhüllende (*UZS*, 211).

One has to unpack this thick, "poetic" passage in order to let the Heideggerian "hermeneutics of nearness" deliver its message and realize that it harbors nothing short of a powerful refiguration of otherness. Surprisingly, such refiguration becomes much more legible through the prism of Levinas's writings on alterity, even though Levinas claims to separate himself from Heidegger,[11] rather than through the traditional hermeneutic concerns, which Heidegger apparently authorizes in *Being and Time*.

According to such a reading of the Heideggerian script, the way in which the world transpires, of course as seen from the perspective of the thought of nearness, is by each being or thing opening itself, in its self-concealment, to the other. The quoted fragment makes clear that openness and concealment have to be thought side by side, together, near each other. In other words, Heidegger's manner of thinking about openness does not preclude or exclude the re-trait, withdrawal, and concealment. On the contrary, openness can be thought as openness only in proximity to concealment and veiling, with the same obviously true for concealment itself. The proximity the passage sketches alerts us to both the focal importance of the notion of the other in it and the direction Heidegger's revision of otherness takes. To that effect, Heidegger's circuitous writing style keeps us constantly aware that any articulation of otherness has to be predicated on the play of openness and concealment. To put it simply, the text underscores the impossibility of conceiving otherness as alone openness or concealment, veiling, blankness. Instead we are asked to look into the mechanics of this proximal exchange between openness and self-concealment and, taking note of Heidegger's word choice and its repercussions, recognize the stakes of this undertaking.

As is usual with Heidegger's texts, their reading depends on the resonance of their key words, as well as the references and implications generated by their deployment throughout his work. Keeping close to Levinasian concerns, one may note, therefore, that the understanding of otherness disclosed by Heidegger's texts on language pivots, on the one hand, on the manner in which a being reaches "itself" by opening itself to alterity and, on the other, on the sense of attentiveness, care, and letting-be implied by this ex-position. It does not take much to recognize that, for Heidegger, reaching oneself (itself) is predicated on extending and maintaining oneself in an exposure to the other. This double movement is encoded into the word *reichen*, which suggests both reaching toward the other and reaching or coming into one's own—both gestures always implicit in Heidegger's polysemic employment of *(er)eignen*. Disrupting and displacing the notion of a stable, self-enclosed identity, the double valency of "reaching" makes a point about otherness whose impact it has become possible to appreciate perhaps only in the context of Levinas or, on the other side of the neighborhood of poetry and thinking, Celan.

Since this point depends on the reading of the extension toward the other, one should keep in mind that Heidegger's texts evidence clearly that reaching oneself has to be always thought in the active, verbal, "essencing" sense. It is perhaps high time to recognize that Heidegger's use of *Wesen* places at least as much emphasis on coming into one's own as on its character of an event, an occurrence, never finalized or complete. As such, it not only does not smack of "essentialism," but, conversely, exposes the ungrounding (*Abgrund*) of any essentiality. What matters for our discussion here is that the comportment toward the other Heidegger outlines never coalesces into an essence but in fact puts in question any desire or illusion of it. Behind the somewhat overdramatized rhetoric of the fourfold lies the invitation to (un)thinking the thing, the one, and the self, along the lines of an originary, that is, essencing, exposition and reaching toward the other. In other words, these texts imply that reaching oneself transpires always as opening and reaching the other. Heidegger carefully notes, though, that this openness does not amount to a disclosure of the content of the other that would simply result in the eventual cognition, thematization, and thus absorption of otherness. Both the other and the one who reaches itself toward the other open themselves as self-concealed (*sich-verbergen*). What enacts and maintains this movement is nearness itself, "which makes them reach one another and holds them in the nearness of their distance" (*OWL*, 104)—not in a dialectics of (re)cognition but precisely in proximity to their respective, non-cognizable, otherness. The other thus remains the other, preserves its alterity precisely in its openness, in its face-to-face.

Obviously the difficulty of this Heideggerian passage lies in thinking openness as retaining and maintaining concealment, not because it falls short of some ideal of cognition but precisely because the other thinking (*das andere Denken*) toward which Heidegger tries to direct his texts should remain attentive to the other. How we envision this attentiveness depends on our reading of the matrix of reaching and on our discerning in it both a relation to the other and oneself and the "constant," always already enacted subversion and questioning of any stability, permanence, or balance implicated in the repetition of this opening. In this context, reaching oneself attains to oneself only as extended toward the other: one is one's own (*ereignet*) as extended, open, exposed toward the other. In other words, one's identity, if it is still the right word to use, is constituted through an ex-positing toward the other. It is in this sense that Heidegger writes about everything remaining itself as extended toward the other, as reaching toward the other's self-concealment or alterity.

In the end, the other is never asked to give up its otherness; in fact, something to the contrary takes place: it is precisely in this reaching that the other's alterity can at all signal itself without losing its self-concealing force, without, so to speak, losing its face. Without this extending and extensive reaching, the other, whether human, animate, or inanimate, could at best be conceived as a dialectical other, with an already reserved and comfortable place in the economy of self-identification. Here lies, perhaps, the significance of Heidegger's contribution but also the cause of much misunderstanding and confusion. In order not to misread Heidegger here, one has to recognize that at stake in his writings on nearness is precisely such a mode of relating to otherness and self that would make the movement of reaching oneself near, almost coextensive with, reaching the other as other, that is, the other understood not as the other of the same, its opposite or its differend, but rather as the self-concealed other, the other whose alterity is noted and heeded. The difficult and self-effacing proximity of both "movements"—and Heidegger's language registers it well in its own convolutions—indeed confuses our thought of difference and strains it in an attempt to take note of the otherness at play.

The matrix disclosed here has the potential of helping us think the paradox implicit in Heidegger's conception of propriation and the role that otherness comes to exercise in *Ereignis*. According to it, the other certainly impacts upon and affects what Heidegger calls coming into one's own to the extent that this entrance into what one is, into identity, reaches toward the content, toward what the other is. The mechanism of propriation or, in more traditional terms, self-identification, thus remains contingent on its continuous openings to what the other can bring, to what the other discloses, or, in fact, to what thinking "lets be." To be its self, everything has to not only avoid closing itself off from the other but, conversely, maintain itself outreached, extended toward the other. Hence the recognition of the other as other forms an originary part of self-identification, a part without which the self inevitably misreads itself. The reciprocity, the face-to-face, of this event underscores the fact that the other likewise extends itself toward and affects the one with what it discloses about itself.

Heidegger makes clear, however, that such reciprocity is always contingent upon reaching its own limit. To be more exact, the passage implies that it is precisely this limit that maintains the reciprocal nature of exchange. Differently said, the reciprocity Heidegger proposes is never the complementarity or the sharing of two exemplars of the same, two things in a generic complicity or two subjects in an intersubjective dialogue, but instead two, in fact always more, others facing their, so to speak, respective alterities. Nearness, therefore, has to be defined through such delimitation, as the limen that inflects propriation and prevents any dialectical completion of the movement. It not only forestalls and averts implicit dialectical "dangers" but in fact disrupts language's tendency to dominate and domesticate the other. The force of the linguistic inflection of nearness is perhaps exactly this: maintaining attentiveness and awareness of the fact that the other's content affecting the one in the exchange of propriation remains the other's. In other words, at the same time that nearness allows beings to come near each other in the movement of propriation (*ereignen*), it also inflects it so that the other's alterity, the singularity that makes it other, remains veiled. The passage I chose as an example for this discussion makes abundantly clear that the limit that maintains the reciprocity of propriation functions as a veil, preserving the other's alterity. The extension by which beings reach themselves reaching toward otherness is *verhüllend*, that is, it shelters and makes clear that the openness in which beings find themselves with respect to one another does not cancel their concealment. To the contrary, it is precisely in nearness that the other can open/conceal itself in its alterity. In a sense, then, propriation and the reciprocity of the exchange that constitutes coming into one's own are the condition of both noting and withdrawing from the alterity of the other, of letting it remain veiled, as Heidegger puts it.

Crucial to this nearing is also the attentiveness and heed that beings grant to one another so that they can "remain themselves." Heidegger employs here two words: *wachen* and *hüten*, which unmistakably allude to the consideration of care from *Being and Time* and "Letter on Humanism." *Wachen* indeed means keeping guard or watch over something, but with the connotation not of control and possessing but instead of keeping awake, staying alert and mindful of the otherness at stake. Similarly, *hüten* suggests protectiveness, looking after, taking care of, tending to (the other). These terms indicating wakefulness and taking care sound remarkably, and surprisingly, close to the terminology of early Levinas, without emphasizing, though, the radical asymmetry that underlies the Levinasian analysis of proximity. This affinity, however, goes deeper than just the proximity in vocabulary, as it underscores the implicitly ethical bearing of Heidegger's elaboration of nearness. This direction manifests itself in the ethical tenor of the terms recurring throughout Heidegger's work, which evidences how important indeed it is to realize that the Heideggerian idiom of taking care, sheltering, keeping guard, or attending to has as much cognitive as ethical significance.

We have, however, to proceed very carefully here in exacting what the ethical might mean in this context, bearing in mind that nearness is both a "language phenomenon" and, as such, a powerful refiguration of otherness. All the more so since Heidegger's own hesitation—in fact, reluctance—in using the words *ethics* or *ethical* and his consistent practice of placing them in quotation marks are well known, especially in the formulation they received in "Letter on Humanism." Heidegger's answer to Beaufret's inquiry about the possibility of ethics, even though it often evokes disappointment and tempts misunderstanding, in fact provides a venue for engaging the problematic of the ethical in the context of thinking and language. In other words, Heidegger's caution in engaging the ethical is motivated not by his inability to write an ethics but instead, as "Letter on Humanism" suggests, by the apprehension about having his thought collapsed into moral philosophy, with inevitably didactic or idealistic overtones. Even more important, Heidegger's circumspect use of terms related to ethics testifies to his unwillingness to separate the "ethical" inquiry from the problematic of language, poetic thinking, and nearness.

This reluctance underscores not a failure or lack of interest but, on the contrary, an attempt at recasting the problematic, evident in Heidegger's idiosyncratic use of language and struggle with terminology throughout "Letter on Humanism." First of all, Heidegger makes forcefully clear that the distinction between ontology and ethics as disciplines is untenable;[12] to the extent that they pertain to the same territory, both terms are no longer suitable, almost invalidated, and in need of displacement. It is almost too easy to mistake this statement for a disavowal of ethical concerns, while in fact it says something to the contrary, underscoring the range that Heidegger gives to the word *ethical*. Coextensive with what can no longer be called "ontology,"[13] even if it is fundamental, such displaced ethics hints at a revision of the parameters of thinking and language, already intimated in our discussion of Heidegger's encounter with poetry and inquiry into nearness. Heidegger calls it *ursprüngliche Ethik*, originary ethics (*W*, 353/*BW*, 235), a term indicative of his interest in determining the "conditions" under which thinking and poetry could at all be "ethical" and make ethics, in any normative or moralistic sense, conceivable. In other words, Heidegger's concerns here, though articulated quite differently, are perhaps not at all far from the Levinasian inquiry and its engagement with what Derrida revealingly called the "ethics of ethics." The originariness that Heidegger underscores, recalling all the figures of "always already" in his thought, wants in fact to implicate all thought in an ethical direction or inflection, without which there would be no possibility of thinking or articulating any ethics. The collapsing of the distinction between ontology and ethics and the eventual displacement of both terms are tied to the elaboration of "an other thinking" (of nearness) as thought that lets the other be in its alterity. In sum, Heidegger does not want to consider ethics as a separate domain of philosophical inquiry, apart or after the "ontological" engagement with the phenomenal. For him, thinking, in order to be mindful of and remember (*andenken*) its own nearness to the phenomenal, must be already in this specific sense "ethical."

While obviously Heidegger's work is not an elaboration of normative standards of moral behavior or even a deployment of guidelines or basic concepts for its inception, it constitutes a consistent and important attempt at inflecting thinking to a degree that would assure that it "lets be" and thus "respects" otherness. What Heidegger's readers do not emphasize enough is that his thought is in fact engaged, from beginning to end, in an exercise of thinking otherness otherwise, through nearness rather than difference, and, furthermore, that the notion of nearness bears with it inescapable ethical connotations. Giving prominence to nearness in Heidegger's work allows us to understand how it wants to approach the other not by thinking it, that is, conceptualizing and "appropriating" the otherness of the other, but rather by coming near it in a way that lets the other be in a manner that preserves its alterity. In other words, at stake is not so much thinking otherness as letting otherness be. This model of thinking, reflected in Heidegger's insistent erasure of the traditional boundary between ontology and ethics, demonstrates in fact the two sides of *Gelassenheit*, or, better, its twofold character: the chiasmic crossing of the onto-logical and the ethical. *Gelassenheit*, if it is to make any sense, "releases" both ontologically and ethically; it releases thinking from the bounds of traditional ontological and ethical inquiry into a thought that approaches the phenomenal in a manner that lets it be. Recalling here the double matrix of "reaching," it becomes clear that for Heidegger any cognitive engagement, if it is to be crit-ical with respect to metaphysics and separate itself from technolog-ical thinking implicated inevitably in the logic of *Ge-stell*, has already and always to think in a way that lets be. *Gelassenheit*, therefore, should be thought in terms of nearness, with its double movement of reaching, taking a "post-ontologico-ethical" course of *das andere Denken*. In other words, the thought of *Gelassenheit* unfolds itself, with its characteristic proximity of the ethical and phenomenological stakes, in the perspective of the inflection pro-duced in language by the nearness of the human to the event of manifestation.

I cautiously call here this inflection by nearness, which underlies Heidegger's problematization of traditional philosophi-cal distinctions, the "ethicity" of language. It is in this precise and specific sense that the words *ethical* and *ethics* are employed in this study, a use never to be confused with a proposition or description of normative system(s) of ethical rules or moral precepts. They indicate instead a peculiar "ethicity" that, according to Heidegger, language always brings with it, a bearing that not only determines the manner in which otherness is "faced" but in fact lets us face otherness in the first place.

My hesitant use of the adjectives *ontological* and *phenomeno-logical* or *phenomenal* should be understood along the same lines, as indicative of the inflection of language's proximity to what it names, a constant Heideggerian concern with bringing thought near the phenomenal and letting it be. The fact that both the "ontological" and the "ethical" stakes of Heidegger's exploration of language have to be explained in terms of nearness accounts for the gradual questioning and erasure of the distinction between ontology and ethics. Let me stress here again that I see this efface-ment not as a sign of the neglect of the ethical by Heidegger but rather as a bypass of the traditional conceptualization of ethics and an indication of the direction in which he wants to take his inquiry into the notion of nearness—toward showing how any type of thought and discourse unfolds within the horizon of *Gelassenheit*, of letting be. Language is obviously prone to veil and forget this "ontological ethicity," or ontological responsibility as

Llewelyn calls it, leading inevitably to the elaboration of the modalities of discourse that become oppressive, intolerant, or, to use Levinas's expression, allergic to otherness. In this context, Heidegger's desire for an other thinking can perhaps be best described as an endeavor to highlight the inflection of nearness, which prescribes language and thinking "ethically." Such pre-scription can be kept in view only at the expense and effort of playing language "poetically," a strategy responsible both for Heidegger's notorious idiom and for his most thought-provoking insights. This is why this idiom of nearness should not be perceived as merely an idiosyncratic linguistic gesture on Heidegger's part but should instead be regarded as inviting a refiguration of otherness with its bearing upon the ethical, political, and social issues. Indeed, a meaningful and accurate engagement with these sets of problems in Heidegger's work should be undertaken with a view to the notions of *nearness* and *Gelassenheit*, which require a rethinking of the very distinction between the poetic and the cognitive, phenomenological, ethical, or political aspects of thought and, importantly, gesture with appreciation toward the language and "thinking" of poetry and its significant contribution to the revision at stake.

I will return to this Heideggerian "hermeneutics" of otherness at the end of this book, to engage specifically the function of the human other in the perspective of Heidegger's understanding of listening and response (*[ge]hören* and *entsprechen*), an aspect of Heidegger's work continuously being opened to renewed debate and critique. So far this study has treated otherness in a rather monolithic way to facilitate the articulation of the specifics of the Heideggerian version of the relationship between nearness, otherness, and ethics. Its last chapter, however, mediated and precipitated by Levinas's insistence on the separateness and distinctiveness of human alterity, will outline the possibility of marking this distinction in the Heideggerian text. Such revisiting of the Heidegger material will be facilitated and contextualized in the meantime by the discussion of the role of otherness in the poetry of Paul Celan, inspired by the Levinasian articulation of the notion of a non-allergic alterity. As befits the entire project, this reappraisal will take place in the neighborhood of poetry and thinking, specifically as an encounter between Heidegger and Celan, restaged through reading several of Heidegger's texts on Hölderlin and their treatment of friendship and Celan's depiction of his own poetics in "The Meridian." The focal issue will be the chiasm of ontological responsibility and ethical alterity, as it has been recently articulated by Fóti's *Heidegger and the Poets* and Llewelyn's *The Middle*

Voice. In particular, the coda will address the question of tracing such a chiasmic version of otherness in Heidegger's work on poetry in the context of his understanding of language. By exploring the possible proximity between Heidegger's approach to poetry and Celan's view of poetic language, the closing chapter will also continue to implicitly refigure the relationship between Heidegger and Levinas and, on a similar note, further develop and specify the stakes of the Heideggerian approach to otherness as they are delineated in his "hermeneutics of nearness."

∾ 3 ∾

SEMANTICS OF PROXIMITY
Levinas on Non-Indifference

The thought of Emmanuel Levinas engages the question of the other as overflowing thinking, as "unthinkable" par excellence, and probes the significance of such otherness for language. It situates itself against the background of the ontological tradition of Western philosophy, which, in Levinas's view, precisely *thinks* the other, and thus inevitably compromises his/her alterity. In the opening pages of *Totality and Infinity*, Levinas characterizes this tradition as the dominion of the Same (*le Même*), of the totalizing thought, which in the process of self-identification subsumes all alterity and makes it merely a necessary part in the self-conscious play of the subject.[1] In distinction from the totalizing modes of thinking, the aim of Levinas's philosophy is to treat the other in such a way that he/she would remain "unthinkable," absolutely exterior and non-thematizable.

Since, as Levinas himself remarks, modern philosophy treats thought as coextensive with, and inseparable from, language (*TI*, 205/*TeI*, 180), the attempt to secure the exteriority of the other as inaccessible to consciousness is interlaced with the question of the "essence" of language. Thus, in a manner parallel to Heidegger, whose endeavor to think the difference between Being and beings becomes the study of the "essence" of language, Levinas's concern for the other turns into a preoccupation with the essential dimension of language, "unheard" in Western thought. This dimension originates as responsibility for the other, irreducible to the difference qua difference as the condition of thinking and thematization. This linguistic dimension is ethics, understood as the condition of the possibility of ethics, as, according to Derrida's formulation, the "ethics of ethics."[2] Such ethics is "empty of content," it contains no ethical prescriptions. Rather, it concerns itself with the relation to the other as the primary ethical command that makes the institution of rules and laws possible. For Levinas, then, language is essentially an ethical burden of responsibility, a relation to the other that

does justice to the fact that alterity overflows (*déborder*) thematization. In contradistinction from Heidegger, Levinas sees the essence
of language not as a play of truth in the aletheic sense but as the
welcoming of otherness, of the visitation of the other.[3] How is it
possible, then, that language, the medium for thematization and
knowledge, which as Levinas repeatedly asserts proceed from the
horizon of Being and establish the domination of the Same, is in its
essence an opening toward the other? Translating it into a post-Heideggerian question: how can there be a signification prior to and
other than the signification of the verb *to be*?

The two guiding notions in determining such a possibility are
saying (*le dire*), as differentiated from the said (*le dit*), and proximity, interpreted by Levinas in terms of non-indifference to the
other. The proximity to Heidegger evident in Levinas's vocabulary
has a strategic significance, allowing Levinas's texts to operate in
the neighborhood of the question of Being with the task of revising not only Heidegger's thought but, with it, the entire onto-theological heritage of the West. As both *Totality and Infinity* and *Otherwise than Being or Beyond Essence* demonstrate, such critique
becomes possible only through a rereading of language, more
specifically, by foregrounding the inflection that the other's excess,
the overflow of his/her alterity, produces in the play of signification. Levinas describes this modulation of meaning induced by the
other's alterity as the saying, which modifies and recasts what is
said. Such inflection, the mark of proximity to the other's alterity,
exposes language ethically, preventing it from becoming non-
indifferent toward the other. As the organizing terms of Levinas's
discourse, proximity and non-indifference also map the course of
his implicit critique of difference as the concept underlying any
and all relations and exchanges with the other and, in the end,
facilitating, even assuring, their eventual collapse into the identity
of the self-same consciousness. The adoption of the term *non-indifference* for explaining the nature of the other's proximity in language illustrates the Levinasian suspicion of difference, as deep as
his mistrust of what he perceives as the essentially violent and
non-ethical, at least according to his terms, discourse of philosophy. This chapter considers the reasons behind Levinas's verdict,
presenting his thought in terms of an underlying concern with the
ethical inflection of language by the other.

The Abrahamic Departure from Totality

In order to explicate his departure from the philosophical tradition, Levinas provides two paradigms emblematic for his thinking:

the first, elaborated in *Totality and Infinity*, describes the rupture of totality by infinity, by the Good that "is" beyond Being; the second, framing his essay "The Trace of the Other," juxtaposes two models of journey that inform the Western tradition, those of Abraham and Ulysses.

As its subtitle "An Essay on Exteriority" indicates, *Totality and Infinity* attempts to secure the exteriority of the other against any totalizing intent of thought. In doing that, it has to place, or rather displace, the other, since the other has no place and is u-topic par excellence,[4] beyond totality. The other becomes thus absolutely exterior, and, as a consequence, the relation to the other is strictly speaking not a relation, since the other cannot be reduced to one of the poles of the I-other relation. The approach of the other cannot be described in terms of "relation," because every relation inescapably constitutes a totality whose elements are ultimately reversible. Since the absolute exteriority of the other precludes reversibility and totalization, there is no "other" pole to form a relation, and, consequently, "toward the other" (*à l'autre*) cannot be grasped as relation. The irreversibility of this "non-relation" does not merely mean that the way the Same goes to the other is different from the way the other goes to the Same: "the radical separation between the same and the other means precisely that it is impossible to place oneself outside of the correlation between the same and the other so as to record the correspondence or the noncorrespondence of this going with this return" (*TI*, 36; *TeI*, 6). This separation can be grasped neither by the Same nor by a third party outside the Same-other "non-relation." In this way, the other absolves itself from the relation, affecting nonetheless the Same. Since for Levinas the ability to relate, to form oppositions, is a necessary characteristic of totalization, the non-totalizable other ruptures totality, albeit "silently," and baffles the security of bipolar thinking.

In order to indicate the radical alterity and heterogeneity of the other, Levinas differentiates between two levels of otherness. The first, merely "apparent" otherness is the otherness present in the play of the Same identifying itself with itself through the necessary detour of the otherness of objects. This otherness, which Levinas always associates with Hegelian phenomenology,[5] is inevitably "compromised" and loses its exteriority (*TI*, 36–37/*TeI*, 6–7). It is this otherness that provides the "other" pole necessary for differing and ultimate sublation: it is reversible and, through the relation to the Same, defines both itself and that Same. Yet that defining results unavoidably in the loss of autonomy: the Same depends on the other as other precisely to seize it, to take possession of it, to represent and think it. However, the second level of otherness, the "non-relation" to the other par excellence is not thinking or representation. If the Same identified itself through the opposition to the absolutely other, the identification would already envelop the Same and the other in a totality. Yet the exteriority of the other allows the other to overflow the play of identification; the other affects or even afflicts the Same without influencing its identity. The other who affects the Same without entering into its self-conscious play of identification Levinas terms the absolutely other, or the Other (Levinas uses the word *Autrui* to stress the singularity and exteriority of that other: *"L'absolument Autre c'est Autrui"* [*TI*, 39/*TeI*, 9]). The absolutely other, *Autrui*, is indifferent to representation and the annulment of alterity that results from it. As radically other, it does not limit knowledge or become the object of thinking.

Levinas finds a similar "understanding" of absolute alterity in Descartes's idea of infinity and Plato's "Good beyond being." Those two conceptions of alterity as the infinite and the Good, alongside references to the Hebrew Bible, inform almost every page of his philosophical writings. The opening section of *Totality and Infinity*, "The Same and the Other," deals primarily with Descartes's conception of the infinite and its relation to language. A similar problematic is elaborated in one of the essays in *En découvrant l'existence avec Husserl et Heidegger* (*Discovering Existence with Husserl and Heidegger*), "La philosophie et l'idée de l'Infini."[6] According to Descartes, the idea of infinity is characterized by two singular features: it cannot be possibly comprehended by the mind hampered by its finite nature, and its *ideatum* cannot be contained by the idea itself. In other words, the idea of infinity, despite its tracing presence in the mind, does not belong to the order of thought, and, unlike with other ideas, there can be no adequation between the idea and its *ideatum*.[7] Rather, the distance between the idea of infinity and its *ideatum* is the non-adequation par excellence. This abysmal distance between the idea and its *ideatum* leads Levinas to affirm that in fact the "content" of the *ideatum* of the idea of infinity is that very distance between the idea and its *ideatum* (*TI*, 49/*TeI*, 20).

At a first glance, this formulation seems somewhat tautological, since it proposes the equation between the *ideatum* and the distance between that *ideatum* and the idea of it. However, this "equation" indicates how otherness should be situated with respect to the Same. In the case of all other ideas, the relation between an idea and its *ideatum* is that of correspondence; in a sense, the idea and its *ideatum* function as two poles in a bipolar relation of adequation. In Levinas's approach to infinity, the bipolarity associated with ideation is ruptured. In bipolar terms, the idea of infinity and the *ideatum*, infinity itself, would be the two poles of the usual paradigm of adequation. However, Levinas emphasizes the fact that the *ideatum* is precisely the distance that initially separates the *ideatum* and the idea and that is normally "adequated" by thought. Therefore, still using the bipolar model, one could talk only about one pole in the case of infinity, that is, that of the idea. What should function as the second pole of the relation, the *ideatum*, becomes the very distance that, because of the impossibility of locating the second pole, remains unspecified, unmeasurable, infinite. The "absence" of the second pole, infinity, depolarizes the hypothetical relation, demagnetizes even what would seem to be the one accessible pole, that is, the idea of infinity itself, and turns the distance between the idea and its *ideatum* into a non-relation: a non-relation without poles, a radical separation, an infinite surplus.

In order to despatialize this non-relation of distance, Levinas, from the very beginning of *Totality and Infinity*, describes it as "desire" (*desir*). He talks about it as the metaphysical desire—here metaphysics is used to mark the departure from ontology conceived as a movement beyond the Heideggerian *physis*, beyond Being—desire without the hope of return (*TI*, 34–35/*TeI*, 4–5). This desire goes "elsewhere," without the hope or need of reciprocation: it is the pure desire for otherness, never answered. It is in the context of desire that the uniqueness of the idea of infinity unfolds itself. Unlike all the other ideas, the idea of infinity does not call for intellection, as it refers to the metaphysical desire par excellence. Obviously the idea of infinity can be thought, yet the only way its *ideatum* can be thematized is in terms of positive or negative infinity. However, for Levinas the metaphysical desire travels beyond thematization, and it is only by desire that the otherness of infinity can be measured, or rather "unmeasured." In other words, despite the fact that infinity makes its "appearance" in thought, thought is no measure for it. In the end, there is a radical difference between thinking and representation as modes of relating to what Levinas calls "false" alterity and the metaphysical desire as the mode of welcoming the other.

That is why Levinas repeatedly stresses the difference between desire and need (*besoin*).[8] Need functions as the basic movement of the ego (*le Moi*); it marks the way the ego relates to the world, the way it "lives from . . . " (*vivre de . . .*). Needs have their basis in lack and therefore can be satisfied. The satisfaction of needs is the subject of Levinas's long description of enjoyment in the second section of *Totality and Infinity*, "Interiority and Economy,"[9] where prereflexive and pre-representational enjoyment marks the formation of the ego, the first process of identification. The primary identification of the ego on the basis of enjoyment proceeds through the fulfillment of needs,[10] where need implies a return necessary for any identification. In the fulfillment of its needs, the ego returns to itself as satisfied and happy: "Need opens upon a world that is for-me; it returns to the self. (. . .) Need is the return itself, the anxiety of an ego for itself, the original form of identification which we have called egoism. It is an assimilation of the world in view of coincidence with oneself, or happiness" (*DEHH*, 192/*DC*, 350). Desire implies an entirely different movement, a different direction, as it does not need to return and cannot ever be satisfied since it feeds on its own hunger. Moreover, desire conceived in this way is neither a lack nor a failure of thought. In fact, there is no thinking that could recompense desire, because desire does not belong to the order of thinking. Instead it overflows thinking; it is a surplus over need and representation, as Levinas often remarks that desire thinks more than it thinks.[11] However, it seems that this surplus cannot be described in terms of thought, since this "more" is not an addition to thought, not some "hyperthinking." Rather, in the context of Levinas's later writings, desire is "otherwise than thinking." Still this "otherwise" functions only with respect to thinking, in the sense that it signals itself through thought as the idea of infinity.

Levinas identifies a similar "otherwise" in Plato's philosophy, which with its idea of the Good reaches beyond being. For Plato, the idea of the Good denotes the highest idea, the one in whose light all the other ideas become intelligible. In this way, the idea of "the Good beyond being" provides a perspective for thinking.[12] What interests Levinas in this Platonic conception of the Good is both its ethical meaning and the fact that, going "beyond being," it provides a perspective for the Same, for thinking and thematizing. "The Good beyond being" implies that thought "thinks" already within the ethical perspective. This ethical direction of thinking, which as direction overflows thinking, constitutes the "beyond," the *au-delà* of Levinas's philosophy. It also explains why the relation to this "beyond" is described through a cluster of ethical terms: responsibility, obligation, assignation, proximity, honesty, uprightness, the-one-for-the-other.

The other paradigm that Levinas provides for the "beyond" of otherness is that of the journey without return. In "The Trace of the Other," he characterizes the domination of the Same in Western philosophy in terms of the journey of Ulysses. He claims that the Same, the representing consciousness, departs from itself with a clear aim "in mind," as it wanders through alterity only to subsume it and thus inevitably return to itself, to its "home"—thought: "consciousness (. . .) finds itself again in all its adventures, returning home to itself like Ulysses, who through all his peregrinations is only on the way to his native island" (*DEHH*, 188/*DC*, 346). In this way, all the movements of consciousness, all that pertains to the subject is ultimately reduced to this return and seen in the perspective of thought returning to its home. For Levinas, this return of the Same to the Same, this self-sameness of thought, implies the necessary reduction of alterity. Within the paradigm of self-consciousness, there is no possibility of heteronomous experience, no signification that "would not be equivalent to the transmutation of the other into the same" (*DEHH*, 190/*DC*, 348). Therefore the other is always autochthonous, inhabits the land of consciousness, and becomes part of the totalizing process of history.

Challenging the history of Western philosophy, Levinas seeks precisely a heteronomy that would not inhabit thought, that "would be an attitude that cannot be converted into a category, and whose movement unto the other is not recuperated in identification, does not return to its point of departure" (*DEHH*, 190/*DC*, 348). He finds such an alternative to the reign of "Greek" conceptuality figured by Odyssean travels in the Judaic,[13] specifically in the paradigm of a movement without return characteristic of the journey of Abraham:

> To the myth of Ulysses returning to Ithaca, we wish to oppose the story of Abraham who leaves his fatherland forever for a yet unknown land, and forbids his servant to even bring back his son to the point of departure. (*DEHH*, 190/*DC*, 348)

The Odyssean journey is characterized by its closure, by the arrival at the point of departure, and hence by the possibility of completion, and ultimately totalization. The Abrahamic journey, in the way Levinas refigures it, is not concerned with its destination; what matters instead is the prohibition to return. In this interpretation, the promise of an unknown land is outweighed by the obligation of no return. Still, that "departure without return" does not go forth into the void, though the land it seeks should remain unknown. While the Odyssean paradigm is based on the return of the movement to its own origin, the Abrahamic journey is, by contrast, a departure from origin without the possibility of recuperation.

However, what is of most importance in Levinas's use of Ulysses and Abraham is the relation between these two paradigms of movement. Even though, in the passage quoted above, Levinas uses the word *oppose* (*opposer*) to describe it, it seems that conceiving this "relation" in terms of opposition or difference would inevitably lead to the subsumption of the Abrahamic journey into the Odyssean pattern: if Abraham is the opposite of Ulysses, his journey can be totalized and recuperated on another level. The Abrahamiad would be then merely the other pole for the Odyssey, the other of the Odyssey, whose alterity could be compromised within the possible Jew-Greek totality. However, Abraham is not a simple opposite of Ulysses. If he were, he would have to seek to return home but eventually fail; he would have to be motivated by the need to return. The return, though, is out of the question in the Abrahamic journey, for Abraham is the radical other of Ulysses, without the mediation, the "infra" that would slide the Abrahamiad and the Odyssey into an opposition. It is as if Levinas, without making the stakes explicit, wanted the name of Abraham to spell an inflection of difference, a hesitation and then a disavowal of the strategy that views the Abraham-Ulysses juncture in terms of an opposition instead of seeing it as the desire to rupture this very modality of thinking.[14] Therefore, only with the Abrahamiad understood otherwise than non-Odyssey can one see the parallel between Abraham's movement without return and the Cartesian surplus in the non-relation to infinity. They both escape oppositional structures and the play of bipolarity; they are "other" with respect to totality, not simply an other world (*arriére monde*), but otherness unmeasurable by the terms of totality and thought.

The problematic of this crucial tension between the Greek and the Hebrew in Levinas's thought is explored by Derrida in his pioneering essay "Violence and Metaphysics," where he immediately links this tension to the question of the essence of language, of the opening of difference and meaning. In the context of the Greek source of philosophy, Derrida questions whether Levinas's thought in its preoccupation with the Judaic can be properly called "philosophical," whether it can sustain its language without ruining its own claims, for in order to be philosophical, Levinas's work has to find its origin within the Greek source. Derrida stresses the fact that the Greek source is not understood historically or geographically: it is rather the awareness that all philosophical questioning begins within the horizon of Greek conceptuality, that the philosophical medium, language as such, is "Greek" (*WD*, 81/*ÉD*, 120). Thus the two most eminently Greek voices since Hegel are Husserl and Heidegger, with the Heideggerian departure from onto-theology marking in fact a turn to the Greek roots, to the Greek element of Being, to "the thought of Being whose eruption or call produced Greece" (*WD*, 82/*ÉD*, 122). Thus Heidegger's questioning of language turns into the recovery of its truly Greek source, dissimulated already in Platonic philosophy and entirely forgotten in the translation of the Greek roots into Latin—the recovering that takes the form of the understanding of language in terms of the redefined *logos*.

According to Derrida, Levinas, in a move opposing Heidegger's return to the Pre-Socratics, attempts to displace philosophy from this Greek origin:

> this thought summons us to a dislocation of the Greek logos, to a dislocation of our identity, and perhaps of identity in general; it summons us to depart from the Greek site and perhaps from every site in general, and to move toward what is no longer a source or a site (too welcoming to the gods), but towards an *exhalation*, toward a prophetic speech already emitted not only nearer to the source than Plato or the pre-Socratics, but inside the Greek origin, close to the other of the Greek (but will the other of the Greek be the non-Greek? Above all, can it be *named* the non-Greek?). (*WD*, 82/*ÉD*, 122)

Levinasian thought calls us away from the *logos*, from the logical speech toward the speech of the biblical prophets. Later Derrida specifies this summons as the desire to kill the Greek father, which amounts to the desire to kill the Greek speech: "But will a non-Greek ever succeed in doing what a Greek in this case could not do, except by disguising himself as a Greek, by *speaking* Greek, by feigning to speak Greek in order to get near the king? And since it is a question of killing a speech, will we ever know who is the last victim of this stratagem?" (*WD*, 89/*ÉD*, 133). Is there another way of achieving the objective of Levinas's thought of speaking Hebrew than to attempt to "kill" Greek language and displace its *logos*? In the analysis that follows, Derrida shows the difficulty of that task, which from the Husserlian perspective amounts to contradictions and from Heidegger's viewpoint folds itself into the problematic of Being. To put it differently, Levinas can never speak "pure" Hebrew; he needs the detour of Greek conceptuality, intelligibility, of the entire heliotropics of philosophical ("Greek") language.[15]

Derrida seems to conclude, therefore, that discourse never escapes violence; it always thinks the other and puts him/her under the light of intelligibility which deprives the other of alterity. On this reading, Levinas's claims to the non-violence toward the other cannot be sustained in the essentially Greek language.[16]

At the end of the essay, Derrida returns to the question of the approach to the dialogue between the Greek and the Jew, to the question of the form of the peace between them. Should it have the form of the reconciliation effected by the speculative logic of Hegel or rather that of infinite separation, of transcendence, proposed by Levinas? Yet it seems that the terms in which Derrida posits the question asked by Levinas can predetermine the answer:

> But the true name of this inclination of thought to the Other
> . . . is *empiricism*. For the latter, at bottom, has ever committed but one fault: the fault of presenting itself as a philosophy. And the profundity of the empiricist intention must be recognized beneath the naïveté of certain of its historical expressions. It is the *dream* of a purely *heterological* thought at its source. A *pure* thought of *pure* difference. Empiricism is its philosophical name, its metaphysical pretention or modesty (*WD*, 151/*ÉD*, 224).

However, one has to ask if Levinas's objective is indeed best served by killing "Greek" language and finding a new speech. For it is possible to read Levinas instead as precisely affirming that language always remains "Greek," and it *must* be Greek for there to be any transcendence of the other.

Already in *Totality and Infinity*, Levinas remarks that the face of the other makes an appearance within totality, within the phenomenological horizon: "The face, still a thing among things, breaks through the form that nevertheless delimits it. This means concretely: the face speaks to me (*le visage me parle*) and thereby invites me to a relation incommensurate with a power exercised, be it enjoyment or knowledge" (*TI*, 198/*TeI*, 172). The face in order to be face has to possess its phenomenological dimension; it has to show itself within the light of thought and submit itself, in one of its "aspects," to the violence of thematization. The face needs language, and it needs language with all its Greek implications precisely to transcend them. Levinas is aware of the fact that trying to "kill" the Greek speech would not mean saving the other from violence but rather condemning the other to the worst, as Derrida himself remarks, violence possible, that of the absolute silence, of the silence about the silence in the face-to-face with the other. The silence of the absence of language would make impossible the trace of alterity; it would exclude the possibility of that other silence before the face of the other, the silence that maintains otherness. And it is the "Greek" language, notwithstanding its necessary violence, that saves us from that worst possibility, for it is still the language one uses to speak to the other, even if it means speaking *about* and thematizing the other. It is true that the other is beyond Greek language, but only as "spoken to" from within and in that language. The "beyond" of the way the face speaks is, therefore, not another language, for example, historically existing Hebrew. Rather it is a certain direction, a "Hebraic" inflection, in which the "Greek" language already unfolds itself.

This is probably how one should read the significance of the Abrahamic journey and of the Judaic prescription of "doing before understanding" from the Talmudic lectures.[17] It is used by Levinas to suggest a direction, a direction without a thematizable destination, without essence or "as such," and yet not an empty one. It is a direction (*un sens*) that "makes sense" par excellence. Without it there would be no meaning, there would be no Odyssey. Therefore it seems legitimate to say that Abraham is not really an opposite of Ulysses, that Levinas's writing is not an opposite of philosophy but rather its inflection, which seeks to ensure an ethical predisposition of thinking. Even though it courts "non-philosophy" and empiricism, Levinas's work does not preoccupy itself in the end with difference, with pure difference or heterological thought. As it becomes clear in Levinas's elaboration of the Cartesian idea of infinity, there is no question of "thinking" the infinite. Infinity is not difference qua difference; it is not difference at all. Rather, the way I read Levinas's remarks in *Otherwise than Being*, it is *non-indifference*, which should be understood as an "an-archic" inflection of difference.

"Non-indifference" immediately underscores probably the most controversial aspect of Levinas's writings, namely, the way of reading them. In his essay "An Ethical Transcendental Philosophy," Theodore de Boer suggests that Levinas must be read ethically. He does not elaborate on this statement, yet from the context it would seem that by "ethical" reading he means reading otherwise than in terms of opposition, perhaps even otherwise than in terms of difference: that is, Levinas's transcendence is not transcendence understood as the opposite of immanence.[18] This is perhaps the most perplexing moment in Levinas's writing: it appears that the otherness he writes about in ethical terms does not belong to the order of difference, or at least not in a simple manner. Such alterity cannot be approached in terms of difference, because then it could be *thought* and thematized, and for Levinas alterity overflows differing and, overflowing it, marks it with this very excess. Thus every difference unfolds itself already with that mark of overflowing, in a direction that "makes sense," in the trace of non-indifference. The "ethical" reading would then mean reading this non-indifference as an inflection, an ethical trace, that marks all language. Difference and all differing would thus be already inscribed in non-indifference, not because non-indifference is a difference, a pure or impure difference, a subspecies of difference, or difference as such, but rather because difference cannot be indifferent to the overflowing, to the surplus, to what Levinas calls *envers*. *Envers* implies a duplicity of meaning important to the way Levinas approaches otherness, as it suggests both the "other side," logically "impossible," of all difference and the "toward" that marks all of Levinas's writing. This "toward" directs to the "inverse" of all differences, of all thinking, the "other side" that can never be reversed and become "this side"; it is the "side" that only "may be" (*peut-être*).

We are thus caught in the double bind of reading Levinas's writing in a "Greek" style, the only one accessible to us, which, as Derrida has shown, leads inevitably and logically to equating his thought with empiricism. In other words, it would mean reading the "Hebrew" inflection in terms of difference, against Levinas's claim that difference as such is always inflected by the trace of alterity to which language cannot be indifferent:

> It has been possible, since *Totality and Infinity*, to present this relation with the Infinite as irreducible to "thematisation." . . . Henceforth the ontological language still used in *Totality and Infinity* so as to exclude the purely psychological significance of the analyses put forward, is avoided. And the analyses, themselves, refer not to *experience*, where a subject always thematises what he is equal to, but to *transcendence*, where he answers for what his intentions have not measured.[19]

The relation to the other is, then, not an experience of transcendence but transcendence itself, transcendence peculiar to language that marks itself as *un sens* of "toward the other" within which thought can think and mean. Thus Levinas's writing demands that one does not read the trace but rather read in the trace, non-indifferently to the other, with this non-indifference of language understood by Levinas as a specific kind of transcendence.

To approach the question of what "transcendence" means in Levinas's thought, it is necessary to return to the problem of his understanding of language. In "Violence and Metaphysics," Derrida remarks that Levinas denounces philosophical discourse for its failure to do justice to the alterity of the other. Still this denunciation does not imply a renunciation or a desire to abandon philosophy. Levinas's critique of philosophical discourse does not aim at a destruction of language; rather, it inverts itself in order not to simply disclaim the validity of thought but to affirm the alterity of the other. The critique that shows how language is unable to render justice to the other does not signify only a failure of language, of "Greek" language. Levinasian analyses do not imply any negativity, any limits for language: the other does not mark the boundaries of intelligibility, and the fact that the other "overflows" does not impose the burden of failure upon language but hints at the other's alterity with respect to language, alterity that can leave its trace only in language. In the last instance, Levinas appears to confirm the powers of language: paradoxically, it is precisely because language can thematize, including the other, that the other can be absolutely other. Looking at it from another perspective, without the thematizing work of language and its resultant violence, there would be nothing the other could inflect, marking the non-indifference against the differential procedures of signification. Alterity therefore does not negate language but, in a perverse move, affirms it with all its ways of saying the other and infinity. Because philosophical discourse places the other within the phenomenal horizon and thematizes him/her, because it "robs" the other of alterity, the other can remain infinitely exterior. Only in this context can Levinas's denunciation of language sustain itself. It is a "positive" denunciation, which, critiquing language, affirms the infinitely other in order then to reaffirm language. Only through this double inversion of Levinas's critique can there be at all a "place," an excess, where the other cannot be "thought," thematized, deposited within difference and thus within language, and yet leave its trace in language.

This double inversion implicitly informs the third chapter of the first section of *Totality and Infinity*, which emphasizes precisely the fact that transcendence can in no way be thought negatively, neither as a negation of totality nor as a negation of language. As Derrida is quick to point out, Levinas cannot then be mistaken for negative theology, which knows and proclaims its own language a failure (*WD*, 116/*ÉD*, 170). The objection that, by affirming the absolute exteriority of the other, Levinas would undermine his own discourse, and with it any possibility of even ascertaining the problematics of alterity, overlooks the inverse affirmation of language implied by Levinas's writings, the affirmation of language as the very "access" to the face. This acceptance results from the fact that while language makes possible the face and its mode of signifying as a trace, and becomes responsible for the other, it also relinquishes any right to the accessibility of the other as such.

The Non-Indifferent Face

In order to reckon with Levinas's claim about the need to read the trace of alterity "ethically" and not "ontologically," we have to infer the reasons for his disagreement and continuous rewriting of Heideggerian terms, even beyond those explicitly cited by Levinas's own texts and, especially, beyond Levinas's unequivocal inscription of Heidegger into the ontological tradition, which disregards Heidegger's express disavowal of ontology. For just as it is important to acknowledge the somewhat restricted scope of Levinas's reading of Heidegger, which never seriously ventures into late Heidegger or recognizes his revisions of the problematic of Being, it is also crucial to delineate the stakes of the Levinasian critique. Levinas's statement about his "profound need to depart from the climate of Heideggerian philosophy"[20] contextualizes his claim to the "priority" of ethics, conceived as "first philosophy," over ontology, even if the latter is understood in the manner of Heideggerian fundamental ontology. What Levinas finds lacking in Heidegger's otherwise necessary and important questioning of philosophy and refashioning of thinking is the absence of concern for the other, which results in the covering up of the question of the ethical.

The recognized difficulty of reading Levinas with and against Heidegger, repeatedly indicated by Levinas himself, lies in the fact that, in spite of Levinas's explicit rupture with Heidegger, there remains a certain analogy between Levinas's critique of Western philosophy of sameness and the Heideggerian destruction of onto-theo-logy. In his critique of philosophy's indifference to alterity and its violent subsumption of the other's difference, Levinas employs much the same strategy that Heidegger uses in his dismantling of metaphysics: he locates the ethical on the "other side," as if anterior to the deployment of the dialectical machinery of thinking, a move reminiscent of Heidegger's characterization of

Ereignis as having "always already" unfolded itself. Yet, as Jill Robbins points out, Levinas "asserts by understatement an analogical importance and precariousness of the two inquiries, but he also leaves open the possibility that his inquiry into the ethical may be 'more' important, 'more' precarious, thereby unbalancing the proportional analogy."[21] Although the ethical and Being trace upon language in an analogical fashion, Levinas maintains the specificity of the ethical and reserves for it the status of "maybe otherwise than being." The fold implied in the maybe, the perhaps of the ethical trace and its demand to be read in a non-ontological, non-Greek manner, constitutes the very difficult difference/otherwise of Levinas's position vis-à-vis Heidegger, the difficulty that is compounded by his relative absence of interest in Heidegger's work from the 1950s and 1960s. I propose therefore to read Levinas and Heidegger in a parallel fashion, focusing on the moments in Levinas's thought where he appears to be responding directly to Heidegger's work. My aim is not to settle or resolve this debate, or even to assess to what extent Levinas reads Heidegger correctly, but instead to provide the context in which Levinas's ethical inflection of thinking and language manifests its significance.

Levinas repeatedly insists that his phrase "toward the other" must be approached in terms of responsibility, the-one-for-the-other, proximity, and direction (*un sens*). The Abrahamic journey and Cartesian infinity not only critique the reduction of otherness in the philosophy of consciousness but also signal a new direction for thinking, only implicit in Heidegger and his preoccupation with listening to others. Although Heidegger frequently stresses the otherness of withdrawing Being, Levinas insists that the ethical significance of the other's alterity cannot be explained in the same terms. Since Levinas's polemic with Heidegger unfolds in the context of *Being and Time* and "Letter on Humanism," one has to keep in mind another possibility of reading the ethical in Heidegger, described in the second chapter in terms of nearness and in the coda as the significance that friendship and listening to others have for language and thinking. For Levinas, though, the alterity of the other's face represents an explicit distanciation from Heideggerian *Mitsein* (Being-with) taken as the primordial manner of relating to others. In the fourth chapter of *Being and Time*, Heidegger, analyzing one of *Dasein's existentialen*, Being with others, remarks that Being-with is equiprimordial with *In-der-Welt-Sein* (Being-in-the-World), and that the analysis of the worldliness of the world (*Weltlichkeit der Welt*) precedes that of *Mitsein* only for structural reasons.[22] Therefore, for Heidegger, *Dasein* is as primordially toward the world as it is toward the other. Its *Existenz* is a primordial ek-sisiting, always directed toward what is beyond *Dasein*. In a Levinasian reading, however, *Dasein* does not relate itself to the other as such but instead understands the Being of the other, which accounts for why Heidegger says that the "with others" is itself a mode of *Dasein*'s Being. By being among others, *Dasein* "identifies" itself with the way they are, their *Auch-da-sein* (Being-there-too),[23] and thus always relates itself to the mode of Being of others, described as another "place" where Being lights itself. In the Levinasian context, the priority of the understanding of the Being of the other implies a certain "uniformity" between *Dasein* and the other, a uniformity with respect to their Being.

Also in "Letter on Humanism," where Heidegger most explicitly addresses the question of ethics, the relation to the other explains itself in terms of Being. Tracing the relation between ontology and ethics back to Heraclitus, Heidegger interprets *ēthos* as the abode (*Aufenthalt*) in which human beings think Being. In its origin, ethics is connected with thinking (*Denken*), with the lighting of Being: since "'ethics' ponders the abode of man, then that thinking (*Denken*) which thinks the truth of Being as the primordial element of man . . . is in itself the original ethics (*die ursprüngliche Ethik*). However, this thinking is not ethics in the first instance, because it is ontology"[24] (ontology in the sense of fundamental ontology, a pre-ontological thinking). In this essay, Heidegger postulates that ethics as a philosophical discipline becomes possible only on the basis of the primordial thinking of Being, of preserving the abode (*ēthos*) in which Being reveals and reveils itself before human beings. However, Heidegger does not determine the way in which the ethical as such is to be thought; he focuses on the primordiality of the thinking of Being and remarks that the other has to be thought as also the thinker of Being, that the relation to the other is mediated by the thought of Being. The relation to the other would have to be explained, then, from the mode of his/her existing.

It is thus possible to say that in his meditation on Heidegger, Levinas opposes a certain threat of uniformity that the relation to the other understood in terms proposed by *Being and Time* may imply. Although obviously the relation to the other becomes possible only in the light of Being, and the other's mode of Being has to be always already "thought," Levinas suggests that the fact that the other is a thinker of Being does not constitute the other's ethical alterity. This postulate of alterity that could not be exhausted by the otherness of withdrawing Being can be seen as a critique of

Heidegger, but it may also be approached as a development in the light of Heidegger's thought, since his "Letter on Humanism" does not specify the meaning of the ethical. Indeed, philosophically Levinas's "ethics of ethics" would not probably be possible without Heidegger's "Letter on Humanism" and its ground-breaking insistence on thinking *ēthos* apart from traditional ontology and its relationship to ethics, as well as from the opposition between *theoria* and *praxis*.

Levinas's radicalization of otherness implies primarily that the other cannot be explained in terms of Being. It is true that Levinas himself uses the word *étant*, yet, if one follows his descriptions carefully, it becomes obvious that the alterity of the other has to be dissociated from both Being and beings. Obviously the other is a being, and its mode of Being comes to light only in the context of the question of Being. Nevertheless, for Levinas the other's face, its absolute otherness, cannot be translated through the meaning of Being. If the other is approached only as a being, then, in the light of Heidegger's analyses, the other is always essentially determined by his/her mode of Being, and thus by Being "as such." In Levinas's eyes, Being-with is, then, not so much the relation with the other in its alterity but with the *Dasein* of the other, with the other as the thinker of Being. For Levinas that would imply too much "uniformity," a parallelism between my *Dasein* and the other's, not a radical asymmetry which he envisions as the relation to the other. In the end, Levinas's dissociation of the other's alterity from Being and beings, from *Auch-da-sein*, reflects his departure from the description of the interaction with others in terms of Being-with.

If Being-with is an ontological reading of the relation to the other, which, in a Levinasian interpretation, remains complicitous with the "allergic" and thematizing tendencies of language, then Levinas's way of changing the stakes to ethical responsibility is the notion of the face. The face, introduced by Levinas in the first section of *Totality and Infinity* as the way in which the other appeals to the Same, is therefore not an object in the field of vision, not the phenomenal face or the physiognomy of another human being. Instead it marks the way in which the other overflows all thought, even the primordial thinking that pre-comprehends Being: "The way in which the other presents himself, exceeding *the idea of the other in me*, we here name the face (*visage*)" (*TI*, 50/*TeI*, 21). The most important characteristic of the face, which Levinas stresses on every occasion, is that it always destroys its own image, its own plasticity; it always overflows and pierces whatever comprehension or representation the Same can have of it. The face can, of course, be arrested in the visual plane; it can be represented and thought, since "[t]he manifestation of the other is, to be sure, produced from the first conformably with the way every meaning is produced."[25] However, what constitutes the otherness of the other overflows representation and meaning. In other words, the face, presenting itself to the phenomenal gaze, ruptures the horizon of Being; it "otherwise than is." This "otherwise than Being" amounts to an ethical call for responsibility, even if no one knows from where, when, and why this demand comes; it is a pure demand, a call toward the other.

The face marks its difference through its mode of presentation, or rather what Levinas calls in the essay "La signifiance du sens" ("The Signifyingness of Sense") from his recent collection *Hors sujet* (*Beyond the Subject*), "apresentation."[26] As Levinas remarks, the face "shows" itself to thinking yet precisely as apresentation; it marks itself within the horizon of Being without being enveloped by it. This apresentation is then aptly called the "secret of the face" (*le secret du visage*).[27] It seems, though, that this secret of the face can be all too easily lost in the English translation. Levinas uses the word *visage* not only to avoid the confusion with "face," the phenomenal face of another human being, but to stress the particularity of the relation to the other hidden in the Latin root of *visage*, in the verb *visere* (to watch, to scrutinize),[28] which implies that, in its relation to the other, the Same is watched, looked upon by the other. The scrutiny that the Same undergoes under the gaze of the other is the primary determinant of the relation to the other. It is not only the case that the Same first sees the other and that this seeing constitutes its relation to alterity, but, conversely, the Same is first seen by the other, and not merely "watched" but by that very gaze called into responsibility for the other. Though the other can be subsequently thematized and thought on the basis of the Same, this calling glance overflows and inflects thinking; its anteriority continues to disrupt the self-same movement of consciousness. It marks a separation so radical that it calls for displacing the other's ethical alterity beyond Being, since within Being that relation would lose its uniqueness and fall under the paradigm of intentionality. This is why the face is the signifyingness of the beyond (*signifiance de l'au-delà*), and why it alone can translate, indicate transcendence: "*Le visage est seul à traduire la transcendance*" (*HAH*, 142).

In *Totality and Infinity*, the face is described as discourse, as the "essence" of language (*TI*, 64/*TeI*, 35). For Levinas, language is the only relation, which, despite consequent thematization, propriation, and self-identification, harbors in its "essence" the possibility of non-violence and respect for the alterity of the other. This possibility is due to the fact that "[s]peaking is before anything else this way of coming from behind one's appearance, behind one's form, an openness in the openness" (*HAH*, 51/*CPP*, 96). Discourse understood as the face is not a modality of thinking, but, instead, it is what makes thinking possible by leaving a sign of direction, *un sens*. For Levinas, thinking, and consequently knowledge, would not be possible without the word from the other (*TI*, 93/*TeI*, 66), who delivers the sign, the face, and is only as that sign, the "sign of the donation of sign." This sign marks the very presentation of meaning that "grounds" language and its primary signification. As Levinas remarks, signification is not the result of signs, but it makes signs possible (*TI*, 206/*TeI*, 181). It is therefore the face of the other, the signification of signification, or signifyingness, that, by overflowing, gives a "direction" to language.

The signifyingness of the face cannot be understood, then, in terms of indication, reference, sign, or symbolization. The face is not a sign of the beyond but its very giving and overflowing. In our reading here, such mode of signifying indicates an ethical inflection of language, repeatedly checking and rupturing the erasure of alterity brought about by thematization and cognition. The way the face signifies, marking itself within signification as apresentation, indicates a beyond, the "sense beyond what a human being can be or show itself as" (*sens au-delà de ce que l'homme peut être et se montre*) (*HAH*, 142). The face, then, is the movement of transcendence, which from within Being and phenomenality points beyond them; its signifyingness is precisely that of a direction that "makes sense," of *un sens*. This sense cannot be reduced to Being and history, cannot be "thought," since, conversely, it is the case that thinking can think Being and history as transcendence only in that direction: the face of the other. In this way, the notion of the face indicates how language can have a primordially ethical sense that is not explained from and through Being, *un sens* that simultaneously provides a direction for what can be called the "ontological sense" as the ringing of the silence of Being.

Levinas's notion of the ethical in language, of "otherwise than Being," should not, however, be simply opposed to Being. Instead, Levinas's position emphasizes the fact that language says Being not only for Being but also, and for Levinas perhaps even primarily, for the other. In this way Levinas underscores another direction for language: the address to the other. Heidegger's phrase *unterwegs zur Sprache*, "on the way to language," indicates a direction, language turned toward the self-veiling Being, toward its otherness. In Levinas, "otherwise than Being" attempts to mean otherwise than this otherness of Being. It does not denote non- or trans-Being, a supernatural dimension, but the fact that as language responds to and says Being, it cannot remain indifferent to the other. Even if what prompts language is Being, as language comes into words, it already shares its saying with the other; it addresses the saying (of Being) to the other. And it speaks *to* the other precisely because he/she remains absolutely other, because, as human beings respond to and say after (*nachsagen*) Being, or in fact its retreat, they cannot "say" the other but instead only address their saying toward him/her. In other words, for Levinas, the withdrawal of Being can be said only in words already marked by the other's irreducible alterity, already "ethical." Levinas's "otherwise" claims that language, the "house of Being," speaks as already "non-indifferent" to the other, since Levinas wants the other's alterity to remain distinct from the withdrawal of its Being; he wants it to trace otherwise. "Otherwise than Being" indicates, then, another fold in the direction of language, an approach that adds itself to, critques, modifies, and radicalizes Heidegger's "way to language," even if this Levinasian ethical modification is implicitly contingent and made possible by Heidegger's move beyond the theory of the subject and consciousness and their ontological grounding. In this ethical approach, the alterity of the other, the face, is the signifyingness of sense (*la signifiance du sens*), which marks a semantics of proximity (*une sémantique de la proximité*).

Semantics of Proximity

The very term *semantics of proximity* indicates that the essential problem for Levinas is the possibility of meaning that would not be determined by Being. This problematics of meaning beyond Being is elaborated most explicitly in two essays: "Meaning and Sense" and "God and Philosophy."[29] Both essays are set in the context of Heidegger's philosophy of meaning, of the illumination of the horizon of Being as the origin of intelligibility: "For Western philosophy meaning or intelligibility coincide with Being."[30] As Levinas remarks in "Meaning and Sense," language in its "essence" does not refer to particular beings, to given sense-data, but it brings to light the illumination of the horizon within which beings are given—Being. Therefore, there is no pure perception without meaning, since to be perceived means already to be and Being is the opening of the paths for language, the origin of meaning. In this way, Being is tantamount to meaning: only what is can signify, since Being is the "movement" of signifying. The question that Levinas poses with respect to this understanding of meaning is whether it does not restrict meaning in such a way that no alterity can remain meaningful without becoming subsumed under the otherness of its being.

To elaborate the possibility of such "otherwise than meaning," which, however, would not amount to nonsense or silence, we need to juxtapose Levinas's discussion of language in *Otherwise than Being or Beyond Essence* with Heidegger's notion of the saying and clarify two of Levinas's most perplexing terms, *le dire* and *le dit* (the saying and the said). For Levinas, the inflection, the trace that the saying marks in the said, illustrates the way in which one can envision meaning that would not be translatable into the terms of Being, where this untranslatability constitutes the characteristic mark of what Levinas names "transcendence." This term not only evokes the religious and the prophetic voice in Levinas's disourse[31] but also points to Levinas's attempt to "transcend" or modify our understanding of meaning, signification, and sense. Since the Heideggerian saying (*Sage*) is always described in the context of *Ereignis*, in order to see how Levinas can affirm meaning beyond Being, it is necessary to compare *Ereignis* and *transcendance*, which mark the crucial moments of Heideggerian and Levinasian thought and are both conceived as "relations" that are no relations at all. In Heidegger's case, the stress in *Ereignis* (disclosive appropriation) falls upon the relating itself, upon the opening of the relating bond, in its preeminently temporal meaning. Analogically, in Levinas transcendence is not a relation strictly speaking, because the related, the I and the other, absolve themselves of the relationship and are neither defined nor totalized by their face-to-face.

As it has been already observed, Heidegger traces his notion of *Ereignis* back to Parmenides' saying about the nature of the relation between thinking (*noein*) and Being (*einai*): "For the Same are thinking as well as Being."[32] The complexity of the relation between *Denken* and *Sein* reveals itself in the polysemous character of *Ereignis*, which, derived by Heidegger from *ereignen*, ties in various meanings etymologically related to *eigen* (own, proper, "authentic"). *Ereignen* means primarily "to occur," yet the way Heidegger uses it in his discourse connects it with identity, with the proper, with "propriation" (various modes of "*-eignung*"). In *Identity and Difference*, Heidegger explicates disclosive appropriation as *Übereignung*, "transpropriation," and observes that transpropriation names the process of nearing of thinking and Being, which marks also the opening of language. In other words, Heidegger claims that Being "is" in such a way that thought and Being are "propriated toward each other," that is, the particular mode according to which humans "are" makes them appropriate for responding to presencing, which in "The Way to Language" he names *Zeigen*—Showing. Transpropriation thus indicates the continuous and never complete movement in which thinking and Being lead each other into their essence, into what is most their own, *Eigene*. As Heidegger clarifies in his essays on language, the "essence" (*Wesen*) of human beings is to be the speakers, to say after Being, where this saying means thinking toward Being in such a way as to voice the saying of Being (*Sage*):

> When mortals are made appropriate for Saying, human nature is released into that needfulness out of which man is used for bringing soundless Saying to the sound of language.[33]

In this way, disclosive appropriation lets the "original" saying be resaid in actual words: through thinking it brings the phenomenal showing into the sounded speech.

Yet this bringing into speech withdraws itself from words, precisely to the extent that it works as the infold, the rift that produces meaning as the result of the fold that thinking marks in Being. The infold is the way-making of language (*Bë-wegung*) in which what shows, and thus "says" itself, is resaid and expressed by thinking. Language is here thought by Heidegger in the "essential" manner, in its primordial relation to the verb *esse*, and its pure verbality constitutes the origin of meaning: "[w]ith its saying, thinking lays inconspicuous furrows in language."[34] In these furrows, continuously opened by the way thinking infolds into Being, meaning originates. For Heidegger, then, meaning in its primordiality has always to be linked with and thought from Being. Therefore, on Levinas's interpretation, also the meaning of the ethical, the relation to the other would have to be explained in the same context. Consequently, the other's alterity would be related to the otherness in *Ereignis* and conceived as the otherness of the other's mode of Being.

With his conception of the distinction between the saying and the said, Levinas questions precisely the primordiality of the link between the alterity of the other and Being and proposes the meaning of otherness that cannot be enclosed within Being and its signification. Intended probably as an inflection of the Heideggerian *Sage*—the saying-event of manifestation—this meaning of otherness is *le dire*, saying, speaking to the other, in whose perspective all linguistic acts take place. This saying, however, needs the said; it requires language in order to mark itself as its "beyond," as its "exception." This saying can mark itself only as said in language, yet, as Derrida remarks, it is said in such a way that the grammatical statement that announces it is at the same time dislocated to make place for a sort of "agrammaticality" of the very offering of language for the other.[35] The said performs, therefore, an ancillary function: thematizing, it lets the saying leave its trace, even if that trace itself becomes immediately thematized: "[b]ut the fact that the ex-ception shows itself and becomes truth in the *said* cannot serve as a pretext to take as an absolute the apophantic variant of the saying, which is ancillary or angelic." Apophansis never exhausts saying; it "presupposes the language that answers with responsibility, and the gravity of this response is beyond the measure of being" (*OBBE*, 6/*AEAE*, 7). One could argue, though, that Heidegger's *Sage* is not the said, because it marks the way to the said, the opening for thematization, and thus comes close to Levinas's *le dire*. Still, Levinas proposes a distinction between the Heideggerian saying and the ethical saying, when, in one of the footnotes in *Otherwise than Being or Beyond Essence*, he differentiates between *le Dire disant un dit* (the Saying saying the said) and the *logos*, *Dire pré-originel* (pre-original saying): "[t]he thematizing logos, the saying stating a said in monologue and dialogue and in the exchange of information, with all the cultural and historical dimensions it bears, proceeds from this pre-original saying" (*OBBE*, 198/*AEAE*, 182). Throughout *Otherwise than Being*, Levinas remarks that language always resounds with Being, with the voice of silence (*Geläut der Stille*) (see, for example, *OBBE*, 135/*AEAE*, 172). This resonance of Being in words, in the said (*le dit*), points to non-said (*non-dit*) or the already-said (*déjà-dit*). However, this non-said, which always remains in the correlation with the said, also does not exhaust the saying (*OBBE*, 23/*AEAE*, 29). Even the already-said, the *déjà-dit*, as the opening of the channels of thematization, which permits what is being thematized to diversify, orient, and polarize itself, is marked with the trace of speaking to the other. What is more, the resonance of Being in the verbality of language is ambiguous, for Being (Levinas uses the term *l'essence* to refer to Heidegger's *das Sein*) resonates in the said always on the point of becoming a name. In fact, it often turns itself into a name, a noun that designates a "being" whose quiddity is the essence of beings.

This ambiguity with which language attends to its own verbality makes Levinas question *Sage* as the exclusive "essential" dimension of language, for as the showing saying of Being *Sage* comes too close to the said, too close to the danger and violence of thematization, to account for the radical separation of the infinitely other. Therefore, though *le Dire* and *Sage* could be translated into English by the same word, *saying*, Levinas suggests that they mean differently. Levinas agrees that the ambiguous mutation of Being into a being, the nominalization of the verb *to be*, the self-veiling unveiling of Being measures pre-ontologically, that is, that it goes beyond the traditional ontological schemes of subjectivity, representation, self-identification, and expression. However, even that "pre-," which describes the invisible furrowing of meaning, does not exhaust *le dire* (*OBBE*, 44/*AEAE*, 55). As Derrida remarks in "At this very moment in this work here I am," Levinas places *le dire* beyond verb and noun, beyond the verbality of language, beyond *symplokè*.[36] The *symplokè* of Being, the interweaving of invisible paths of verbalization and nominalization is marked with the "toward the other" beyond verb and noun.

In Levinas, the saying signals itself through the said, but not as Being; it signals itself from within Being as "otherwise than Being" (*autrement qu'être*). In other words, even though *le dire* signals itself in terms of Being—that is, the manifestation of Being is the primary event: "If being and manifestation go together in the said, it is in fact natural that if the saying on the hither side of the said can show itself, it be said already in terms of being" (*OBBE*, 43/*AEAE*, 56)—the saying of the saying in terms of Being does not account for the saying as the relation to the other. In order to preserve its status on the "hither side" of the said (*en deça* or *à l'envers*), the saying has to immediately unsay itself: "The *otherwise than being* is stated in a saying that must also be unsaid in order to thus extract the *otherwise than being* from the said in which it already comes to signify but a *being otherwise*" (*OBBE*, 7/*AEAE*, 8). What, without silencing the ethical, prevents this mutation of the ethical signification of otherwise than Being into the horizon of Being is the particularity of the trace, which will be discussed later. Levinas's analysis of language makes clear that he intends his saying to signify beyond Being, beyond the verbality of language, its way-making, which makes Being vibrate in words (*faire vibrer l'essence*) (*OBBE*, 35/*AEAE*, 44). For Heidegger, this vibrating is the very arranging (*fügen*) that readies the structures that can be filled with meaning. It is this arranging understood as the very call for arranging that Heidegger names *Sage*. While Heidegger can be said to focus mostly on the arranging, on the gathering of *Sage*, Levinas's primary concern lies with the direction in which the gathering of saying (with human responding [*nachsagen*] already inscribed in it) gathers—the other.

This difference in emphasis between Heidegger and Levinas becomes evident in the role otherness plays in their approach to language. For Heidegger, otherness is always at play in the transpropriation of *Ereignis*, where it is determined by the fact that, as Gianni Vattimo observes in *Les aventures de la différence*, humans and Being are free from the determinations given to them previously by metaphysics, that is, those of subject and object.[37] What Heidegger thinks through *Ereignis* is the very process of "propriating" between thinking and Being. Since "propriating" is understood in an eminently verbal sense, thinking and Being near each other in such a manner that they never completely come into their "own." As Derrida remarks in *Spurs*, the proper is never fixed, it lifts itself and carries itself away (*"s'elève et s'emporte—de lui-même"*).[38] Hence there is no absolute identity, it is never fully posited, rather it is being reciprocally "guided." This mutual "guiding" is perhaps best visible in the Heideggerian fourfold (*Geviert*): mortals, gods, earth, and the sky near each other, and in this nearing they are on the way to their "own." In an analogous way, humans and Being are in the process of constant passing into each other; they are continuously coming mutually into their own, and it is this coming, this approaching one's identity, which interests Heidegger most. This passing into the other makes explicit that in Heidegger's thought alterity is always present, since it is only through the other that identification becomes possible; in fact, identifying itself is the nearing of the other.

Taking the transpropriation between human beings and Being as the only way in which Heidegger addresses/abandons the question of ethics, Levinas points to the necessity of a more radical approach to the ethical significance of the other's alterity, which would claim a sense beyond that of Being. For Levinas, such sense is inscribed in the ruptures of self-identification induced by the other's alterity, in the dislocation and exposition of the subject to the other, which Levinas calls "subjectity" (*subjectité*). This subjectity should never be confused with the subject proper, as it always precedes the subject and inflects its modality of self-sameness into ethical openness and responsibility. In other words, subjectity denotes a pre-subjective modality of exposure to the other, one's subjection (*sujetion*) to the other. Unlike the subject, subjectity is not characterized by its opposition, ultimately recuperable, to objectivity, as the subject-object opposition usually implies the possibility of identification, the process of coming into one's own.

For Levinas, subjectness, in the sense of sub-jection, implies precisely dispropriation, the impossibility of identification and identity, an irrecuperable rupture of subjectivity.[39]

Differently put, the other is not there for the subject to mark itself against it; rather one is prevented from ever becoming a subject by one's subjection to the other, and, consequently, one (*l'un*) is there always for the other (*l'un-pour-l'autre*). As Levinas remarks, the-one-for-the-other does not constitute the way one expresses oneself or gives a sign; rather it is that very sign itself, the sign of responsibility for the other (*OBBE*, 49/*AEAE*, 63). Derrida observes that this "giving of the very giving of giving" (*donner le donner même du donner*) is neither a thing nor an act, and therefore what gives is not an ego (*un moi*), not a subject in the usual sense.[40] Instead the meaning of the-one-for-the-other is that of the Abrahamic departure without return, a departure toward the other, which marks also a departure from Being, a radical "disinterestedness." Since for Levinas Being, *esse*, means always *interesse*, the depositing and de-situating of the-one-for-the-other "is the very modality of dis-interestedness" (*dés-intéressement*) (*OBBE*, 50/*AEAE*, 65). This "structure" that characterizes subjection makes possible the abandonment of ontological terminology: subjectness is not only *dis-inter-esse* but also responsibility.

According to Levinas, the one (*l'un*) is incontrovertible and irreducible to a verbal form, that is, it cannot be described in terms of Being or beings: "This nominal form comes from somewhere else (*d'ailleurs*) than the verbalness of essence" (*OBBE*, 53/*AEAE*, 68). Since self-identification leads ultimately to the concept of the subject, to the elaboration of the genre of "human beings," in Levinas's reading the subject not only does not preserve an individuality but in fact loses its singularity in this process of universalization. Against the background of this semi-mechanical generalization, Levinas claims that it is precisely the subjection, the subjectness, to the other that guarantees the singularity of "my" ethical responsibility against the universalizing power of representation. This peculiar mode of singularization, however, does not individualize one's identity but rather ensures the uniqueness of its exposure to the other, disrupting the complacency of any generalized or shared burden. Because the subjection to the other becomes also "election," the responsibility of the-one-for-the-other is singular par excellence: nobody can take my place; no one can relieve me of my responsibility for the other. In the responsibility of subjection, the uniqueness of the responsible "me," anterior to any variant of philosophical I, secures its essential singularity. In this way, Levinasian subjectity can never become a subject, for its exposure to the other prohibits a self-gathering necessary for the notion of the subject. The saying that delivers the sign of the-one-for-the-other before telling anything consents infinitely and pre-voluntarily and always signifies a consent for the other.[41] Yet the singularity of *l'un* cannot be approached in terms of identity. In fact, the essay entitled "No Identity" makes clear that the responsibility for the other is the primary dispossession of *l'un*, as there is no identity that precedes the subjection to the other, and the one always means "the-one-for-the-other."

For Levinas, the-one-for-the-other also indicates a meaning different from Heidegger's *Existenz*. To the extent that *Dasein* happens as *ek-stasis*, as a continuous transcendence toward the world, it always transcends in and toward Being. Moreover, *Existenz* is marked by reciprocity; it is an existence that in nearing Being comes, in a sense, into its own without ever coming into its own. The-one-for-the-other, on the other hand, means "no identity" but an an-archic displacement of subjectivity. In this notion of subjectity as subjection one can perhaps see a distinction between Heideggerian nearness and Levinasian proximity. As is the case with *Sage* and *le dire*, though translatable into English by the same word, *proximity* or *nearness*, *Nähe* and *proximité* differ in their emphasis. Keeping in mind that Heideggerian nearness cannot be collapsed into the proper without a reserve or a remainder, Levinasian proximity can be taken as underscoring and radicalizing the ethical significance of nearness, implicit in Heidegger's work. Due to this modification, Levinas's proximity indicates a transcendence beyond Being, a movement "from within" Being that cannot be totally converted into modalities of *einai*.[42] This "from within" points to the complexity of thinking the non-phenomenal from within the phenomenal, the complexity that for Levinas defines the essence of language, the face. This complexity reflects the direction of the *entre-tiens* with the other, in which the world is offered as a theme (*TI*, 95/*TeI*, 68). Thus the way the other faces becomes the offering of a direction for the invisible furrowing of meaning described by Heidegger, the offering that can itself be thematized only inasmuch as the other faces phenomenally. Even if language turns itself to the face as already thematizing it, as trying to keep the face within the light of phenomenality (*TI*, 195–197/*TeI*, 169–172), the face, though it originates language, signifies "beyond" it (*au-delà*).

Levinas claims that the direction of offering precedes in an inverted manner disclosive appropriation (*Ereignis*), for it is only from within the opening that one can think the overflowing of the opening. Yet by overflowing, that which overflows, as the absolutely anterior, *passé non-thèmatisable*, transcends even the very order of primordiality. In the verb *to be*, Being resonates in such a way that it not only does not muffle the echo of the ethical saying (*le dire*) but "helps" it deliver the signal, which imprints its trace upon thematization as dethematization (*OBBE*, 46–47/*AEAE*, 59). What is of most importance here, then, is the way in which this imprinting dethematization modifies the self-veiling of Being, the manner in which *proximité* might be "different" from *Nähe*— the trace. I see such possibility opened by the two key terms in which "The Trace of the Other" characterizes the trace: *droiture* (straightforwardness, uprightness) and *irrectitude*.[43] In spite of the apparent contradiction, the juxtaposition of these two words reflects what Levinas calls transcendence. If *droiture* designates the way the trace enters the light of phenomenality, then the trace is never a mask or a false appearance behind which the "true" other is hidden. On the contrary, in the trace the other appears "naked," expresses itself, yet not in the manner of correlation between the sign and the signified, not in the manner of "rectitude" that would comply with the differential economy of signification. The apparent contradiction is produced precisely by the peculiar manner in which the other's alterity signifies "laterally" and turns the trace into the very "irrectitude" of signification.

The irrectitude of the trace that signals the proximity of the other as the opening of language provides a hint as to its difference from "nearing." Heideggerian nearness is characterized by transpropriation in which thinking and Being are made appropriate for each other. The self-veiling of Being belongs to transpropriation as that which preserves the oscillation between identity and alterity. Yet the fact that Heidegger characterizes nearness as *sparende*, as always retaining, reserving, and thus preserving alterity, means also that, by reserving itself and remaining other, that which comes near "influences." The withdrawal characteristic of Being "identifies" *Denken* as the thinking of withdrawing, of reserved and veiled alterity. Therefore, nearness is marked by a mutual influence through the self-veiling reserve of thinking and Being which come near each other. The "same" of thinking and Being can then be described as a "magnetic" drawing near, an encounter in which one feels the power of drawing. Thus thinking and Being "magnetize" each other without surrendering their identity; they propriate without becoming fully proper.

According to Levinas, the proximity of the other cannot, however, be thought as drawing together but rather as irrectitude.

What Levinas questions in the Heideggerian understanding of language through nearness is the implied unicity, the drawing, the *Zug*, which, though disengaged from subjectivity and non-dialectizable, contains a residue of sameness. For Levinas, this residue, however faint, varied, and marked with otherness, does not seem to do justice to the absolutely other. That is precisely why there is no "propriation" in the Levinasian proximity, why the ethical alterity of the other is declared as not affecting identity at all. Levinas characterizes this proximity as "non-allergic" (allergy: the other-effect, from the Greek *allos* [other] and *ergon* [activity, effect]), which suggests that the other has "no effect" on thought, that he/she neither limits theoretical knowledge nor influences it but instead overflows it. Because of the irrectitude of the trace, thought, though "noticing" the trace, encounters no resistance, no limit. In other words, while transpropriation is marked by the affecting "toward the other" of thinking and Being, which steer each other into their essence by "magnetizing" the direction, the trace lets thought lose itself in the direction without affecting or limiting it. The meanings of *trans* in transpropriation and transcendence appear therefore to be different: in Heidegger *trans* means reciprocity, "each other," and a possible allergy, while in Levinas *trans* indicates irrectitude, not verticality as opposed to the horizontality of transpropriation, but the trace as direction without limit—infinity. Thus it becomes obvious that for Levinas alterity in transpropriation, the reserving in *Ereignis*, is not absolute or ethical alterity. In Levinas's eyes, the reciprocity of transpropriation harbors a "trace" of allergy, a mutuality of drawing, of leading *each other* into essence. And, in Levinas's interpretation, the other has to be infinitely other, has to be "overlooked" and have no "effect"; not because he/she "is not," rather because, due to the irrectitude of the trace, the other overflows "laterally," infinitely non-allergic.

The Trace

The non-allergic character of otherness implies the ingratitude on the part of the one, since gratitude would be a response, a return into the inevitability of totalization. Beside making impossible any par excellence "thoughtful" response to the other, non-allergy points to a twofoldness of the trace, to its marking itself within language and at the same time erasing itself from it. Thus the trace is possible only as the trace of the trace, as the erasure of the trace (*OBBE*, 91/*AEAE*, 115). It is the trace as the erasure of the trace that articulates the controversy at the center of Levinas's philosophy, the possibility of displacing or dislocating the "essence" of language in such a way that, despite its "beyondness," or rather because of it, it would mark the "Greekness" of language with the trace of "Hebraic" alterity: the trace that erases itself in such a manner that its erasure becomes "unerasable," that it remains (probably) a tracing erasure, at least as a possibility, a "maybe" (*peut-être*).

Since the relation to the other is beyond *symplokè* "otherwise than" the interweaving of the language paths, the trace marks itself as a rupture of *symplokè*, a rupture simultaneously interwoven into *symplokè*, yet interwoven in such a way that it inflects the interweaving. Levinas elaborates this, one is tempted to say, double rupture at the end of *Otherwise than Being*, with a particular stress laid on the twofoldness of this rupturing:

> This discourse [of Western philosophy] will affirm itself to be coherent and one. In relating the interruption of the discourse or my being ravished into discourse I connect its thread. The discourse is ready to say all the ruptures in itself, and consume them as silent origin or eschatology. . . . Are we not at this very moment (*en ce moment même*) in the process of barring the issue that our whole essay attempts, and of encircling our position from all sides? (*OBBE*, 169/*AEAE*, 215)

> And I still interrupt the ultimate discourse in which all the discourses are stated, in saying it to the one that listens to it, and who is situated outside the said that the discourse (*discours*) says, outside all it includes. That is true of the discussion (*discours*) I am elaborating at this very moment (*que je suis en train de tenir en ce moment même*). This reference to an interlocutor permanently (*d'une façon permanente*) breaks through the text that the discourse claims to weave in thematizing and enveloping all things. (*OBBE*, 170/*AEAE*, 216–217)

These two "moments" in Levinas's discourse, though they happen at the very same moment (*en ce moment même*), best describe the twofoldness, the two "moments," of the trace.

The twofoldness of this inscription/erasure comes under a very detailed and penetrating scrutiny in Derrida's interpretation of the trace in "En ce moment même dans cet ouvrage me voici." As Derrida explains, the relation between these two moments is not that of distinction; rather, the "second" moment has, in the manner of metalepsis,[44] an infinite "advantage" over the "first" one. While the first moment belongs to dialectics, it returns to the same and interweaves the trace into the totality of discourse, the second one makes the first one possible and, by making it possible, overflows it infinitely and beforehand.[45] In this way, the two moments constitute what Levinas calls transcendence, which, in terms of this study, functions as a specifically ethical inflection of language. For Derrida, these two moments also imply a "series," a repetition without which Levinas would not be able to offer the "probable" essence of language as the relation to the other. One can always treat this "series" in the sense usually attached to this word, but then the beyond of the series characteristic of Levinas's writings, the *hors-série*, would be disregarded.

The *hors-série* of the series in question results from the fact that the series comprises not the threads, the paths that interweave the mesh of language, but the interruptions of the threads. Even though the trace, the saying, interrupts the weaving of the linguistic threads only to be simultaneously rewoven into the "torn" mesh, this reweaving does not amount to a simple relinking of a torn thread, as the new "knot" is not woven out of threads but out of the very interruption of the threads. In other words, the series beyond series does not weave threads but the interruptions, the intervals of hiatus between them (EM, 39–40). Thus this absolute series is strictly speaking without a single knot, because it links a multiplicity of interruptions without threads (*sans-fil*) which let open the interruption among interruptions. These serial interruptions Derrida calls *sériature*,[46] a seriasure characterized by *destricturation absolue*, which points to the absence of the destination of the trace, to the impossibility of return. The "absolute destricturation," the impossibility of stricture, has to be, however, always mediated through the stricture of language; it has to be, as Derrida remarks, negotiated in terms of stricture and series (44). This contamination is not "negative"; it does not detract from the trace but rather constitutes the very process of tracing. Yet the necessity of negotiating the trace makes one interruption, one trace, insufficient for guarding the alterity of the other. There must be (*il faut*) a series (of erasures), a seriasure.

Seriasure characterizes such an interweaving of the trace that lets the trace abandon its trace, absolve itself from it and remain other. Seriasure is therefore not only an interweaving, an interlacing (*entrelacer*), but also an "entracing" (*entracer*); it is the very performing of what Derrida calls *l'entr(el)acement*.[47] *L'entr(el)acement* is the letting-the-trace, which, as it wants to say and do nothing, announces itself on its own basis, not on the basis of Being. The letting-the-trace (*laisser-trace*) implies the abandoning, the leaving, of the trace, which does not insist on a sign but effaces itself only to let the trace of a trace. Therefore the letting-the-trace performs "otherwise" than letting-be (*Seinlassen*); it marks a meaning beyond Being. As Derrida remarks, seriasure is based on the principle of repeating itself in dislocation without return (*se répéter . . . pour se dis-loquer sans retour*) (EM, 33/RL, 22). He stresses the fact that this iterability is of a strange and unusual kind; nevertheless, it is an iterability which lets "this very moment" differ and distance itself with respect to itself. Yet, though Levinas writes about the "interrupted discourse," the rupture that he has in mind seems to be more of a permanent, continuous rupturing. Although Derrida is absolutely right that the reference to an interlocutor pierces the language mesh serially, Levinas nevertheless insists that the effects are, in a manner of speaking, permanent (*d'une façon permanente*) (*OBBE*, 170/AEAE, 217). Both *façon* (manner) and *permanente* (permanent) are decisive in this context, for, whenever Levinas writes about the face or the trace, he indicates the unique manner in which they signify with the use of the words *en quelque façon*. *Façon* refers specifically to the inverse, the other side signified by the trace, and, since in *Otherwise than Being*, Levinas implies that the inverse signifies permanently, it appears that the *façon permanente* describes the very laterality of the trace elaborated in "The Trace of the Other."

It is indeed the laterality of the trace that provides the context for Levinas's "metaphors" of threads, knots, and ruptures, as it also accounts for the non-allergic facing of the other. But, if the other is non-allergic, then he/she does not really rupture language, or at least, the rupture is not violent. As Levinas often remarks, the other does not break the order of language, she baffles it (*desarçon-ner*). Then, there seems to be no need for an actual reweaving, since nothing is torn, maybe (*peut-être*) only the language mesh is ruffled by the passing-by of the other. Can we then say that the trace of the passing is otherwise than rupturing, weaving, and rerupturing? If so, then its tracing is guaranteed not only by seriasure but primarily by its "permanence," a strange kind of permanence that only "may be" permanent and thus can be indicated exclusively through a series of erasures. Series implies a split in "this very moment," an iterability of "at this very moment" (*en ce moment même*). However, that iterability, this "split," is, as Levinas remarks, "inoperative without a second time, without *reflection* on the condition of the statement that states this signification" (*OBBE*, 156/AEAE, 199). The iterability is operative only after the fact (*après coup seulment*), and it is the *après coup* effect that, according to Levinas, necessitates seriality and the repetition of ruptures. For Levinas, the iterability, characteristic more of the said, can itself operate only already in the "permanence" of the trace. It seems, therefore, that for Levinas language goes through a series of silent and invisible ruptures only when it already unfolds in the trace of the other, which, signaling itself serially, nevertheless signifies laterally, and, in *en quelque façon*, continuously.[48] Laterality does imply absolute separation, but a separation that already designates an "obligating" direction. This direction lateralizes the said in a manner radically different from polarization, for lateralization implies not only difference but the enveloping in non-indifference. It is lateralization that makes all language, all atoms of the said (EM, 50/*RL*, 38), at each and every moment, marked with the saying, with the non-indifference toward the other. The Abrahamic direction implies a lateral sense, which compels not only to reading the trace and the entracing but to reading them already *in* the trace.

The laterality of the trace also accounts for the notion of the an-archic, inoriginal, absolutely past other. The other obligates "the one" in a lateral manner; that is, the obligation precedes any demand, any call on the part of the other, "an obedience that precedes the hearing of any order."[49] Laterality marks the way in which the other entraces itself upon language as absolutely and irreversibly past, yet past in such a manner that it permanently "lateralizes" language in the ethical direction. This lateralization can be approached as a minimal linguistic inflection, untraceable by words but nevertheless affecting them and endowing language with a sense of ethical obligation.

The laterality of the trace also points to another Levinasian departure from Heidegger. In *Ereignis*, as Heidegger makes it clear throughout his writings, thinking is always a response, co-presencing with Being's call for thinking. Because of this infold of thinking into Being, Being always retains a sense of primordiality, but a co-presencing primordiality of the call for thinking. The Levinasian trace marks itself laterally with respect to history and Being; therefore, responsibility toward the other cannot be characterized through the "ontological" term of "response." It is a responsibility that overflows the terms of Being, responsibility anterior to the call.

This particular atemporality of the trace is given special attention in Derrida's exploration of the phrase "*il aura obligé*" (he will have obligated) from "En ce moment même." The future anteriority implied by the phrase characterizes the mode of tracing as "other" with respect to presence and absence. Levinas at one point describes it as "non-absence," at other points as non-synchronizable diachrony. Just as it is not a present, presence, or presencing, it is also not a total absence or a negative but instead an an-archy, the beyond of any origin, always reducible to the terms of Being. As Derrida explains, the future anteriority of *il aura obligé* does not "decline a verb saying the action of a subject in an operation that would have been *present*" (EM, 49/*RL*, 37). The trace can be approached neither in terms of verbality nor nominality; instead, as Levinas quite often points out, it has to be understood as "accusativity" or "vocativity." In *Otherwise than Being*, the saying is described as "pure vocative" (*OBBE*, 150/*AEAE*, 191), and in "God and Philosophy" as accusative.[50] Such saying means therefore the extra-verting of subjectity (as "the-one-for-the-other"); it turns one into *me voici*, indicative of one's subjection. This accusative or vocative precedes the nominative; it directs all nominalization. As Levinas puts it, the saying is like silence. It can even be easily "misheard" as the *Geläut der Stille*, as the "rustling of *il y a*"; yet, though it comes without words, it does not come with empty hands. Those "not empty hands" imply the accusative beyond and prior to all nominative, the accusative of the one "seen" by the face, a subjectity that cannot avoid responsibility by simple nominalization and a turn into an I, the specimen of a genre, or a universal.

The declaration of responsibility, *me voici* (here I am), becomes possible because of the "in-originality" of the trace (*OBBE*, 97/*AEAE*, 123). Levinas remarks that the trace cannot be approached in terms of originality and primordiality, for the "height" from which the signifyingness of the other "lateralizes" language is beyond the hierarchy of origin and primordiality. The "in-originality" of the trace marks what Levinas calls its "enigma," which, despite an obvious reference to Heidegger, probably needs to be understood differently from *Geheimnis*, characteristic of the reserving withdrawal of Being. The enigma of the Levinasian saying does not simply add itself to the signification of Being but "deranges" it; it directs it to a "track" different from the tracks of Being.[51] Thus the Levinasian enigma marks another "derangement" of many of Heideggerian terms, a lateralization of the enigma of the trace with respect to the mystery of Being.

For Levinas, the laterality with which the enigma of the trace signifies indicates a modality different from that of Being and certitude, the modality of "otherwise than Being or beyond essence," the modality of "maybe": "The signifyingness of an enigma comes from an irreversible, irrecuperable past which it has *perhaps* [in this context, rather *maybe* (*peut-être*), modification mine, K.Z.] not left since it has already been absent from the very terms in which it was signaled ("perhaps" [may-be, *peut-être*] is the modality of an enigma, irreducible to the modalities of being and certainty)" (*DVI*, 214/*CPP*, 71). The enigma of the trace, though it announces itself in terms of Being, cannot be explicated in those terms. As Derrida writes in "En ce moment même," the "perhaps," "maybe," and "probably," which proliferate throughout Levinas's writings, do not imply anything empirical or approximate about the rigor of Levinas's discourse (EM, 33/*RL*, 23). Since the saying does not belong to the discourse upon the said, and it does not express itself in terms of statements and certainties, the enigma does not define or refuse to define anything that could be approached in terms of the language of "being present." Although the use of *peut-être* affects all the assertive statements of Levinas's work, it does not enfeeble them; instead, it points to the fact that the "maybe" of the enigma makes language possible, that language gets under way only within the ethical direction. As Derrida remarks, "[w]ithout that [ethical] responsibility there would be no language, but it *is never sure* that language surrenders itself to the responsibility that makes it possible (surrenders to its simply probable essence)" (*RL*, 23).[52] This remark captures the way the enigma of the trace "directs" language: the trace of ethical responsibility precedes the origin of language in such a manner that language can neither affirm it as its own "essence" nor suppress its "maybe."

It is precisely this "maybe," marking with its rhetorical "seal" Levinas's work, that lets him maintain the claim to a discourse "otherwise" than through Being. In other words, the unerasable insecurity of the "maybe" marks the ethical language of "otherwise than being" apart from Being by disallowing any settlement or resolution of its precarious mode of signifying. On this account, the enigma of the trace differs from the mystery of Being: Being, letting beings be, veils itself and retreats as the clearing for "what is." The enigma, on the other hand, never veils itself, it is "nakedness par excellence," the absence of any image, even that of self-veiling; it is absolute alterity, which as alterity, is imageless, a trace. Moreover, as Levinas remarks in *Hors sujet*, the ethical modality of the trace "precedes" any rhetoric, as it is only through the relation to the other that underlies language that rhetoric receives a meaning, *un sens*.[53] For Levinas, the new modality of "otherwise than being" implied by the notion of enigma secures a meaning, *un sens*, beyond the otherness associated with Being: "What is essential here is the way a meaning that is beyond meaning is inserted in the meaning that remains in an order, the way it advances while retreating" (*DEHH*, 209/*CPP*, 66). Levinasian trace, its lateral signifyingness, allows his discourse to "maybe" have a meaning beyond Being, without contradicting itself or detracting anything from the argument. At the same time, it is only in the context of Heidegger's question of Being and meaning that Levinas's philosophy can show its full significance, or should one say, in order to remain "responsible" for his discourse, its full signifyingness.

Usually ethics is thought apart from, or at best as part of, properly or purely philosophical, that is, ontological or epistemological, discourse. Even "Letter on Humanism," despite the radicalization of both the ethical and the ontological problematics, still places ethics within the horizon of Being. For Levinas, Heidegger, to the extent that human beings, as the "shepherds of Being," have their essential determination in resaying Being, makes the ethical contingent on the esse-ncing (*Wesen*) of language. Therefore Levinas insists that what he takes to have been thought by Heidegger as a purely ontological issue, that is, the question of Being as Being, must be shown as already immersed in the ethical signifyingness. This is why Levinas sees ethics not simply in the dimension of *praxis*, actual rules and imperatives— though, as he often remarks, the face as the proximity to the other has a direct link to the empirical event of obligation to another[54]—but rather as inscribed in the very essence of language, as traced in the very unfolding of thinking.

This complicated Levinasian approach to Heidegger should not be taken too quickly as a pure and simple critique of Heidegger's conception of language that would postulate a different "essence" of language, for, when considered against the backdrop of Heidegger's work on language, it makes possible an amplification of the ethical concerns echoed in Heidegger's own texts. Levinas is clear on the point that the relation to the other is not the essence of language, and that it is, at best, as Derrida remarks, a "probable" essence of language. In other words, the relation to the other is beyond essence, yet not as a higher essence, but rather as a direction that provides meaning for the invisible furrowing of signification, for the way thinking infolds into Being. As both *Totality and Infinity* and *Otherwise than Being or Beyond Essence* make clear, Levinas acknowledges the "essence" of language as the vibration of Being. Still, this acknowledgment does not mean that the ethical, the *ver l'Autre*, does not lateralize this vibration by leaving its trace. In this way, Levinas wants to give the Heideggerian approach to language an "other" direction. Only through this "derangement,"

clearly stressed in the last paragraph of *Otherwise than Being,* can
the importance of Levinas's ethics be grasped:

> In this work which does not seek to restore any ruined con-
> cept, the destitution and the desituating of the subject do not
> remain without signification: after the death of a certain god
> inhabiting the world behind the scenes, the substitution of
> the hostage discovers the trace, the unpronounceable inscrip-
> tion, of what, always already past, always "he," does not enter
> into any present, to which are suited not the nouns designat-
> ing beings, or the verbs in which their essence resounds, but
> that which, as a pronoun, marks with its seal all that a noun
> can convey (*OBBE,* 185/*AEAE,* 233).[55]

The trace is the pronoun, the pre-name, which irrecusably marks
all language, and, as the seal of otherness with which Levinas remarks language, it introduces an irreversible change into philosophy. With Levinas, philosophy can no longer think ethics apart
from the "purely philosophical," from Being qua Being, from difference and differing as such. It is in fact possible to read Levinas as
saying that difference can never be "pure," not only because as
such it is unthinkable but primarily because it is always marked
with non-indifference.

It is indeed in the notion of non-indifference, in its modality
of "maybe," which "perhaps" inflects language ethically, that I see
Levinas's most valuable contribution to the debates about language and otherness. To see its significance, it is necessary to
underscore Levinas's reluctance to describe ethical alterity in terms
of difference, which inevitably and interminably involves the
other and weaves his/her alterity into the play of signification. In
other words, in a Levinasian interpretation, difference fails to render justice to ethical alterity; only when it is "an-archically"
inscribed in non-indifference and thus pre-scribed ethically, can
difference be at all sensitive to otherness. In Levinas's view, it is
possible to discern otherness, and thus also difference, only in the
perspective of non-indifference, which has already dislocated and
ex-posed the machinery of language. As ethically inflected, language, despite its continuous thematizing of otherness, its compromising of the infinity of the other, reserves a possibility of non-
indifference to alterity.

The significance of this ethical inflection of language comes
best into view against the backdrop of Heidegger's concern with
language and with the saying of Being. The juxtaposition of Hei-

deggerian and Levinasian terms brings them into relief and under-scores the specificity of each thinking and a difference of emphases. It must be remembered, though, that to the extent that in Heidegger's approach to language thinking "listens" not only to Being but also to others, it is possible to claim that a sense of expo-sure or non-indifference to others surfaces already in Heidegger's discussions of poetry and language. Obviously, it is Levinas who, via a different route and set of concerns, emphasizes and elaborates the specificity of the ethical inflection of language, precisely as jux-taposed to the notion of language as the saying of (the retreat of) Being. That is why it is in the context of Levinas's thought, in the aftermath of his polemic with Heidegger, that one is perhaps better prepared to read the ethical concerns in Heidegger's texts. In an interesting way, Levinas's insistence on seeing language as exposed to the other and marked by an ethical sense and direction, as the double meaning of *un sens* suggests, provides a perspective within which Heidegger's own pronouncements about otherness can be better heard. As a result, the encounter of those two thinkers underscores the significance of the twofold or chiasmic otherness that influences and inflects language: the enigmatic character of giving in *Ereignis* and the entraced ethicity of language, its exposi-tion to the other.

᪆ 4 ᪆

THE OTHER NOTATION
Stevens and the Supreme Fiction of Poetry

Wallace Stevens could be called a philosopher('s) poet, in the sense that his poetry often explicitly engages philosophical ideas, themes, and concerns, evolving a poetics that has not simply a literary but also a philosophic value and relevance. And if we were to name one particular thinker in this context, it would be, without doubt, Heidegger, even though Stevens, in spite of his interest in the German philosopher, probably never read any of his works. Without claiming any direct influence, it is enough to take a look at the amount of literary scholarship linking Stevens's poetic concerns with Heidegger's question of Being to appreciate the relevance of this connection for contemporary literary and theoretical debates. Most, if not all, of those accounts employ Heideggerian ideas as a background against which it becomes possible to recognize and articulate the stakes and the importance of Stevensian poetics. I adopt here a different approach, which, while it certainly argues for a "Heideggerian" reading of Stevens, also regards his texts as a poetic counterpart of Heidegger's exploration of language, which corroborates and reinforces the latter's insights. To the extent that the Heideggerian refiguration of otherness is motivated by his engagement with poetry, Stevens's work can be considered Heidegger's neighbor, and its poetics, a contribution to the problematic relation of thinking to what Stevens himself most often calls "being." The emphasis on this proximity does not simply question or enlarge the canon of "Heidegger's poets" but instead enters the neighborhood of poetry and thinking on the poet's side. If Heidegger's texts on poetry work on the model of a thinker responding to the poem and developing his insight in its proximity, then this chapter, as well as the subsequent ones on Celan, presents poetic developments of language as an exchange with philosophers, as a prism that inflects, enlarges, and contextualizes their concerns.

Our discussion here will focus specifically on how Stevens's late poems, revising the earlier articulations of his poetics through the optics of the divide between mind and world, approach the relation of poetic language to reality as the problem of figuring and marking the otherness of Being, the effect that its withdrawal produces in poetry. Stevens refers to this otherness as "a poem that never reaches words,"[1] indicating a structure of linguistic transfer perhaps as complex as the Heideggerian "way-making" of language, where the saying (Sage) of manifestation traverses into "the sounded word" only in the form of what Heidegger calls the unsaid (Ungesagte). In Heidegger, this volatile affinity between the phenomenal and the linguistic can be explained as the infold of thinking into Being, a nearness that motivates and structures the language-event. For Stevens, the proximity and the reserve of Being that inaugurate poetry present themselves, in terms proposed by "Notes toward a Supreme Fiction" and "A Primitive like an Orb," as nativeness and inhabiting. Reminiscent of the pre-ontological understanding of Being from Being and Time, Stevensian "poetic nativeness" does not signify a simple familiarity but rather an involvement with otherness structurally similar to what contemporary thought, from Heidegger to Derrida, has identified as tracing. In other words, it is a familiarity with the unfamiliar, a mark of what erases itself, a habitation in otherness.

The poems that follow "Notes toward a Supreme Fiction," moving beyond the apparent post-Romantic poetics of the earlier texts, tie the inception of poetry to the retreat of Being from words. As in Heidegger, in Stevens's poetry the possibility of thinking this otherness from which language unfolds hinges upon a discourse, a poetic idiom, which, rather than mapping the relation between the self and the world, demonstrates their common habitation, in which their difference marks itself in the first place. In the context of the complex interrelation between various poetics in Stevens, this chapter foregrounds precisely the dependence of this moment of disclosure upon a reserve of otherness, and the proximity of this Stevensian figure to Heidegger's infold. It shows how Stevens regards all that transpires in a poetic text, its idiom, imagery, and themes, as motivated and regulated by the degree in which language can be seen as native to Being. Reading this sense of indigenity in the context of language understood as disclosure, my argument elaborates what might be called the "poetics of notes" in Stevens's late poems. Since this aspect of Stevens's poetic language finds its exemplary expression in "Notes toward a Supreme Fiction," the chapter deals in detail with parts of this long "manifesto," as well as with several poems written in the same period of time. It also argues that the title phrase "supreme fiction" becomes Stevens's vehicle for discussing the equivocal inscription of otherness in poetic language.

Exploring the limits of the familiar interplay of the mind and the world, Stevens's poems often refer to an other, unnameable poem, for which they themselves are merely preliminary "notes." This recurring theme of a poem that eludes words, a "non-poem" withholding itself from writing, maps Stevens's continuing interest in what remains other with respect to the text of a poem. This otherness is never obtrusive; on the contrary, it often disappears behind the spectacular word- and sound-play of Stevens's language, with its elaborate rhythmic, rhyming, and stanzaic patterns. What, then, is the status of this other "poem," this other *of* the poem, and how can this otherness, which makes "place" for poetry, be indicated in poetic language or critical discourse that follows it?

Poet on the Dump: Stevens's Reckoning with the Romantic Legacy

Interested in rearticulating the difference between imagination and reality, self and other, Stevens explores the legacy of poetic figurations of these schemas, consciously involving his work, both its rhetoric and its thematic, in the post-Cartesian debates on duality and difference. To appreciate the complexity of Stevens's treatment of the issues of difference, oppositionality, and binarism and to foreground the modification introduced into these discussions by his idea of "the poem that never reaches words," it is important to review the critical responses to Stevens's work, in particular those that address its representation of otherness. The intricacy and difficulty of Stevens's engagement with consciousness and its attitudes toward its other finds its expression in the often antithetical interpretations of his work, readings that, in most cases, either stress the novelty of his "post-Cartesian" language or relegate him, by criticism or by praise, to the rank of an epigone, however excellent, of Romanticism. What decides about this "critical divide" is precisely the reading of the poem that, as "Notes toward a Supreme Fiction" puts it, does not reach words, and in other places bears the name of the "central" and "grand" poem, or simply "the poem" (*CP*, 440). In fact, it is possible to maintain that most of the critical discourse on Stevens hinges upon the reading of the otherness of this "wordless poem" and its function in Stevens's poetry.

Since Stevens himself draws attention to the various poetics explored or at work in his texts, it is both difficult and unproductive to simply privilege one of them, for only their entire spectrum offers an appreciation of Stevens's complexity. We have, then, on the one hand, critics like Bloom and Vendler,[2] who inscribe Stevens into the Romantic tradition, taking the "central poem" as an invocation to the centrality of the self and poetic imagination. Marjorie Perloff, a critic of the echoes of Romanticism and Symbolism in the twentieth-century lyric, and a scholar of the "Pound era" in American poetry, also reads Stevens, to the extent that his poetry accomplishes itself in the play of self and other, within the Romantic paradigm of subjectivity. According to her reading, the images in Stevens's poems function as symbols of his emotional states, and the world, in a typically Romantic move, becomes the exteriorization of the lyrical I, the mirror of the poetic self.[3] Its otherness becomes subsumed into the correspondential relation between the symbolic sign and the symbolized, and the "beyond" to which Stevens's texts allude becomes definable within the symbolic paradigm. What is symbolized may be determined from the symbol itself, though not in terms of an ideal realm of essences. Perloff concludes that, although Stevens refers to indeterminacy, the forms of his poetry become determinable in terms of symbolic correspondences.[4] Otherness in Stevens's work can be explained, then, through reference back to the poet's self, to the creating mind, characteristic, for Perloff, of the lyrical form.

In his early reading of otherness in Stevens's poetry in *Poets of Reality*, J. Hillis Miller inscribes it into a teleological schema, where the central poem describes the ideal toward which Stevens's poems strive, the "perfect poem."[5] However, the poetic perfection remains unattainable, and the "progression" of Stevens's poetry condemns itself to failure; it becomes utopic. Otherness in Stevens's texts is again explained through a traditional, this time Platonic, paradigm structuring the history of metaphysics. In a similar vein, Joseph N. Riddel's *The Clairvoyant Eye*, though it carefully demarcates Stevens's theory of imagination from its Romantic parallels, interprets Stevens's work in terms of self-expression. Like Miller in *Poets of Reality*, Riddel approaches Stevens's poetry in evolutionary terms, through a change in the poetic theory underlying the poems. For Riddel, though, the development of Stevens's style reflects his self, the growth of his sensibility. Dealing with the problem of Being in Stevens, with the way "man experiences his is-ness,"[6] his argument remains within the metaphysical categories of self and world. Consequently Being is approached as beingness, as the way things "are," and the "central" poem becomes an attempt to regain a lost unity, a past in which the mind and the world could be synchronized.

Gerald Bruns and Thomas J. Hines, who read Stevens in the context of Heidegger's meditation on Being, also describe his poetics in terms of unity as the central category of interpretation.[7] In *Modern Poetry and the Idea of Language*, Bruns suggests that both Heidegger's and Stevens's conceptions of language can be approached through what he calls the Orphic paradigm, with the Orphic language defined as the speech of Being that unites the mind and the world in their presence. Stevens postulates the unity between the word and Being;[8] the poetic text discloses then the world as it is, and affirms its presence through words. Hines likewise, pointing out parallels between Heidegger's and Stevens's "theories" of poetic language, employs the rhetoric of unity, unison, and unification to describe the stakes of Stevens's poetry. In his interpretation, Being becomes the "source" of both the world and the mind, and, in its temporal dimension, it merges the interior and exterior time.[9] For both Bruns and Hines the "central" poem in Stevens, the poem that hesitates on the verge of words, would have to be read in the context of this unity. Thus, whether otherness in Stevens's poetry is explicitly described as post-Romantic or analyzed from the perspective of Heidegger's philosophy, otherness, the "beyond" of this poetry, is regularly interpreted in terms of presence, substance, subjectivity, the unity of word and Being. Such readings illustrate how closely indeed the idea of the "poem without words" engages and plays upon the Romantic or Symbolist paradigms, foregrounding the question of the fundamental unity of Being underlying the Cartesian dichotomy of the self and the world as its other.

This variety of interpretations has its source in the implicit doubling of Stevens's poetry into poems and their "central," "grand" poem "that never reaches words," a duplication that has often been interpreted exclusively in transcendental or Symbolist terms, without enough attention paid to the fact that these indications of doubling do not function as merely figures or symbols that point to another "order" or to the unity of the intelligible and the sensible in the intentional act of the mind. It is obviously true that both Stevens's poetry and his essays show a continuous interest in what one could indeed call a post-Romantic poetics. As Marjorie Perloff remarks, Stevens "rejects one form of Romantic dualism, that between natural and supernatural, the 'real' and the transcendent worlds, [but] remains committed to the other, perhaps more central Romantic and Symbolist dualism between the 'I' and the other, self and world."[10] The variations of the relation between self and world, which appear in a number of Stevens's poems, most notably in "Man with the Blue Guitar," result in different views of poetic language:[11] in a mimetic balance between the representation and the represented: "A tune upon the blue guitar / Of things exactly as they are"; in the interpretation of the imagination as the creative force that imposes its own laws and order and thus changes the reality exterior to the mind: "Things as they are / Are changed upon the blue guitar" (*CP*, 165); or in a disclosure understood as the unfolding of the unity of self and world in their Being: "And being would be being himself again" (*CP*, 255).

Thus Stevens's poetry often involves an interplay or a dialogue between various, sometimes opposed, theories of poetic language. In the Stevens chapter of his more recent book, *The Linguistic Moment: From Wordsworth to Stevens*, J. Hillis Miller has attempted to classify them under the rubric of three strategies that inform the entirety of Stevens's work: the mimetic, the aletheic, and poetry as creation.[12] Miller traces both mimetic and aletheic poetries back to Aristotle's *Poetics* to point out their mutual dependence and interconnections. The mimetic approach to poetry contends that language corresponds to reality and can adequately mirror it in a poetic statement. The aletheic theory of poetry, which Miller associates with Heidegger's "The Origin of the Work of Art," regards poetry as a revelation, a disclosure of reality through and in words. According to the third theory, poetry functions as a "metapoetry, a poetry of grammar, with the stress on the play of words among themselves."[13] With the evidence of many individual poems that either expressly describe or perform these theories, Miller's distinctions indeed account for a variety of Stevensian "poetries," poetries that can on the whole be derived from the main theme of Stevens's work—the relation between the mind and the world—and the various forms it assumes at different stages of the poet's career.[14]

The complexity and multiplicity of levels in Stevens's poetry thus validates different, even seemingly contradictory, approaches to his poetic language. Still, as recent criticism has made clear,[15] it is possible, especially in the context of the later poems, which attempt to move away from the binary oppositions and dualisms that structure the early poetry, to approach Stevens's work more radically, in a way that may put in perspective Stevens's preoccupation with different poetic attitudes to language. For his late poetry does not simply move toward a unity that would resolve the oppositions and leave a sense of balance achieved through a unifying concept; on the contrary, it underscores the remainder, a residue of distinct otherness, however unnameable, which because of its ineffable character resists any unification. Such implication of a "beyond," of a poem that never reaches words, cannot, then, be explained or interpreted in traditional metaphysical terms which inform the critical categories used to describe Romantic and post-Romantic poetry. Notwithstanding the "echoes" of the Romantic poetics, this most elusive otherness disrupts the paradigms and figures in which Stevens's poetry casts and explains itself, drawing attention to what, having brought poetry into words, remains other for them. Discussing the three prevalent poetic theories in Stevens, J. Hillis Miller points to this "disruptive element in Stevens's poetry," which cannot be integrated within those underlying poetics, and links it to "the essential poem at the center of things, which may be neither named, nor seen, nor possessed theoretically."[16] In "Metaphoric Staging," Joseph Riddel, revising his earlier assessment, elaborates this otherness in Stevens's poetry as the impossible origin, as the absence of the beginning and the deferral of the closure of the book, which "could never have preceded language or been exterior to it."[17]

One has, then, to delineate carefully the contours of this "central" poem and the way it underscores the indebtedness of Stevens's texts to an otherness, which does not enter the grand thematic or rhetorical schemes of his poems or even explain itself through the paradigms that their language explicitly provides. It is much less "spectacular" than the play of words or ideas, and yet its silent import increases in Stevens's later poems. As the analysis of "Notes toward a Supreme Fiction" demonstrates, this otherness plays for Stevens's language a role similar to the infold in Heidegger's thought, as it refers to a singular engagement between thinking and Being. This otherness has implications for Stevens's language and poetics similar to those that the otherness of self-veiling Being in *Ereignis* has for Heidegger's approach to poetry and language as such. For Stevens, it determines the workings of language and indicates its intimate link with Being, with the "strange relation" of the "is" that arranges language and the poetic text. Stevens's poetry, with its own elaborate set of terms and notions, illustrates how otherness, which Heidegger claims as the most singular inflection of language, manifests itself as a transfer between two stages of poetic language—the poem and its supreme fiction, or, in other words, "the poem that never reaches words."

If this comparative proximity of Heideggerian and Stevensian idioms seems almost "natural," it is at least partially because of an astonishingly close parallel between some tenets of Stevens's work and the writings of Hölderlin, and their catalyzing role in Heidegger's dialogue with poetry.[18] For both Hölderlin and Stevens, poetry becomes its own theme, as their poems reflect upon themselves and often thematize the origin and essence of poetic language.[19] To the extent that Heidegger chooses Hölderlin as the poet of poets expressly for this very reason, Stevens can be regarded as Heidegger's "neighbor"; for him, too, poetry becomes first and foremost a concern with language. As Beda Alleman remarks, one of the important characteristics of Hölderlin's poetry, which informs Heidegger's discourse on the holy, is its experience of the absence of God (*Fehl Gottes*). It is in fact this distance and the remoteness of the holy that lead Hölderlin to a critique of Romantic dualities and unities. Significantly in this context, Stevens's poetics also gets its incentive from the disappearance of gods: "to see the gods dispelled in mid-air and dissolve like clouds is one of the great human experiences. It is not as if they had gone over the horizon to disappear for a time; nor as if they had been overcome by other gods of greater power and profounder knowledge. It is simply that they came to nothing."[20] And again in "Notes toward a Supreme Fiction": "The death of one god is the death of all" (*CP*, 381). In Stevens, the disappearance of gods leads to the decreation of the ideal and transcendental orders, and later to the poetics of the act of the mind.

Yet the most significant parallel between Stevens and Hölderlin comes from their attitude toward Romantic poetics. As Alleman explains, Hölderlin's work, when understood in relation to the systems of German idealism for which it at first provided the inspiration and incentive,[21] demonstrates how later Hölderlin distances himself from the synthesis of idealism, because of its exclusion of any real difference and the subsumption and appropriation of otherness: *Aufhebung* implies that difference is possible only as inscribed in the synthesis. In Alleman's view, Hölderlin moves beyond idealism, and the way he approaches the work of art cannot be grasped in idealistic terms.[22] What is more, Hölderlin can play such an important role in Heidegger's thinking not as a result of the suppression of the idealistic moment in his writing but rather because what interests Heidegger is that, remaining within metaphysics and the metaphysical determinations of Being, Hölderlin's poetry points beyond metaphysics; it is double in its intent, both metaphysical and post-metaphysical.[23]

A parallel double gesture is at work in Stevens's poetics: even though numerous of his pronouncements, poems, and critical statements operate within the well-defined metaphysical schemes and exploit Romantic and Symbolist dualisms, his poetry plays those opposites against each other and alternates various conceptions of poetic language in an attempt to radicalize poetics, to

investigate and uncover the origin of the familiar poetic, or philosophical, paradigms. The moment in Stevens's work when it points
toward the other of the poetic tradition in an attempt to disclose
what Stevens might call the central, "wordless" poem is closely
related to his exploration of the fold between language and Being,
and its influence on the scene of representation. As "Notes toward
a Supreme Fiction" makes clear, for Stevens poetry originates out of
the difference that human beings and their thinking introduce
into reality: "From this the poem springs: that we live in a place /
That is not our own and, much more, not ourselves" (*CP*, 383).
Poetry arises out of a difference; it is an awareness of the difference
between human beings and the world in which they live. In other
words, poetry begins at the moment the mind realizes that there
exists an exteriority, otherness, "not ourselves," which cannot be
subsumed under consciousness.[24] This otherness not only cannot
be explained in terms of the unity of self and world but rather
should be seen as itself precluding any possibility of such unification. For what Stevens's work discloses is a difference at the origin
of language, difference between thinking and Being, more fundamental than the one between the mind and the world.

In a way recalling Heidegger's texts on dwelling, Stevens
approaches this relation not only in terms of difference but primarily as a sense of inhabiting and nativeness within which language
unfolds. Describing the "essential poem at the center of things," "A
Primitive like an Orb" highlights precisely the sense of habitation
and of being native, which envelops Stevens's poetic language: "a
nature to its natives all / Beneficence, a repose, utmost repose, /
The muscles of a magnet aptly felt" (*CP*, 442). Language arises
through human beings out of their sense of being native, from the
repose that thought finds in Being. Here the relation between
thinking and Being expands into a place of habitation, a magnetic-
like binding between the human mode of Being—thinking—and
Being itself. Stevens's poetry elaborates how such "magnetic"
forces that maintain thought as native to Being also arrange poetic
idiom, how these invisible "muscles" allow language to unfold and
pre-structure the disclosure of the world. It also intimates that the
nativeness of thought to Being marks the place for language that is
not yet "affected" by difference but rather makes room for it. Differently put, only because thought is native to Being can it at all
become aware of the specificity of its difference.

The significance of this linguistic dwelling becomes visible in
"Description without Place," which, as Hines remarks, outlines the
Stevensian poetics of disclosure:

> Description is
> Composed of a sight indifferent to the eye.
>
> It is an expectation, a desire,
> A palm that rises up beyond the sea,
>
> A little different from reality:
> The difference that we make in what we see
>
> And our memorials of that difference,
> Sprinklings of bright particulars from the sky.
>
> The future is description without place,
> The categorical predicate, the arc. (*CP*, 343–344)

The difference "we make in what we see" originates language as disclosure, not of things or their images but of Being. Thus "place" in this poem denotes not simply a point in space but a place where language is born, where thought, describing an arc toward the future, makes the "linguistic" difference. The fact that this description as the manifestation of the native character of thinking takes place "without place" makes obvious that also the "place" from "Notes" is without place, that it cannot be understood in spatial terms. The "place" of the difference originating poetic language cannot be conceived in spatio-temporal terms; in fact, as the second part of "Notes," "It Must Change," clarifies, time and space originate from "an immenser change" that thought describes in Being. The paradox of a "place without place" and the displacement of the word's meaning suggest that the origin of language can be approached only through a distanciation from the established patterns of signification. The discovery that Stevens attributes to poetic language does not refer to the disclosure of the world as the spacetime in which thinking exists. Instead, poetry reveals the "place" of its own origin beyond the parametrical framework of space and time and its corollary modes of representation.

Only "after" this disclosure, this opening of language, can one talk about the relation between the inside and the outside, self and world. In Stevens's formulation, such poetry of discovery attempts to describe the "essence"[25] of poetry, the first moment or the "first idea" of poetic discourse, antecedent with respect to the above paradigms. Thus it is not strictly speaking a poetics but rather a "topology" of language, exploring the place of its origin and the inscription of its otherness in poetry. In this context, the poetic theories at play in Stevens's work in a sense rely on this originary disclosure, on the very *topos* for language. Thus those theories and discourses, though they inform a large part of Stevens's oeuvre, must be seen in the perspective of the "disclosing" moment from which "the poem springs"; all the more so since, as "Notes toward a Supreme Fiction" explains, they are possible only because "we reason of these things with later reason" (*CP*, 401). In a sense, the proximity figured by Stevens as nativeness to Being charts the field within which language unfolds its differential paradigms of signification and makes possible the difference between the world and the mind as well as the poetries contingent upon it.

Notes toward Otherness: A Supreme Fiction?

Stevensian insights and numerous refigurations of the scene of representation gain a new momentum once we take them on an ironic note as a question directed at the possibility of marking the other in language. His use of traditional formal devices and Romantic rhetoric, often at odds with the avant-garde poetic scene, acquires a new meaning then—an additional complication in Stevens's attempt to foreground the already elusive, "wordless" poem. It also brings to a high pitch the strain between Stevens's language and its own disfigurement, visible most sharply in the way his texts indulge in and then strip away the conventional connotations of words like *idea, fiction, essence, abstraction*, etc. It is as if Stevens deliberately placed his ideas in familiar surroundings, easily interpretable according to the worn-out scenarios of difference, opposition, identity, only to prepare an ironic surprise, ironizing, perhaps unwittingly, not only our reading habits but also the fiction of an unproblematic and clean break with them.

The poetics of disclosure, which Stevens suggests as perhaps capable of at least noting the otherness that underlies the unfolding of language, finds its most complex presentation in "Notes toward a Supreme Fiction," which questions most radically the figurations of the relation between the mind and its object regarded as par excellence constitutive of poetic language. Attempting to reground poetry, Stevens turns specifically toward the fold thought marks in Being, toward the "in" of this fold. The poems become a description of the "in," of the way thought "cuts" into Being; and, since Being is no-thing, and cannot be described in spatio-temporal terms, the description changes into a "description without place." It is, then, no accident that when Riddel describes Stevens's poetics as a formulation of the impossibility of closure or completion of the book, and suggests that such poetry inevitably dismantles metaphysics and its grounding oppositions (subject/object; mind/world), he turns to "Notes" as the paradigmatic text.[26]

Stevens's own "notes" on the possibility of non-metaphysical poetry—that is, poetry no longer grounded in but instead inaugurating the division into the mind and the world—become possible after a long period of examining and challenging the traditional structures of poetry and thought, a process which Stevens calls "decreation." The first step of such decreation, the "disappearance of gods," signifies the rejection of the ideal, transcendental notions, and the focusing on "bare" reality perceived by the mind. Consequently, the poems of *Harmonium* become variations upon the interaction between the mind and the world, with either the mind imposing its a priori structures upon the world or the world numbing the mind with the exuberance of its details. As Hines contends, though, Stevens, in a Husserlian move, quickly takes his poetry beyond idealist and realist notions to investigate the very act of the correlation between the mind and the world. This type of poetry necessitates a severe thematic reduction, an evolution toward poetry reflecting upon itself as "the act of the mind," with many of Stevens's poems falling into this pattern (for instance "Of Modern Poetry") and functioning as "the poem of the act of the mind" (*CP*, 240). In order to make such poetry possible, Stevens progressively reduces both elements of the correlation, the mind and its object, often narrowing the field of the poetic vision to only one object, as in "A Study of Two Pears," with the object itself being actually less important than the manner of its perception. As Stevens's poetry brackets the rest of the world, it also limits the lyrical I to only this one act of perception and makes poetry a meditation on its own act of "poetizing," on the way it describes its own object.[27]

After "decreating" poetry toward the minimal structures of perception, Stevens eventually comes to undermine even this apparently primary poetic intentionality, which in its bare form should exhibit the originary movement of thought and language. It is this move, so characteristic of Stevens's late poetry, that makes his enterprise parallel to Heidegger's departure from metaphysics. Recognizing poetry as an initial disclosure of the world, Stevens shifts his focus to the origin of language in the incision that thought makes in Being, a moment when differing commences. In "Notes toward a Supreme Fiction" the presentation of the postulates for such poetry takes the form of three axiomatic statements: "It (Supreme Fiction) Must Be Abstract," "It Must Change," and "It Must Give Pleasure." Critics usually see in these axioms a stipulation of a new aesthetics that could accomplish the writing of a "supreme fiction." However, since Stevens attempts to "write" his "central poem" non-metaphysically, one has to refrain from explaining this poetics of discovery in teleological terms. For supreme fiction does not stand for perfection of the poetic art, at least not when perfection means an ideal poem that would capture the essence of reality.[28] A more thorough explanation of supreme fiction has, however, to be deferred until the three axioms of "Notes" have been carefully elaborated. Provisionally, one can say that supreme fiction and its attributes of abstractness, "changing-ness," and pleasure are tied to Stevens's understanding of the "essence" of language as the "poem that never reaches words."

The otherness that Stevens tries to figure in the rhetoric explicitly allergic to it is described in the first part of "Notes," "It Must Be Abstract," as "the first idea." The notion of the first idea appears in virtually every canto of the first part, and the four initial cantos open with different descriptions of it:

> Begin, ephebe, by perceiving the idea
> Of this invention. (CP, 380)

> It is the celestial ennui of apartments
> That sends us back to the first idea. (CP, 381)

> The poem refreshes life so that we share,
> For a moment, the first idea. (CP, 382)

> The first idea was not our own. (CP, 383)

Paradoxically, the accessibility of this "first idea" is predicated upon ignorance: "You must become an ignorant man again / And see the sun again with an ignorant eye / And see it clearly in the idea of it" (CP, 380). However, ignorance here does not postulate a dismissal of knowledge but indicates that the first idea precedes knowledge as it is customarily associated with perception and understanding. The first idea cannot, then, be confused with the operation of the perceiving mind, for it is not a result of perception or intuition. In fact, in a typical Stevensian double play, "idea" in "Notes" brings with it and at the same time disavows its traditional meanings. It is not a Platonic idea, since Stevens has already cut himself off from any ideal or transcendental orders. The first idea should not also be mistaken for an empirical idea, which would constitute a part in the chain of associations. What is more, it does not refer to an invention of the mind, an imposition of a priori structures upon the field of perception: "Never suppose an inventing mind as source / Of this idea nor for that mind compose / A voluminous master folded in his fire" (*CP*, 381).

Even the idea of the sun in the first canto of the poem cannot be substituted for the first idea. Though the sun traditionally serves as the first trope, the source of visibility that makes seeing and understanding possible, the opening stanza of canto 1 makes clear that the first idea has to be dissociated from the traditional paradigm of visibility and knowledge. The first idea means instead seeing the idea of the sun and the world as "invented" upon this idea: the world, the mind, knowledge, and understanding are all "inventions" of the idea of the sun; that is, the sun, the opening of visibility makes possible the world and the mind that apprehends it. "Notes" indicates that the first idea should be understood as a continuous questioning of the idea of the sun, a reappraisal of the self-representation of the conditions of thought:

> There is a project for the sun. The sun
> Must bear no name, gold flourisher, but be
> In the difficulty of what it is to be. (*CP*, 381)

At this moment, "Notes" explicitly connects the project for the sun, the inquiry about the ground of knowing, with the question of Being. Characteristically for Stevens, this question is here dissociated from knowledge and from naming, from language as it is understood in its empirical dimension: speech and writing. For the difficulty of "to be" lies precisely in maintaining a distance that has already been suggested in a non-spatio-temporal understanding of place, a distance that would make a "description without place" different from descriptions of the world and of the real.

In this distanciation, one can begin to see the particulars of Stevens's conception of poetic language and the importance of the otherness of Being for it. Its essential dimension differs from naming, from words and the verbal content of the poem, and this distanciation is indicated in the double movement of the first idea:

> The poem refreshes life so that we share,
> For a moment, the first idea. . . . It satisfies
> Belief in an immaculate beginning
>
> And sends us, winged by an unconscious will,
> To an immaculate end. We move between these points:
> From that ever-early candor to its late plural. (*CP*, 382)

Instead of indicating an essence, perhaps even the very essence of essence, the first idea is described here as a distance, a "between" that sends the reader from "that ever-early candor to its late plural." In other words, instead of securing a stable identity, it displaces substantiality, subjectivity, and meaning away from a center, core, or ground. It is "visible," present only to the extent that it moves into "its late plural," into words and poems, but at the same time it is veiled and lost in this plurality:

and yet so poisonous

Are the ravishments of truth, so fatal to
The truth itself, the first idea becomes
The hermit in a poet's metaphors,

Who comes and goes and comes and goes all day. (*CP*, 381)

Displacing the conventional meanings, this passage characterizes the first idea in predominantly temporal terms, as "coming and going." As it "comes," as it appears in poetry, the first idea also "goes," disappears into or in between the words. Therefore the disclosure in Stevens's poetry implies also a disappearance, a simultaneous departure. Riddel points out that the first idea marks "an origin that inaugurates every poem but has its be-ing only in the poem."[29] Reflecting the ambiguity and duplicity that structure Stevens's poetics,[30] this "coming and going" could be read in principle as the Stevensian version of the play of (un)concealment, delivering what it has to say, like Heidegger's *Sage*, only at the expense of erasing the transfer itself.

   This simultaneous disclosure and disappearance of the first idea foregrounds also the structure of the metaphorical transfer characteristic of the poetry of notes. In fact Riddel calls the first idea the first metaphor,[31] a "metaphoric staging" not so much denoting the impossibility of escaping metaphor or the necessity to always be in a metaphor and as metaphorized but instead referring to the very movement of instituting metaphoricity. Hines in turn explains this ambiguous metaphorization in the context of the play of concealment and unconcealment in the Heideggerian approach to language. The concealment that lies at the essence of language results from the infold of thinking into Being. As thought thinks Being, it breaks into language paths or tracks (*Bahnen*), along which signification becomes possible. However, with the appearance of words, the tracks are immediately covered, obliterated by the production of language. This covering of the language tracks, the inevitable overflowing and otherness of Being, its inaccessibility to thought, constitutes Being's "protective" concealment from thought. Hines identifies a similar pattern of tracing otherness in Stevens's treatment of metaphor as degeneration. In Stevens's poetry, metaphor becomes a continuous displacement of referents, without the possibility of fixing their literal or metaphorical meaning.[32] The impossibility of a fixed meaning indicates a concealing character of the metaphorical transfer, the covering of the structure that enables the very differentiation between the poles of metaphorical language.

In his essay "Le retrait de la metaphore," Derrida deals with a similar problem connected with the status of metaphorical language in Heidegger. Especially in the works following *Being and Time*, Heidegger often uses expressions that are metaphorical at first glance but, he claims, are nevertheless exempt from the usual play of meaning associated with the metaphorical transfer. Probably the most obvious example is the phrase "*das Haus des Seins*" ("the house of Being"), which, as Derrida explains, speaks neither literally nor metaphorically but instead challenges, through its depiction of Being, the very schema of metaphorical language.[33] "The house of Being" indeed invalidates any application of the categories of literality or metaphoricity to it. The difference between the literal and the metaphorical, in fact the notion of transfer that lies at the heart of metaphor, is legitimate only with respect to entities, to beings; that is, in Heidegger's idiom, it works on the ontic level. The attempt to transfer it to the ontological level of Heidegger's analysis becomes fraught with problems. Since the house of Being characterizes language in its "essence," as it emerges from the infold of thinking, it resists the categories that describe beings. The phrase "*das Haus des Seins*" works, then non-literally and non-metaphorically; it is instead a quasi-metaphor, a transfer not *between* words but *into* words, which characterizes language on its way to expression. Derrida concludes that this Heideggerian saying opens in its design, in its incision into Being (*entame, Aufriss*), the space for the conceptual network. Consequently, such quasi-metaphoricity performs the linguistic transfer into the difference between the literal and the metaphorical, where the transfer, the *phora* associated with metaphor, becomes possible as a result of a quasi-transfer, itself already in retreat (*retrait*), tracing and retracing, marking a mesh of traits (*retrait, Gezüge*).

Stevens's poem "Metaphor as Degeneration" highlights a similar quasi-metaphorical transfer:[34]

> The swarthy water
> That flows round the earth and through the skies,
> Twisting among the universal spaces,
>
> Is not Swatara. It is being. (*CP*, 444)

The poem attempts to thematize the quasi-metaphorical movement associated with Being;[35] yet such a description cannot be simply "without place." It has already its place in language, and Being has become a "mere" metaphor; it has "degenerated," in an allusion to Heraclitus, into the image of a river:

> the flock-flecked river, the water,
> The blown sheen—or is it air?
> . . .
> And the river becomes the landless, waterless ocean?
>   (*CP*, 444)

The metaphor of the Swatara river shifts from water, to air, and to "the landless, waterless ocean." As Hines suggests, it switches its referents and cannot settle on one metaphorical meaning that would properly illustrate the literal. The poem, then, is not simply a case of a metaphor becoming ill-functional or degenerating but instead inevitably suggests that language functions as metaphor that is always "degenerated"—an uncontrollable transfer between two words, or rather two meanings. As the title indicates, metaphor becomes degenerated as a result of an anterior transfer, not between but into words, a transfer possible only as its own effacement, as a degeneration into metaphor.

When tied to the "between" of the early candor and its late plural from "Notes," the treatment of metaphor as degeneration becomes emblematic of Stevens's conception of language as the transfer from "the poem that never reaches words" into the poetic text itself. The obvious proximity between Stevens's terms and Heidegger's distinction between *Dichtung* and *Poesie* or the reserve of the unsaid in the saying (*Sage*) underscores the scope and philosophical relevance of Stevens's view of language for changing the parameters of the discussion of otherness. The transfer at work in Stevens's poetry makes clear that the "essential" dimension of poetry lies beyond the verbal content, beyond what is customarily referred to as the poem.[36] It marks a singular otherness, which, indissociable from language, lets it unfold at the expense of remaining wordless itself. Language as such is "a speech only a little of the tongue" (*CP*, 397), a little to the extent that the first idea already "degenerates" into words. This is why canto 4 of "It Must Be Abstract" begins with an emphatic statement, "The first idea was not our own," and an earlier poem, "The Creations of Sound," talks about a "speech we do not speak" (*CP*, 311). In these poems, language no longer designates exclusively the human faculty of speech, since human presence and thought, though indispensable for language, for the difference from which language springs, do not function as the source of language: "There was a muddy center before we breathed. / There was a myth before the myth began, / Venerable and articulate and complete" (*CP*, 383). In other words, myth created by human imagination is possible only as a result of a myth that does not enter words and instead makes words and meaning possible, that is, *muthos* as the "essence" of poetry.[37] Since the line preceding the above quotation explicitly warns against any Platonic parallels—"But the first idea was not to shape the clouds / In imitation" (*CP*, 383)—"essence" should be read here perhaps similarly to the first idea, for example, along the lines of Heidegger's reading of *Wesen*. The transfer that the first idea performs between the early candor and its late plural does not involve imitation, the production of a lesser, inferior representation of what came beforehand. Instead, the "beyond" is transferred into language only by disappearance and degeneration, by effraction or tracing. In this way, *muthos* becomes the re-covered origin of poetry, retreating behind or between spoken or written words.

Because of this retreat, *muthos* as "the essential poem at the centre of things" (*CP*, 440) cannot be properly named, even though one can find throughout Stevens's work numerous words that refer to *muthos* as the myth that precedes language. Thus, tempting a quick metaphysical solution, *muthos* becomes either the central or the essential poem, with the proviso that neither the concept of centrality nor that of essence can account for *muthos* as presented in "Notes," for the Stevensian "essential" poem is not really a poem, a spoken or written text, as it points to what makes the text possible without directly appearing in words. It therefore "precedes" essence, and the adjective *essential* is, on Stevens's reading, another instance of degenerating into metaphor.

The way *muthos* in opening language separates and withdraws itself from words explains the title of the first part of "Notes": "It Must Be Abstract." Hines contends that this title implies that the first idea as it is named inevitably slips into abstraction.[38] This is undoubtedly true, and increasing abstractness, which thinking entails, is reflected in Stevens's treatment of the "late plural" of language. However, if it were the case, the first *must*, unlike the other two, would describe a necessity that is imposed on poetry, and not one dictated by it. In truth, the way Stevens uses the term *abstract* indicates also another meaning, which becomes better visible in the etymology of the Latin cognate *abstractus*. According to *O.E.D.*, the word is etymologically composed of two parts: the prefix *abs* (off, away) and the root *tractus* (drawn). Thus its etymological meaning is "drawn away" or "withdrawn," and among the English uses the dictionary lists: "1. drawn, derived, extracted 2. withdrawn, drawn away, removed, separated." Just as much as it indicates derivation or extraction, *abstract* signifies also withdrawing, removal, and separation. Therefore, the postulate that supreme fiction must be abstract does not simply mean that it is subject to abstraction in the sense of generalization or deduction. Instead, it indicates the "between" characteristic of the first idea, which, transferring the "essence" of poetry into words, simultaneously disengages itself from them; it tears itself away from the poem. This tear reflects the distance between beginning and end, the early candor and its late plural. In the context of the first idea, abstraction designates, then, the act of withdrawing characteristic of the "essence" of poetic language, with the abstractness of the first idea implying its necessary slippage away from knowledge and poetic vision. In this specific sense, the tearing away and separating indicates the irreducible otherness of the first idea, with its enigmatic inscriptions in the language of the poems.

The implicit an-archic temporality, to use Levinas's idiom, of this withdrawal comes to the fore in the second part of "Notes" and its axiom "It Must Change." This part links the first idea with the notion of withdrawing, retreating, "sending back" as Stevens calls it: "It is the celestial ennui of apartments / That *sends* us *back* to the first idea" (*CP*, 381, emphasis mine). From these two lines it may seem that the first idea is merely a thing of the past, which has already been completely lost in the late plural of the poem. However, can one indeed say that the first idea belongs to the past, in the sense of the past opposed to the "now," the presence of the present? Canto 4 of "It Must Be Abstract" precludes such an easy conclusion: "The first idea was not our own. Adam / In Eden was the father of Descartes / And Eve made air the mirror of herself, / Of her sons and of her daughters. They found themselves / In heaven as in a glass; a second earth" (*CP*, 383). As Hines points out, Adam, naming objects and animals in Paradise, already performs the split between the mind and the world, and Descartes merely codifies this division, which has implicitly structured language, elaborating it in philosophical terms. But what is even more important, those two stanzas suggest that the first idea cannot be understood within usual temporal schemes. Since there was no mythical time, no golden past, in which language was pure, and consequently no fall of language, the first idea cannot be comprehended within teleological or temporal paradigms. It is not an ideal that was lost at some point in history, nor an ideal that could be claimed back some time in the future, at a point when language would achieve its "purification," the clarity enabling it to penetrate to the ideal.

Complicating the temporal structure of representation, "sending back" in "Notes" not only does not designate a point in the past but in fact reverses the movement between the early candor and its late plural, making poetry a remembrance, a recall of what has never passed and has never been properly present. Such twofold structure of poetic language finds its parallel in Heidegger's "way" of language, in which the worded language becomes only the "last stage" of language, its "end-product." For Stevens the poem, unable to retain and envelop the first idea in its own temporal structure, can only "send us back" to it, in the same sense in which for Heidegger language is a response sending us back as *Andenken* to the already veiled saying-event of manifestation. Like Heidegger's *Ur-sprung*, this "sending back" reaches beyond the usual division of time into the past, the present, and the future, not by transcending to an atemporal dimension but rather by tracing the unfolding of time itself.

Notwithstanding the numerous images and poetic figures illustrating traditional linear or cyclical models of time in the second part of "Notes," its title in the end refers to the quasi-metaphorical movement, an invisible linguistic change called by "Description without Place" an immenser change:

> There might be, too, a change immenser than
> A poet's metaphors in which being would
>
> Come true, a point in the fire of music where
> Dazzle yields to a clarity and we observe,
>
> And observing is completing and we are content,
> In a world that shrinks to an immediate whole,
>
> That we do not need to understand, complete,
> Without secret arrangements of it in the mind. (*CP*, 341)

According to this poem, Being "would come true" only in an "immenser change," not an effraction of time or a distance that has elapsed on the temporal axis but the unfolding of temporality as such. For this change is not simply an immenser change but "a change immenser than / A poet's metaphors." If metaphor is a transfer, an ex-change between two words, possible because the two words are in a relation, an "embrace,"[39] the immenser change of the first idea precedes and arranges that exchange. To that extent, this immenser change cannot be effected simply by the mind; in fact, it takes place "without secret arrangements of it in the mind."

The change that makes poetry possible could be called a pre-metaphorical change, immenser and more important than metaphors themselves, as it is a change that allows language to flow into words and transfers thought's response to Being into language. In "Notes toward a Supreme Fiction," this change is referred to as "changingness": "In the uncertain light of single, certain truth, / Equal in living changingness to the light / In which I meet you" (*CP*, 380). As in "Description without Place," where it comes true in the change immenser than metaphors, here Being is related to what the text calls "changingness." This coining is not an arbitrary gesture on the part of Stevens, a word play or an attempt to name change in a more active manner, to indicate its verbal character. Changingness, especially in the context of the poetics of "Notes toward a Supreme Fiction," refers to change as the "between," the transfer of the first idea into words, which makes changing and differing possible. If changingness functions as the rupturing otherness that produces words and their configurations—the poetic text in its narrow sense—this rupture itself and its withdrawal become the poetic text par excellence, the poem that never reaches words.

The axiom of changingness articulates the dependence of differential and oppositional paradigms structuring language—general/particular, literal/metaphorical, content/form, etc.—on changingness, an immenser change that language introduces into Being itself. In "Primitive like an Orb," this change is referred to as "an inherent order active to be / Itself" (*CP*, 442). This extraordinary image not only shows how close Stevens's understanding of language comes, though unwittingly, to Heidegger's thought but also sheds light on its effort to capture the way Being attempts to work itself into words. For Stevens, such saying is nothing more than an exercise by an inherent order to be itself. Being is nothing more than an activity to be itself, with no sense of progression or development but rather with an emphasis on the sense of having come into the present, already obscured by the notion of presence and its implications for the conceptualization of time. As in Heidegger, language needs human beings to come into words; it needs their "native" thinking. This dependency constantly inflects Stevens's language, defamiliarizing its own constructions of this relation in terms of differences, oppositions, or divides running between mind, imagination, self, consciousness, on the one hand, and world, reality, object, other, on the other. In the end, in spite of the totalizing and stabilizing inclinations of Stevensian rhetoric, the elusiveness of this change immenser than metaphors prevents his language from too easily inscribing itself in one of the handy explanatory paradigms it itself provides.

Read along the same lines, the third part of "Notes" emerges as a Stevensian polemic against aesthetic approaches to poetry and the conception of beauty associated either with the musical, sonoric, and rhythmical elements of poetic language, or with the universality of the poetic message:

> To sing jubilas at exact, accustomed times,
> To be crested and wear the mane of a multitude
> And so, as part, to exult with its great throat,
>
> To speak of joy and to sing of it, borne on
> The shoulders of joyous men, to feel the heart
> That is the common, the bravest fundament,
>
> This is a facile exercise. (*CP*, 398)

For Stevens, the beauty of the poetic text does not follow from its musicality or universality but arises from the pre-musical aspect of language: "To find of light a music issuing / Whereon it falls in more than sensual mode" (*CP*, 398). The "more than sensual mode" is not simply the intelligible as opposed to the sensible but suggests an undercutting of the dichotomy itself and connects the more than sensible music with the operations of the first idea: "But the difficultest rigor is forthwith / On the image of what we see, to catch from that / Irrational moment its unreasoning" (*CP*, 398). The "unreasoning," unraveling the rational categorizations of poetic language, claims for poetry the possibility and force of "discovering," so much underscored also in Heidegger's "neighborly" relations with the poets. Stevens not only ironizes the equation of the poetic with the irrational but, more important, regards the unfolding of the world as essentially poetic:

> But to impose is not
> To discover. To discover an order as of
> A season, to discover summer and know it,
>
> To discover winter and know it well, to find,
> Not to impose, not to have reasoned at all,
> Out of nothing to have come on major weather,
>
> It is possible, possible, possible. It must
> Be possible. (*CP*, 403–404)

Beyond the rhythmic, rhyming, and other musical qualities, the beauty of the poetic text lies perhaps in the "unreasoning" of the moment produced by poetry, in its disclosive effect. It is this sensation of discovery, the "beauty" of its unfolding into words, that "gives pleasure,"[40] but this satisfaction is probably no longer measurable by the aesthetic faculties of the mind.

It is perhaps in this exact sense that one would also have to read Heidegger's brief mention of beauty in the epilogue to "The Origin of the Work of Art" in terms of unconcealment:

> Truth is the unconcealedness of that which is as something that is. . . . Beauty does not occur alongside and apart from this truth. When truth sets itself into the work, it appears. Appearance—as this being of truth in the work and as work— is beauty. Thus the beautiful belongs to the advent of truth, truth's taking of its place. It does not exist merely relative to pleasure and purely as its object. The beautiful does not lie in form, but only because the *forma* once took its light from Being as the isness of what is. (*PLT*, 81)

Questioning implicitly the Hegelian judgment about only the past relevance of art for the occurrence of truth and challenging the aesthetic categorization of the beautiful as a non-theoretical activity, Heidegger points to a concealed, "peculiar confluence of beauty with truth" (*PLT*, 81). As confluent with unconcealment, beauty is not simply a category of aesthetic perception but in fact an effect of disclosure, of a Stevensian chancing upon a "major weather," with which works often classified as beautiful according to aesthetic criteria evince no familiarity.

Perhaps Other: Stevensian Notes on Difference

Providing a schematic representation of the poetics informing Stevens's late work, the three axioms from "Notes toward a Supreme Fiction" suggest that language has a sort of a double structure, operating as an exchange between the poetic text and the first idea, understood as the originary dimension of language that abstracts itself from the text. To the extent that the first idea can be said to have the positivity only of a trace, disrupting the text by means of its absence and otherness, its modality is always that of a maybe or a perhaps. It is such play on the assertiveness of linguistic formulations that can possibly explain Stevens's notion of supreme fiction, as a supreme "may-be," important even if permitted only the status of a quasi-fiction.

"Supreme fiction" is often quoted in Stevens criticism as an example of his debt and commitment to post-Romantic poetics, a word both interesting and troubling with its metaphysical connotations for any contemporary reading. Marjorie Perloff accurately identifies *fiction* as one of the most often used, highly charged terms in Stevens's poetry: "A concordance of Stevens's criticism, if there were such a thing, would probably show that the following words had a very high incidence: *being, consciousness, fiction, reality, self, truth.* These are, of course, Stevens's own words, and the poet's advocates have adopted them quite naturally. But it does not follow that they have some sort of absolute value as nodes of critical discourse."[41] This absoluteness has to be questioned also because Stevens's own writings make this idiom problematic. For example, the postulates of abstractness and changingness make clear that supreme fiction cannot be reduced to a fiction of the mind, as "Notes" emphasizes the fact that supreme fiction is "not ourselves" and hence not compatible with the categories of subjectivity. In this specific sense, it does not belong to a post-Romantic poetic or critical vocabulary, which would have to be explained in terms of the dichotomy of self and world, consciousness and its object, be it natural or supernatural. To borrow a term from philosophy, which, as Stevens remarks elaborates on different parts of the same whole that poetry does,[42] supreme fiction spells a resistance to and an inflection of metaphysics as well as the conceptuality and imagery contingent upon it. Within the always metaphysical language, supreme fiction marks a retreat, an "abstraction" from words, a poetics of perpetual displacement of language from its self-figurations.

This abstention of supreme fiction, its teasing modality of the possible, illustrates perhaps the most critical point made by "Notes toward a Supreme Fiction." Because of its formal qualities—a very symmetrical division of the poem into three parts and of each part into ten cantos; the elaborate, repetitive stanzaic patterns—the poem presents itself as a structural unity, which would fall in place with the Romantic-oriented interpretations of Stevens's poetry. However, this symmetricality is disrupted by another "formal" aspect of the poem: the poem is nothing more than a collection of notes. The format of notes, apart from dispelling the promise of some unifying center, illustrates a characteristic, for Stevens, critique and inscription of the poetries engaged by his texts in the problematic of supreme fiction. In this context, the title "Notes toward a Supreme Fiction" does not simply indicate that the poem is a preliminary sketch, a preparation for a fully developed poetics, but rather that a complete and final poetics of supreme fiction is not possible—not because of the necessary historical and temporal change but because supreme fiction does not conform to teleological schemas. "Notes" is not a stage on the way to supreme fiction but a formulation of a broader poetics of notes, which stresses the fact that the poetic text can only indirectly point toward its retreating source, undecidable finally as to its presence or absence. Thus "Notes" becomes very important for Stevens's writings, since in its context all other poems become "notes," that is, texts that try to negotiate their own debt to the non-textual(izable) supreme fiction, which remains unnamed, abstracted from the text.[43] The second stanza of "A Primitive like an Orb" is almost emblematic of this note-like character of Stevens's language:

> We do not prove the existence of the poem.
> It is something seen and known in lesser poems.
> It is the huge, high harmony that sounds
> A little and a little, suddenly,
> By means of a separate sense. It is and it
> Is not and, therefore, is. In the instant of speech,
> The breadth of an accelerando moves,
> Captivates the being, widens—and was there. (*CP*, 440)

The stanza opens a distance between "the poem" and "lesser poems," contending that "the poem," although intimated, "noted," in these poems, possesses "a separate sense," not translatable into either the mechanics or the products of the semantic processes. This sense, explicitly described as Being, or to be exact as "is," separates itself from the terms of the opposition is/is not, presence/absence, turning poems toward their "origin."

Can the repeated examination to which Stevens's texts submit various poetic paradigms, then, be ascribed to an implicit dissatisfaction with the way they (dis)figure what Stevens regards as poetry's "native" proximity to Being and its "separate sense"? If this holds true, then "Notes" articulates an insight fundamental to understanding Stevens's work: no matter what poetic theory a given poem seems to espouse, entertain, or displace, they all function as markers, as notes pointing toward supreme fiction, that is, to the proximity to Being that inaugurates language and yet can be recuperated only in a modality of "maybe." What this poetics of notes constantly underscores is the difference that for Stevens underwrites the possibility of language and poetry: the difference that thinking opens in Being, the difference that derives its meaning from the native relation of thought to what it purports to understand. Even if Stevens himself does not formulate this insight explicitly, the way his texts establish, leave, and repeatedly return to various configurations of the divide between self and other, implies the incompatibility of the idiom of difference with the sense of nativeness characteristic of poetic language. To this extent, noting the difference that matters for it, Stevens's poetry "sends us back" to what lets language discern and thematize difference as such—the nativeness of thinking to what Stevens call the text of the world.

For just as Heidegger characterizes *Ereignis* in linguistic terms, Stevens regards the happening of the world as essentially linguistic, to the extent that it takes place only in conjunction or engagement with thinking. Stevens's phrases from "An Ordinary Evening in New Haven"—"words of the world are the life of the world" or "a new text of the world"—describe not the synthesis of the subject and its object that language performs through the conceptual network but instead an indebtedness of language to the text, in Heidegger's idiom, the saying, of the world. "Two Illustrations that the World Is What You Make of It," ironizing its own title, maintains that the source of language remains outside of the mind: "he thought within the thought / Of the wind, not knowing that that thought / Was not his thought, nor anyone's" (*CP*, 513). Since these late poems follow the implications of the poetics of "Notes," it is important to remember that world does not function here as an opposite of self but as a non-spatial and proto-linguistic "place" of the inception of language. Stevensian "new text of the world" indicates precisely the quasi-linguistic nature of this place, its character of a supreme fiction, a poetic text par excellence—a possibility of poetry. What therefore makes us native is the linguistic nature of the world, which allows for the proximity or nativeness from which language (poetry) unfolds. This translation, though, is never complete; the "separate sense" of this proximity cannot be brought to words without being articulated as a difference and transposed into one of the relational paradigms contingent upon it. This "separate sense" does not strictly speaking become part of the economy of signification but instead functions as the linguistic space that this economy inhabits, to which it is native, without being able itself to signify this proximity.

The insight we can gather from Stevensian poetics of notes is indeed uncommonly close to Heidegger and, elaborated in its own terms, illustrates the poet's side of the neighborhood of poetry and thinking, providing means of intervening into the Heideggerian text and reinforcing its claim about language's debt to ontological proximity. If Heidegger's conception of the way-making of language can be seen as an attempt to depart from the onto-theological tradition and its conflation of the other and the same, then Stevensian poetic notes provide a way of reckoning with the poetic figurations of otherness and their essential complicity with the reversible and collapsible metaphysical structures, projected and sustained by the self-same activity of poetic consciousness and its language.

Since Heidegger insists that what matters for the other thinking (*das andere Denken*) and what matters for poetry are the "same"—"Saying is the same element for both poetry and thinking," with the peculiarly Heideggerian reading of sameness not as equality or identity but rather extreme proximity—then the "hermeneutics of nearness," which we have seen at work in Heidegger's texts, constitutes itself in an exchange with poetry. This encounter should not be construed as simply a thinker's open-mindedness about a poet's insights but rather as a proposition that thought "thinks" only in proximity to its other, only with an ear turned to its neighbor—in Heidegger's view—poetry: "the most urgent issue . . . is, to seek out the neighborhood of poetry and thinking" (*OWL*, 82). As Heidegger puts it in "The Nature of Language," what is expedient for a thinking experience with language is the neighborhood of poetry, "for the two belong to each other even before they ever could set out to come face to face one to the other" (*OWL*, 84). Questioning the myth of the self-sufficiency of philosophical inquiry and the desire for the self-sameness of its reasoning, Heidegger conceives thinking as fundamentally insufficient, in need of a neighbor that thinks otherwise (poetically?). Stevens's poetry makes a similar gesture toward thought, openly engaging, modifying, or even parodying the philosophical idiom. His language indeed underscores and exemplifies his statement about poetry and philosophy dealing with the same problems in their respectively different discourses. Where Heidegger articulates the need for "another thinking," Stevens responds with the poetry of notes, declaring each poem a fragment, a piece in the irregular puzzle of supreme fiction. Even the longest among his poems, notwithstanding the degree and sophistication of their formal arrangements, function as the notation of the proximity of language to Being.

Like Heidegger's texts, Stevens's poetry is almost painfully aware of the difficulty of introducing such notation into the "essentially" metaphysical language, of the strain that it puts on poetic diction. We have noted the polysemic folds of Heidegger's language and Stevens's persistence in invoking and canceling the accretions of meaning in his key words. Such poetic labor not only complicates permanently Stevens's stance toward the aesthetics of high modernism but foregrounds the difficulty of any notation of otherness. For it is possible, perhaps even necessary for keeping a balanced view of Stevens's poetics, to read those complexities of Stevensian discourse in terms of a refiguration or rather a renotation of otherness. The failure of Stevens's rhetoric, its almost constant relapse into the metaphysical language of self and other (as self), brings home precisely the problems that language experiences in noting otherness.

If Heidegger finally disclaims the possibility of overcoming metaphysics and wants to leave it to itself, Stevens's work illustrates perhaps even more vividly the extent to which language is enmeshed in its own heritage and dependent on its metaphysical provenance. There is no talk in Stevens about a new poetry, at best only notes, delivered by the poet on the "dump" of poetic images, toward something that may be fiction anyway. For this fiction is not so much an ideal, a transcendental principle that could reground poetry, but instead an ironic near-linguistic quasi-transcendental. It is as if Stevens were teasing us with the suggestion that language can note otherness only as a supreme fiction, or, even more forcefully, that the very attempt to note otherness is itself a supreme fiction. In other words, Stevens the ironist indicates that the notation of otherness in language is only a possibility, a possibility that, as "Notes" puts it, must be possible, but only in a modality of "perhaps." It is no accident that the notion of otherness as "native" proximity can only have a discursive status of a possibility, a maybe, visible in Heidegger's analyses of the modalities of Being in terms of possibilities or in the Levinasian "perhaps" trace. Supreme fiction can, then, be read as the Stevensian notation of otherness, perhaps only a poetic fiction, whose "maybe" is constantly exposed by the self-sameness of its language. And yet this supreme fiction cannot quite be dispelled; its notation remains in the text, if only as a reminder that the poem is just "a note toward . . . " Such notation of otherness, even though or perhaps precisely because it is easy to (dis)miss in the midst of familiar figures of the self, can lay claim only to the rank of an inflection; not an opening or making room for a new articulation nor a "positive" conception of the other, but instead a rupture of the figures and images which language has accumulated and regenerates in the efforts to spell the other otherwise.

The peculiarity of this Stevensian notation manifests itself in its return to the notion of nativeness and inhabiting. The confusion that such notation sends through Stevens's language is partly due to the fact that Stevensian indigenity does not explain itself in terms of belonging to some substance or ground that is common, known, or familiar. It is not being native to that which confirms and completes the self's identity but instead a nativeness to otherness, to "not ourselves." In "Lebensweisheitspielerei," Stevens connects this idea of nativeness with the sense of indigence, the insufficiency of "light," which functions as the token of otherness:

> The proud and the strong
> Have departed.
>
> Those that are left are the unaccomplished,
> The finally human,
> Natives of a dwindled sphere.
>
> Their indigence is an indigence
> That is an indigence of the light. (*CP*, 504–505)

The recognition of what it means to be human is tied here to the "dwindled sphere" of decreased transcendental orders and to the consequently reduced scope of intelligibility. The indigence of light, even though it spells a lack in cognition and introduces the undertone of disappointment, also intimates the possibility of otherness outside or beyond the range of intellection. In other words, the indigence of light bespeaks the indigenity, the nativeness, to what remains other. Here it is not simply a question of Stevens throwing his support behind the idea of deferral and the impossibility of closure but of an attempt to explain the capacity for discerning and thinking difference. To Stevens, human beings mark and recognize the difference of thought in Being because they are natives to otherness. It is because we are indigenous to otherness that difference can at all be an issue for us, that it can become both a matter of thinking and its regulatory principle. Here lies perhaps an "iconoclastic" side of Stevens—an ironic extraversion of indigenity from sameness to otherness, a flip that allows Stevens's poetry, in spite of its continuous aesthetic and cognitive systematizations, to "note" otherness.

The fact that we are native to otherness and indigent of light ironizes the image of a self-identical subject, for whom the other comes as a surprise, a threat (the monster from "The Man with the Blue Guitar"), and an indication of the limit placed on the household of consciousness. For if otherness can indeed disrupt the apparent peace of self-sameness, it is only because alterity is native to identity, a sort of "internal paramour" as one of Stevens's poems suggests.[44] Even if this poetic notation of otherness is a fiction, a "failure," and the form of notes toward . . . does not effectively invert the direction of language, the very possibility of this default appears to be predicated on language's native place in what it tropes as other. The paradoxical appearance of Stevensian nativeness to otherness articulates the critical tension of his poetry, a strain that eventually collapses the very idea of construing the relation to otherness on the principle of an opposition, a divide, a difference. If difference "matters" because poetry/thought are native to otherness, then language, with its differential paradigms of signification, can measure this indigenity only on the scale of fiction and rank it supreme.

∞ 5 ∞

CHIASMUS OF OTHERNESS
Reading Celan and His Interpreters

Perhaps the single most characteristic feature of Paul Celan's poetry is its concern with the other, with the possibility of speaking to him/her, of addressing the other in what constitutes his/her alterity for language. This preoccupation with acknowledging the unrepresentable alterity of the other, of his/her suffering, pain, and death, finds both its source and its haunting force of expression in the catastrophe of the Holocaust and Celan's personal experiences of persecution, suffering, and the loss of family. Already the early poems of *Mohn und Gedächtnis*, unfolding the characteristic motifs of Celan's texts—the memory of the Holocaust, death, destruction of the other—speak often to or in the voice of those who, like Celan's parents, died in concentration camps:

ESPENBAUM, dein Laub blickt weiss ins Dunkel
Meiner Mutter Haar ward nimmer weiss.

Löwenzahn, so grün ist die Ukraine.
Meine blonde Mutter kam nicht heim.[1]

ASPEN TREE, your leaves glance white into the dark.
My mother's hair was never white.

Dandelion, so green is the Ukraine.
My yellow-haired mother did not come home.[2]

we drink it at noon and at daybreak we drink it at night
we drink and we drink
we are digging a grave in the air.[3]

In his Bremen address and in "The Meridian," Celan defines his poetry in terms of a search for a bearing, for an encounter with the other that would happen, paradoxically, both *in* and *despite of* or *against* language. He has in mind, of course, the German language,

133

the language of his parents, and hence his mother tongue, but, in the same breath or turn of breath (*Atemwende*),[4] also the language of their murderers: "language. In spite of everything, it remained secure against loss [*unverloren*]. But it had to go through its own lack of answers, through terrifying silence, through the thousand darknesses of murderous speech."[5]

Celan's poetry thus combines its response to the Holocaust with the problem of the critique of language, reinforcing the latter's claims with the ethical concern for the violence that language, images, and the dictates of representation can inflict on the other. In this way, at stake in Celan's continuous return to death in concentration camps, reinforced by the recurrent images of smoke, ashes, and burnt hair, is the intertwining of the task of remembrance with the question of poetic figurations of otherness that would both recognize the other and preserve his/her alterity. For as Theo Buck suggests, Celan's poems attempt to grasp the responsibility for others ("*Verantwortung für andere wahrzunehmen*"),[6] to address the very possibility of an ethical relation to others in language. To that extent, Celan's poetry follows the trend of the literature of the Holocaust that, as George Steiner shows in *Language and Silence*, links it to "the critique of language in philosophy, literature, and art; the tendency toward silence inherent in modern literature; and the relationship between political events and the work of art."[7] This is why Celan's late poetry focuses more and more on the textual inscriptions of alterity, foregrounding the relationship between poetic language and the ethical meaning of otherness.[8] Celan's explorations are accompanied by a sharp sense of the historical time in which he writes, illustrating the need both to understand the historicity of the poetic text[9] and to grasp how the experience of the atrocities of the war defines our views of poetry, language, and otherness. Celan's acute awareness of the linguistic dimension of this problem is reflected in the complexity of his language—its dislocated syntax, splintered words, broken and fragmentary images—which continuously unworks the poetic text and keeps it open to the signification of otherness. Thus the significance of the Holocaust for Celan's poetry and its involvement with the other, that is, its ethical inflection, are perhaps best understood in the context of what Levinas describes as the concern for the other's death, a concern that overrides even the preoccupation with the self and irrevocably marks its language with ethical prescription.[10]

This link between the Holocaust and the problem of the trace of the other in language may account for, on the one hand, Levinas's interest in Celan and the ethical possibilities of poetry and, on the other, for Celan's own need to continue, despite or maybe because of the disappointment with Heidegger's silence, his conversation with Heidegger's ideas about poetry and language. Accentuating and measuring this ethical dimension of the poetic text, Celan's poetry deliberately breaks with traditional imagery and conceptuality and, inverting them, not only makes the text alogical but forces it to turn against itself, to become, as Celan remarks in "The Meridian," a counterword, *das Gegenwort*, the word that, conscious of its insufficiency and distortion, displaces itself from itself, finds a crack in itself, to allow the other to remain other and yet be signaled in language. Celan's poems, through numerous instances of coining, paronomasia, enjambement, and splitting words into two lines, force language to open its familiar syntactic and semantic paradigms to otherness. Such poetic strategy draws attention to the unwritten of language, which, although present visibly only as whiteness and audibly as silence, preserves the trace of the other's inflection of language.

It is therefore not surprising that Celan's poetry has become a meeting ground for literary critics and philosophers interested in approaching otherness from various perspectives: subjectivist, rhetorical, deconstructive, or ontological and ethical.[11] It is enough to mention here the readings by Levinas, Derrida, Menninghaus, Lacoue-Labarthe, or Hamacher to realize the scope and pertinence of Celan's work to current debates about language, otherness, and ethics. This variety of readings seems to be induced by the indeterminacy and often hermetic character of otherness at play in Celan's work, whose scope or direction cannot be readily inferred from the ruptured and self-displaced idiom of his texts. Celan's poetry indeed provides a constellation of concerns of critical importance to current inquiries into the possible meaning and signifcance of the figurations of the ethical, concerns reinforced and made concrete by Celan's personal and historical circumstances, the Jewish background and the haunting memory of the Shoah. This chapter proposes to take a look at these critical encounters, with a view to their helpfulness in articulating a chiasmic fold running through Celan's figuration of otherness, a proximity between what might be called ontological otherness and ethical alterity.[12]

It follows in the footsteps of Derrida's influential and rich study, *Schibboleth*, devoted to the issues of otherness and difference and their function in the overall organization of Celan's texts.[13] Evoking Celan's work, Derrida's text is written in such a way as to precisely avoid summary and schematization, as it continues to find more links between Celan's images, metaphors, and principal terms and plots new passages between them that, in turn, require another shibboleth, another "key-word." Derrida achieves this effect by weaving and reweaving together three tropes, passageways, or operations by way of which Celan's writing comports itself toward otherness: date, shibboleth, circumcision. These figures all describe a similar movement of splitting, differing, and opening language, of dislocating it toward the other, yet, at the same time, each of them has a different valency, a distinct set of associated images and significations. Date or dating, seemingly the most neutral of these tropes, marks the relation between the event of writing in the singularity of its circumstance and the possibility of its repetition, of the reiteration of what remains "universal" in the text in spite of its coded uniqueness. The second term, shibboleth, brings in social and political connotations, indicating both the possibility and the passage between, on the one hand, alliance and community and, on the other, exclusion, persecution, even extermination. Circumcision, which Derrida, via Celan's poem "Einem, der vor der Tür stand . . . ," refers to the problem of circumcising, incising, and inscribing the word, plays on the relationship between body and language, emphasizing Celan's strategies of "wounding" and opening language in an offering of the poem to the other.[14] The style of presentation Derrida adopts conveys best the range of meaning and various contexts in which otherness marks Celan's work—the polytropy of the encounters with the other (whether as date or through the work of shibboleth or circumcision), meetings that hold open the passage for textual, linguistic, historical, and political differences.

Perhaps the best example here is the "double edge" of shibboleth itself, its polarization between identification, belonging, community, on the one hand, and exclusion and discrimination, on the other: "the word turned *Shibboleth* . . . reminds us also of what I will call the *double edge* of every *Shibboleth*. The mark of an alliance, it is also an index of exclusion, of discrimination, indeed of extermination."[15] Derrida thus keeps open and in question the value and the meaning of the otherness at stake, as well as the uses to which difference can be put, indicating instead linguistic, textual, and poetic passages, datings, and cuts that regulate inscriptions of alterity. For what in effect underlies and organizes Derrida's exposition is the overall "mechanics" of giving (*datum*), in its historico-political, poetico-textual, and ethical dimensions, together with its nodal points in Celan's work: date, shibboleth, signature, circumcision. Derrida has in mind here the general sense of giving that inaugurates writing, that gives dates, places, and words, opening (and maintaining) the passage (of difference) and thus allowing language to address the other.[16]

In the context of this non-conventional, non-calendaric dating, which, working as part of the general organization of the text ("with that dating which, leaving nothing over, is utterly confounded with the general organization of the poetic text"),[17] gives words and at the same time dislocates and circumcises them toward (for) the other, I want to focus on the "ethical" dimension of Celan's work, of its invocation of the personal other and the effect this memory/address has on Celan's language. How does the invocation of the other, the name, the shadow, the "you" (*Du*), which cuts across datation—the event of the poetic text (its dates, places, passages, code words; its wounds, traces, and cinders)—affect Celan's understanding of poetic language? Does Celan's talk of two kinds of strangeness, of double alterity and its perhaps untraceable difference, mark an inflection of language that underwrites the entire event(uation) of the poem, its occurrence on the scission, the passage, the shibboleth between the giving and the given? Is this fold, then, what Celan considers to be the poetic (*Dichtung*)? What will both permit a sharper delineation of this twofold otherness and contextualize its implications is the exchange between two other philosophers reading Celan's work: Lacoue-Labarthe's "Heideggerian" discussion of Celan in his book-length *La poésie comme expérience* and Levinas's miniscule, especially by contrast, three-page "note," which declares the need of reading Celan "otherwise."[18]

The Unwritten Text and the Name of the Other

Celan's poetics of otherness or of the other, as one might call it, is expressly formulated in "The Meridian," the speech that addresses the question of art in Büchner and treats it as an inroad into the problematics of poetry and, specifically, Celan's definition of poetic language. "The Meridian" underscores Büchner's radical questioning of art ("*In Frage-stellung der Kunst*"),[19] especially his critique of Romantic conceptions of art, and suggests that art performs a distanciation from the I, from the subject: "The man whose eyes and mind are occupied with art—I am still with *Lenz*—forgets about himself (*der ist selbsvergessen*). Art makes for distance from the I (*Kunst schaff Ich-Ferne*). Art requires that we travel a certain space in a certain direction, on a certain road" (*GW* III, 193/*P*, 44). For Büchner, art not only does not express the subject but instead "forgets" it; it moves away from the I. In effect, it opens a distance from the I, a distance that furnishes a direction, a road that art traverses. Celan's own questioning continues precisely within this opening, in the direction suggested by *Lenz*. As a consequence, Celan's poems do not preoccupy themselves with the beautiful, for, as he writes in "Reply to a Questionnaire from the Flinker Bookstore, Paris, 1958," "[i]ts [poetry's] language has become more sober, more factual. It distrusts 'beauty.' It tries to be truthful."[20] The stress falls here on truth, which, in the context of both Celan's poetry and his prose pieces, especially "The Meridian" and "Conversation in the Mountains," should not be identified with truth as *adequatio*, as knowledge belonging to the subject, but instead approached from a Heideggerian perspective, in the sense of truth as an opening, an unconcealment of what is. In "The Origin of the Work of Art," Heidegger defines poetry (*Dichtung*) as a projection, an *Ur-sprung*, the originating leap into language. *Dichtung*, therefore, is an originary distance, a way to language. "The Meridian" defines art in very similar terms, for Celan, like Heidegger, also introduces the opposition between *Dichtung* (poetry) and *Kunst* (art), a distinction presented as a way, a road, which poetry traverses through art. In fact, as Celan specifies, this way denotes a distance between poetry and art, distance that poetry travels into art: *"Dann wäre die Kunst der von der Dichtung zurückzulegende Weg"* (*GW* III, 194). *"Zurückzulegende Weg"* implies an essential difference between art and poetry, an understanding of *Dichtung* as preceding poetry and art, reminiscent of Heidegger's differentiation between *Poesie* and *Dichtung*. As in Heidegger's writings on language, also for Celan *Dichtung* describes an originary poeticity of language, the opening for words, which traverses not only poetry but all art—it makes art possible.

The "way" from poetry to art opened by Celan's reading of Büchner becomes the focus of his poetics. This distance, as "The Meridian" maintains, indicates an opening of the subject to otherness, to *"Ich-Ferne."* The estrangement of the I from itself results most importantly in breaking open the way for the other: "Perhaps, along with the I, estranged and freed *here, in this manner,* some other thing is also set free?" (*P*, 47).[21] With the distanciation of poetry from the subject, the other is allowed to appear as other, and the poetic text turns itself toward the other, across the distance of strangeness (*das Fremde*). The significance of this turn is immediately underscored by Celan: "Perhaps after this, the poem can be itself . . . in this now art-less, art-free manner." (*"Vielleicht ist das*

Gedicht von da her es selbst . . . auf diese kunst-lose, kunst-freie Weise" (*P*, 47/*GW* III, 196). It is through that turn toward the other that the poem may be itself, freed from art and aesthetic concerns. Here again Celan refers to the difference between *Dichtung* and *Kunst*: the poem at the moment of its origin is "art-less"; it is not poetry in the sense of configuration of words, rhythm, meanings; it has to be distanced from art and from its aesthetic categories. This "art-less" and "art-free" poetry functions instead as the opening toward otherness, in which art, "art-ful" poetry, originates.

Such poetry, the "art-free" poem, the originary *Dichtung* as "The Meridian" puts it, is "lonely and on the way" (*"einsam und unterwegs"*) (*GW* III, 198), that is, on its way to the other: *"Das Gedicht will zu einem Andern, es braucht dieses Andere"* ("The poem intends another [better 'an other'], needs this other) (*GW* III, 198/*P*, 49). This "intention upon the other" finds its expression not simply in the poem's thematics: *"Jedes Ding, jeder Mensch ist dem Gedicht, das auf das Andere zuhält, eine Gestalt dieses Anderen"* ("For the poem, everything and everybody is a figure of this other toward which it is heading") (*GW* III, 198/*P*, 49). In other words, the other does not appear merely as a theme, an image or a series of images in the poem, but, conversely, all aspects of the poem, its imagery, meaning, rhythm, point toward the other.[22] Such otherness, taken as perhaps a focal moment, though not a center, of the poem, implies the necessity of making place in critical discourse for a plane, a dimension, without forgetting that all spatial categories are incompatible with what Celan intends as the other, which lies outside aesthetics and is essentially "art-less." Derrida's *Schibboleth* surveys this field, mapping its linguistic, poetic, and temporal displacements with the notions of shibboleth, signature, date, cinders, and circumcision. Celan himself calls this dimension the "narrowness" of art when, dismissing the idea of enlarging art (*"Elargissez l'Art!"*), he postulates that poetry should take art into its innermost narrowness, to bring this narrow edge of otherness into focus so that it can silently and invisibly cut through the poem: *"Die Kunst erweitern? / Nein. Sondern geh mit der Kunst in deine allereigenste Enge"* (*GW* III, 200). In this context, *Dichtung*, poetry in its primordial or originary sense, describes the edge, the narrowness of the poem, the thin region where language addresses the other.

"The Meridian" characterizes this narrowness in a very provisional manner: for Celan, the increased awareness of this narrowness of poetry manifests itself in a strong tendency toward silence (*"eine starke Neigung zum Verstummen"* [*GW* III, 197]). Attempting to address otherness, to bespeak it, the poem already silences itself, refrains from words, from naming and compromising the other. This silence, the reticence of modern poetry, and the resulting obscurity "ha[ve] been bestowed on poetry by strangeness and distance (perhaps of its own making) and for the sake of an encounter" (*P*, 46). The encounter (*Begegnung*) becomes possible only in silence, yet in silence in a sense produced or induced by words, the silence corresponding to the "narrowness" of the poem. Only this silent narrowness, the fissure of language, can, without ever saying it, bespeak, or more precisely un-speak, the "altogether other" (*ganz Andere*). In order to respect otherness, this narrowness has to be "utopic," without proper place or meaning: "*Und einmal waren wir auch, von der den Dingen und der Kreatur gewidmeten Aufmerksamkeit her, in die Nähe eines Offenen und Freien gelangt. Und zuletzt in die Nähe der Utopie*" ("And once, by dint of attention to things and beings, we came close to a free, open space and, finally, close to utopia") (*GW* III, 200/*P*, 52). In Celan's words, the "narrowness" of poetry is eminently utopic: it does not have a center, a place; it cannot be grasped or located. This utopic character of otherness indicates that it cannot be associated with words themselves, images, meaning, or any other formal, semantic, or aesthetic qualities of the poetic text. For the poem as such can only point through poetic devices, paronomasia, breaking words into their etymological components, literally opening cracks in them, etc., to its "edge," to the narrowness that "meets" the other.

At stake in this chapter is the way one can understand the otherness traced in Celan's poetry, specifically, whether it can be approached in ontological terms, pertaining to the other's Being and its significance for language, in textual terms, as the otherness of the unwritten, or in a specifically ethical way, as the unspoken ethicity of language—a linguistic inflection. Celan's engagement with Heidegger, both in his thematic and linguistic concerns, indicates that at the center of his poetics lies the question of twofold otherness in language—the fold between Being and the ethical and their chiasmic propensity for crossing into each other. It becomes manifest that Celan attempts to mark in his poetry the specificity of the ethical inflection of language against the backdrop of ontological concerns—a way of both following the chiasmic otherness implicit in Heidegger and emphasizing the distinctness of the ethical.

In order to bring this distinctness of the ethical into relief, it is helpful to survey briefly how both critics and philosophers interpret in various ways Celan's poems and his interest in what withholds itself from language, and how their readings already suggest a bifurcation, an emergent twofold direction of this poetry. Werner Hamacher, for example, in his essay "The Second of Inversion: The Movement of a Figure through Celan's Poetry,"[23] places the stress on otherness understood as the unwritten of language, the uncontrollable irruption in writing that brings words and yet itself does not enter them. It is possible, then, to see his reading as an elaboration of what Celan himself refers to as the narrowness of poetry, its splintering and separation from itself, which "wounds" language and opens it to the other. Hamacher's text focuses on the figure of inversion, which in the Hegelian tradition marks a turning of nonreality, absence, and death into being. Such inversion, which negativizes the negative, stems from the conception of time "determined as the continuum of negativity referred to itself and furthermore as the negative unity of the differentiated" (SI, 285). Hamacher maintains that the figure of inversion was to guarantee the semantic function of language under the conditions of finitude (SI, 292). Reading a line from Celan's poetry, "*Wo sie nie war, da wird sie immer bleiben*," Hamacher points to the fact that such an inversion turns absence, a nothingness, into presence, where the inverted "nothing" becomes a substantial being, and in this way absence can be transferred into language and turned into a presence, a word. Celan's poetry radicalizes such notion of inversion and ultimately rejects it (SI, 302), for otherness in Celan's poems cannot be inverted into presence but instead indicates a place "of an absence . . . unattainable for . . . the presence of our own language" (SI, 284). Therefore, inversion in Celan becomes an interruption of language, a splitting of meaning, a distance between the written and the unwritten. Frequent instances of inversion and paronomasia, pointing to the essential inability of language to come to itself, to retrieve the fullness of its presence and meaning, show how Celan's work abandons itself and goes toward the "unwritten"—the other of the text, whose only trace is the whiteness of the written page.

Analyzing the figures of inversion like "*Ich bin du, wenn ich ich bin*," and the ubiquitous paronomasia of Celan's writing, Hamacher contends that Celan's poems separate themselves from themselves, create a cleft, a fissure between the written and the unwritten. Such a cleavage is suggested by the figure of the "second," where "*die Sekunde*" written with a dash between "*se*" and "*kunde*," separating the word into two lines, can be also read as "*diese Kunde*" (this message) (SI, 292). In this way, the word itself performs the inversion; it creates semantic ambiguity, and, moreover, it suggests that the message of the poem is the very inverting, the crossing over from the written to the unwritten which the poem enacts. The "second," etymologically derived from Latin *secare*, "to cut," cuts the second between the ambiguity of meaning, and it severs language from the possibility of unambiguous meaning (SI, 292). The cut and inversion, usually stabilizing the subject through linguistic recuperation of presence, in Celan makes the stability of the subject impossible and suspends the determination of the "you." This in turn leads to the indetermination of discourse as such, to language that interrupts and mutes itself. Hamacher claims therefore that Celan's language not only does not invert nothingness into being but rather converts "its literary being, compositionally and semantically, into nothing" (SI, 296). Announcing the nothingness of the root of language, poetry also turns the encounter with the other, the "you," into the impossibility of speaking and inscribes the other into the uncontrollable transformations of the text, where the encounter with the you and its alterity "comes about only as this im-parting and this partitioning of the speech" (SI, 302). Inversion, often tied to the idea of return and the restitution of the self, a figure for the subject's relation to itself, is disassociated in Celan's poems from the subject. It becomes a figure for the poem, for language coming back to itself as nothing, as an other (SI, 304). Referring to the figure of boomerang in "Wurfholz," Hamacher remarks that the poem never comes fully back to itself, it remains separated from itself, a boomerang that does not reach the same point, a distance indicated by Celan in the phrase "*Ich-Ferne*."

Through the frequent instances of paronomasia, a minimal alteration of a graphic or phonetic form, Celan's poetry causes the disappearance of the monosemic body of the word and, as Hamacher puts it, "ex-posits" language to the unwritten. Poetry becomes "the trace of a discourse [*Spur einer Rede*]" that encodes what remains hidden in it, what has not come into language (SI, 309). Thus the unwritten enters the poem only in the form of a rupture, an interruption and intermittence of the text. Celan's inversion becomes the inversion of inversion, the figure in which the poem abandons itself without the possibility of recuperation. In this way, Celan's poetry always ascribes itself to otherness, to the unwritten, the unsaid in language. This is why Hamacher can finally assert that none of the topoi or tropes of Celan's poetry, neither its form nor content, can fix, determine, or describe the path his text takes. The poem remains therefore without a direction, without a center; it can never recuperate its meaning.

Winfried Menninghaus, by contrast, in *Paul Celan: Magie der Form*,[24] reads the unwritten otherness of language in subjectivist

terms. His interpretation focuses on the word *Name* as the pris-
matic word in Celan's poetics: "*Es begegnet, von den sonstigen Verän-
derungen in Motivik, Metaphorik und Sprachform unberührt, quer durch
alle Gedichtbände Celans*" (*MF*, 9) ("It reappears, unaffected by the
other changes in motifs, metaphoric, and language forms,
throughout all the collections of Celan's poetry" [trans. mine]). To
put it differently, it is the word *Name* that, despite its indetermi-
nateness, gathers all the elements of Celan's poetics and exposes its
reflection upon the inner forms of language. Following Benjamin's
notion of "*Intention auf die Sprache*," Menninghaus contends that
Celan's poems through their themes, motifs, and metaphors
intend the inner form of language beyond the verbal content. For
Benjamin, "*Intention auf die Sprache*" means the principle of forming and shaping language, toward which every text is directed in
its inner form: "*das 'Prinzip' von Sprachgestaltung, nach dem eine Rede
(Text) in ihrer (seiner) inneren Form 'gerichtet' ist*" (*MF*, 13). In Celan's
poetry, the equivalent of the inner forming of language beyond
words is what Menninghaus calls "*Intention auf den Namen*," which
as the principle of "language-shaping" (*Sprachgestaltung*) functions
as the focal point of Celan's poetics.

Menninghaus's reading shows that through his poetry Celan
attempts to disengage *Sprachgestaltung* from the semiological difference between the signified and the signifier. However, Celan's
opposition to the semiological difference does not mean that he
opts for the atomistic motivation of signs, as Menninghaus argues
that for Celan language is not a re-presentation of things, and the
sense of presence comes from the correlation between the form of
language and the constitution of the subject: of "*der 'Gestalt' einer
'Person'*" and "'*Gestalt und Richtung und Atem' ihres 'Sprechens'*" (*MF*,
35). This inner correlation, which makes language possible,
announces itself in Celan's use of *Name*, which, as Menninghaus
maintains, refers to the correspondence between language and the
subject. The essence of such language does not therefore realize
itself in the verbal content but instead makes itself known through
or in the shadows of words (*MF*, 43). It is this non-verbal form of
linguistic presence that points to an essential coherence of language beyond the semiological difference. Expectedly enough
Menninghaus calls it *semiologische Indifferenz*, semiological indifference (*MF*, 46).

Menninghaus repeatedly stresses the fact that this metalingual
aspect of language is not only not abstract or ahistorical but, conversely, eminently historical. In his interpretation, he underscores
the parallel between the arbitrary modes of signification, of the rela-

tion between the signifier and the signified, and the killing of human beings by physical power. The metaphorics of burning, ashes, burnt hair, and death, which hauntingly reappears throughout Celan's poetry, establishes this correlation between the annihilation of Jews by fascism and the distancing from the blinding light of semiological difference. For Menninghaus, the difference between the signifier and the signified, with its play of arbitrariness and indeterminacy, obliterates the "presence" of the *Name*, of the essential coherence at the root of language. Only the exposition of the unsaid in language can counteract the effect of semantic arbitrariness.

The interfacing of language and silence, which appears in Menninghaus's reading of Celan's poetry as *"Intention auf den 'Namen',"* has been stressed by many critics. However, Menninghaus's book shows carefully how this intertwining becomes nonverbal, and the *Name* non-significative. He points to the "lines," poetic curves (*Gedichtkurven*), which run through Celan's poetry, between its words, themes, and metaphors, and "order" them in the direction of the *Name*. Yet it is precisely this ordering and the reading of *Name* that seem to be problematic in Menninghaus's engaging study. Without doubt, *die Enge*, the "narrowness" in which poetry inverts upon itself can, and perhaps has to, be read in terms of *Name*, a non-verbal, non-significative direction of language. Yet if *Name* points to the interfacing of the subject and language, *Sprachlichkeit* then guarantees, in essence, the subject's silent dominance over language: apart from arbitrary and uncontrollable semantic properties of words, the inner form of language would have the shape corresponding to the subjective structures. From the very origin language would be "controlled" by the subject, even though this control could never be explicitly brought into words. Moreover, such conception of language inscribes the other in Celan's poetry into the subjectivity of *Sprachgestaltung*, where, inevitably, the other would have to be read in subjective terms; his/her autonomy and otherness would thus be reduced, even compromised. In other words, for Menninghaus, the imprint of subjectivity would pre-set the poetic curves along which Celan's work addresses the other.

However, the singular fixation of Celan's language on the other has to put in question Menninghaus's presupposition that *Name* refers to a silent, almost "magical" correspondence between subjective and linguistic structures, which would affirm the unvoiced affinity between subject and language, and instead point us in the direction opened by Hamacher's reading and its insistence on the indebtedness of Celan's poetic figures to alterity.

Indeed, in Celan's poetry the word *Name* indicates, clearly in most cases, the *du*, the "you" to whom the poems direct themselves. For example, "With Letter and Clock" represents words themselves as the wax with which poetry attempts to seal what remains unwritten—"your name":

> Wachs,
> Ungeschriebnes zu siegeln,
> das deinen Namen
> erriet,
> das deinen Namen
> verschlüsselt. (*GW* I, 154)

> Wax
> to seal the unwritten
> that guessed
> your name,
> that enciphers
> your name. (*PPC*, 107)

The "wax" and "sealing" refer perhaps to the manner in which the words point beyond themselves to the non-verbal and try to preserve, to "seal," the name. More important, the poem links *Name* to *du*, as it claims to preserve *deinen Namen* (your name). Paradoxically, this non-verbal name can be "sealed" only when it is deciphered, and, at the same time, encoded—a riddle. "Mit allen Gedanken" describes the necessity of leaving the world, of abandoning words with their reference to objects, things, persons, in order to encounter this you: "*MIT ALLEN GEDANKEN ging ich / hinaus aus der Welt: da warst du*" ("WITH ALL MY THOUGHTS I / went out of the world: and there you were" (*GW* I, 221/*PPC*, 167). The you can be found only beyond the world, beyond the words, and there, as the poem later suggests, lies the possibility of a name ("*so gut wie ein Name?*"/"as good as a name?"). Thus what lies "between" the words does not so much reflect an unvoiced "presence" of the speaking person, the subject, but instead marks the silent encounter with another person, figured in the pronoun *you*.

The importance of this correlation between the other and the name for the deployment of poetic language is indicated in "Schieferäugige," where the you becomes enlivened by the breath of the name:

> Du hier, du: verlebendigt
> vom Hauch der im frei-

geschaufelten Lungengeäst
hängengebliebenen
Namen.

Zu
Entziffernde du. (*GW* II, 98)[25]

As in "With Letter and Clock," the "splinter-eyed you" remains to be deciphered, for it is not accessible to the language of the poem; its only trace can be found in the breath of the name, and strictly speaking not even in the name itself but rather in the "wake" left by the name, in the direction it marks. Even though these are only a few examples of the link that Celan's poetry establishes between "name" and "you," they all suggest that *Name*, rather than referring to the subject's presence in language, presence that would overcome the distance of the semiological difference, points to the subject's radical openness to the you. In fact, a great majority of Celan's poems can be described as addressing the you in an attempt to find a name that would both signal the you and let it remain other. The insistence with which the poems point to the you leaves no doubt that the name, the you, marks a way leading beyond words and names, into the non-verbal plane of language as the only place where language can encounter "you."

It still remains to be seen, however, what status the you entertains in poetic language. The words used by Celan to indicate the subject, *ich*, and the other, *du*, as Emmanuel Levinas remarks, are reminiscent of Martin Buber's *Ich und Du*.[26] Can, however, the you be read as another subject and the poem as an attempt at an intersubjective dialogue, communication, conversation between I and you? Yet Celan's poems clearly deny any possibility of a conversation, in fact of an intersubjective exchange predicated upon the similarity of the participants. The poem "Erhört" emphatically dismisses any similarity between "I" and "you": "*Dir, / . . . war / ich nicht ähnlich*" (*GW* II, 87) ("to you, / . . . / I was not similar" [trans. mine]). In "Hafen," the you is compared to an astral flute sounding from beyond the edge of the world: "*du, wie die / Astralflöte von / jenseits der Weltgrats*" (*GW* II, 51). As in "Mit allen Gedanken," the you is placed beyond the world, beyond the limits of what can be seen, and what can be named by language. It cannot, therefore, be a partner in a dialogue, another subject, because it does not enter the "world" within which such an interchange could possibly take place.

A further confirmation of the position that Celan does not view poetry as a dialogue with another subject comes in a poem from *Schneepart*, "The Half-devoured":

ein weiterer Name
—du, du beleb dich!—
muss eine Ziffer
dulden,

Unzählbarer du:
um ein Un-
zeichen
bist du ihnen allen
voraus. (*GW* II, 384)

another name
—you, you come to live!—
must endure
a number,

you, never-to-be-counted:
by one null-
token
you are ahead of
them all.[27]

This poem could be easily presented as an example of the obscurity and unreadability of Celan's late poetry. However, in the context of Celan's preoccupation with otherness, the poem yields important clues about the complexity of its "non-image" of the other. As the poem suggests, the other comes to live in a name, a "farther" (*weitere*) name, to modify the translation, and must endure the number, even though the other remains "uncountable" (*Unzählbare*), with the mathematical references indicating that Celan disengages the other from the totalizing concepts of a people or a genus. To borrow Levinas's remarks on this issue, for the other to be absolutely other, there can be no generic concept that would inscribe all people. As Hamacher suggests, Celan's poetry, a painful testimony to "the murdered race," points to the pervasive complicity between the violence of the Holocaust and the violent erasure of alterity and difference characteristic of generalizing concepts. Like Adorno's or Benjamin's critiques of Enlightenment, Celan's texts become an accusation of the totalizing tendency of Western thinking to subordinate alterity and difference to sameness. This reappraisal of our practices of conceptualizing the relation to others may explain Celan's need to put in question the abstract notions of a human species, a race, a common language (SI, 297). This radical dismissal of generalizing concepts is illustrated in "Der halbzerfressene," which claims that even though the you should not be counted, measured, or classified under a common category, it has to bear the mark of (mis)reading it in universal or generic terms. "You" is only a name, which is at the same time an "un-sign" (*Un-Zeichen*), and the severing of the word into two lines clearly indicates that Celan points here to a "non-sign," a non-significative, non-verbal name, which can say the other without measuring and inscribing otherness under the generality of concepts. The root of *Unzählbare* echoes the word *erzählen*, "to ac-count," "to tell," implying that the name that the other bears says her/him, it accounts for the other in such a way that it does not count the other as another exemplar of a genus, another human being among all the people. For only such a name, an "un-sign," a farther name, removed from other names and words, can respect the you as the totally other, as *ganz Andere*. It is because of this name, that the other precedes all words (*"um ein Un- / zeichen / bist du ihnen allen / voraus"*), with the distance between linguistic signs and the un-sign as the name of the other constituting *die Enge*, the narrowness that traverses the poem and directs it to the other.

The linguistic status of the you in Celan's poetry—its being apart from signs, between words or in their shadow—indicates that it should not be approached in terms of a dialogue, that the ethical specificity of this poetry mandates another approach. The Celanian ethical concern can be seen instead as an inflection of language, whose mechanism cannot be known or described, because the sense it generates does not belong within the cognitive or semantic fields. It marks itself in language only indirectly by inflecting and directing it toward the other; that is, it can be discerned only to the extent that one recognizes that language finds itself always exposed to and aware of the other, that it has already become an address to the other. Since the you plays the role of the other, who only leaves its trace on the edge of language, this other cannot, therefore, be seen as a participant in a conversation; rather, the other must be seen as the very condition of dialogue, an opening of a direction in which the subject can "address" the poem:

Aus seiner Krume
knetest du neu unsre Namen

. . .

einer Stelle, durch die ich
mich zu dir heranwachen kann,
die helle
Hungerkerze im Mund. (*GW* II, 12)[28]

The poem indicates that the other's absence can be traced in its influence on words, in the way the other "magnetizes" language.[29] As the poem focuses on the movement away from words and the subject, on the direction into which it extends, piercing through names and words, the lyrical subject can merely "feel" the words, in an attempt to locate a place, a fissure through which it can "awaken" toward the other. In addition to the literality of starvation, the image of "a bright candle of hunger" manifests the desire for the other, the desire that is already present in language and never satisfied because of the inaccessible alterity of the other.

Another poem from *Atemwende*, "To Stand," presents a similar image of waiting for the other:

> STEHEN, im Schatten
> des Wundenmals in der Luft.
>
> Für-niemand-und-nichts-Stehn.
> Unerkannt,
> für dich
> allein.
>
> Mit allem, was darin Raum hat,
> auch ohne
> Sprache. (*GW* II, 23)

> TO STAND in the shadow
> of the scar up in the air.
>
> To stand-for-no-one-and-nothing.
> Unrecognized,
> for you
> alone.
>
> With all there is room for in that,
> even without
> language. (*PPC*, 225)

Poetry awaits the other, under a scar, a knarb, an incision the other makes in language. This waiting constitutes the aim, the *raison d'être*, of poetry, to stand for the other, "no-one" and "nothing," since this other cannot be named, known, or spoken about. The incision that the other has already made in language becomes a space (*Raum*), a room opened through language, in its "shadow," and yet "without language," without the possibility of signifying this alterity.

This distanciation of the other from language defamiliarizes the you in Celan's poems, inverts it, as in "Conversation in the Mountains," into a neuter "other." In their conversation, two Jews called by Celan "Klein" and "Gross"[30] talk about language of the neuter, of the third person: "not for you, I say, is it meant, and not for me—a language, well, without I and without You, nothing but He, nothing but It, you understand, and She, nothing but that" (*P*, 19–20).[31] Ultimately, then, the language addressed to the other dismisses the first and second person, the categories connected with the notion of dialogue and intersubjective space, and turns itself toward the other, he, she, or it, the category indicating strangeness, foreignness, the unknown. The alteration to the third-person pronouns excludes the other from the familiarity of conversation; it gives the other a "farther name," and makes her/him a stranger to language. The context of the conversation, the images of the mountains, glaciers, snow, the folding and cracking of earth ("The earth folded up here, folded once and twice and three times, and opened up in the middle" [*P*, 19/*GW* III, 170]), evokes the poems with similar imagery, especially from *Atemwende* and *Schneepart* and in particular, perhaps, "*Etched Away*," in which the other inhabits the hospitable glacier rooms[32] and the other's sign, the crystal of breath, can be found in the "time crevasse." The analogous location of the other in the time crevasse and the language from "Conversation in the Mountains" in the opening of earth indicates that the language of "he, she, and it" indeed refers to the you, the other, in the poems. All these signals about the "other" status of *du* in Celan's poetry make obvious his distanciation from the conception of a dialogue with the other. For Celan poetry can become at best only a "desperate conversation" (*verzweifeltes Gespräch*) (*GW* III, 198), dispatching messages not even to but rather toward the other, without expecting a response. In other words, Celan's poetry does not concern itself with what becomes known about the other person in a conversation, with what can be asserted about the other as another subject, but instead it directs itself toward the other's alterity, namely, toward what makes the other other, inaccessible to thought, knowledge, and language.

"Two Kinds of Strangeness":
Celan on the Possibility of Signifying the Ethical in Poetry

Having shown how Celan's poetry foregrounds the inflections of its own language induced by the other's alterity, it remains to be seen what significance, "ontological," "ethical," or both, should be ascribed to them. Any extended reading of both Celan's poetry and prose pieces makes clear that at stake in his work is a twofold otherness in language: on the one hand, the otherness of Being and, on the other, the other's alterity—which marks language with a specifically ethical inflection, an exposure to others that has a sense other than that of Being.[33] The word *chiasmus*, which perhaps best describes this doubling, underscores the instability and fragility of this distinction, the proximity between two aspects of otherness and its proclivity to a cross-over and the erasure of the fold. This chiasm characteristic of Celan's texts resonates particularly well when we juxtapose two readings of Celan's poetry proposed by Lacoue-Labarthe and Levinas.

In *La poésie comme expérience*, Philippe Lacoue-Labarthe proposes a Heideggerian reading of the other in Celan, since as he argues: "*la* poésie *de Celan est tout entière un dialogue avec la* pensée *de Heidegger*"[34] ("all of Celan's poetry is a dialogue with Heidegger's thought" [trans. mine]). This perspective of a dialogue with Heidegger becomes visible already in the title of Lacoue-Labarthe's study, where "experience" refers to the Latin *expeiriri* (traversing a danger) and Heidegger's explicit foregrounding of *Erfahrung* as a journey, a way (*fahren*), a move, which proleptically characterizes Celan's poetry as being on its way (*en route, en chemin*) toward its own source. In this view, Celan's poetry presents an experience of traveling toward the origin of poetry, a description familiar from Heidegger's discussion of Hölderlin's poems and the way-making of language.

In "The Meridian" Celan writes about the *Unheimliche*, which Lacoue-Labarthe reads as an attempt to go beyond the human, a turn toward Being itself. In their desire to undo the proper, the self, the I, Celan's poems push toward the limit of language: "*la poésie advient là où cède, contre toute attente, le langage.*" Thus poetry becomes a spasm of language, an irruption of silence: "*la poésie est le spasme ou la syncope du langage*" (*PE*, 74). Lacoue-Labarthe makes clear that the caesura, the syncope, cannot be read as the other of art since it happens beyond any dialectics. Therefore this silent place is "*le lieu étranger lui-même*" (the foreign, other place), the moment when the self becomes irrecuperably displaced toward otherness (*PE*, 77). This turn toward the other, transpiring between discourse and silence, becomes possible, however, only as the gift of the other: "the totally other is the gift of the other as the possibility of the same, that is to say, as the possibility for the same to constitute itself in *différance*").[35] This formulation explains the impossibility of dialectizing the movement between the I and the other: the self does not transcend itself in order to return to itself, but instead the very movement of self-definition and self-consciousness becomes possible through the previous gift of the other. Lacoue-Labarthe argues convincingly that the radicalization of terms in the course of "The Meridian," from *Unheimliche* (uncanny) to *Fremde* (strange) and finally *Andere* (other), reflects Celan's concern with the possibility of dialectizing the "gift": while the exchange between the self, the proper, and the strange is reversible, the movement of the self within the gift from the other transcends the bounds of any dialectic. This gift, as Celan remarks in "The Meridian," takes place in the mystery of the encounter, and, as Lacoue-Labarthe explains, *mystery* in German, *Geheimnis*, implies both something unfamiliar and something familiar, intimate (*proche*)—*heim*. The mystery, then, suggests at the same time a proximity, a nearness, to what remains other; it is being at home in otherness, perhaps on the order of Stevens's nativeness.

Lacoue-Labarthe argues that the "intimate" transcendence of the gift resembles the withdrawal of Being in Heidegger, and therefore the otherness of the other should be read in terms of the other's Being. He therefore dismisses Levinas's proposition from *Noms propres* to approach the gift of the other as "otherwise than Being" as too precipitous: although poetry addresses itself to a singular "you," "this address to you is the address to the alterity of you—of this other—it is the address, mysteriously arising from the intimity [from the intimate difference], to the Being of the other, who always 'is' and cannot 'be' except as a being").[36] Even though poetry marks an openness to the other, an acceptance of the gift of her/his otherness ("*accepter cette parole, au coeur même du poème . . . comme le don de l'autre*" (PE, 95)/"to accept this speech, at the very heart of the poem . . . as the gift of the other"), addressing the other is tantamount to responding to Being. In other words, when Celan's poetry attempts to find *Un-zeichen* in order to "describe" the other, that un-sign refers nevertheless to the other's mode of Being, or at least has this signification inscribed in it. Lacoue-Labarthe claims then that what in fact constitutes the other's alterity and difference from the subject, is the way the other "is": "the 'saying of you,' the naming of poetry is a mode of 'saying Being' different from the one properly belonging to thought, but it is still a mode of 'saying Being'").[37] Even when the poem expressly addresses the other, it actually does not speak her/his otherness; it can only speak Being. The space of otherness, or the "other space" as Lacoue-Labarthe puts it, opened in poetry can in no way be placed beyond Being: "*L'expérience du toi, la rencontre, n'ouvre à rien*

d'autre qu'à l'expérience d'être: du rien d'étant" (PE, 98) ("The experience of you, of the encounter, opens onto nothing else but the
experience of Being: of the absence of beings"). To the extent that
the mystery of the encounter with the other is the mystery of
Being, of the absence of entities or beings, the other's alterity
becomes identified with what makes beings possible and yet does
not belong to them: the opening, the void, the rising, the presencing of what is. In other words, Lacoue-Labarthe reads Celan's other
in terms of the ontological difference, as a being whose mystery
lies in the way in which it exists, in its *Dasein*. Otherness in Celan's
poetry should therefore be pursued along the lines of the otherness
of Being, as the link between language and the opening of a space
for what is.

Lacoue-Labarthe is absolutely right that both Celan's poems
and prose writings indeed present themselves as a dialogue with
Heidegger's thought: not only poems like "Todtnauberg," crediting
Celan's visit with Heidegger, or "Tübingen, January," paying trib-
ute to Hölderlin's poetry, but especially "The Meridian," whose
argument evolves around words that ring with Heideggerian connotations: *Dasein, Begegnung, Entwurf, Geheimnis, Entsprechung,
unterwegs,* and *Erfahrung.* Most important, Celan's poetics hinges
upon the distinction between *Dichtung* and *Kunst,* reminiscent of
Heidegger's argument in "The Origin of the Work of Art." There
can be no doubt, then, that Celan's project points in the same
direction as Heidegger's: it aims at the very origin of poetic language in Being. Nevertheless, in his approach to language, Celan
forks this direction to stress the possible separateness of the other's
alterity from the otherness in the withdrawal of Being, to indicate
a chiasmus as fragile as the turn of breath, *Atemwende,* from "The
Meridian" and from the collection bearing this very title.

After speaking in "The Meridian" about the importance of
direction (*Richtung*) in poetry, the direction along which the poem
"travels" and experiences (*erfahren*) the world, Celan discloses an
essential "twofoldness" in the poem's concern for the origin of language: "*Aber es gibt vielleicht, und in einer und derselben Richtung,
zweierlei Fremde—dicht beieinander*" (GW III, 195) ("But there may
be, in one and the same direction, two kinds of strangeness next to
each other" [P, 47]). Here, in a manner similar to the rhetoric of
peut-être through which Levinas introduces "otherwise than
Being," Celan implies a possibility of a fold in otherness, essential
yet almost indiscernible. This postulation of double otherness
appears in the context of Celan's discussion of obscurity (*Dunkel-
heit*) in modern poetry, suggesting that at least part of this obscu-

rity comes from the involvement with the question of Being and the other, and a possible chiasmic crossing between them. That issue surfaces again in "The Meridian," when Celan stresses the necessity of differentiating between two kinds of strangeness: *"vielleicht gelingt es ihr [Atemwende] hier, zwischen Fremd und Fremd zu unterscheiden"* (GW III, 196)/"it is perhaps this turn, this *Atemwende*, which can sort out [differentiate] the strange from the strange" (P, 47). "The Meridian" points to *Atemwende*, the turn of breath, the interval between words, as a possible place of differentiation between the otherness of Being and the alterity of the other.

This chiasmus is at work again in the title poem of *Sprachgitter*, where Celan indicates the difficulty of distinguishing the twofold otherness, since the otherness of Being often overlaps and covers the alterity of the other:

> Augenrund zwischen den Stäben.
>
> . . .
>
> Shräg, in der eisernen Tülle,
> der blakende Span.
> Am Lichtsinn
> errätst du die Seele (*GW* I, 167)
>
> Eye's roundness between the bars.
>
> . . .
>
> Athwart, in the iron holder,
> the smoking splinter.
> By its sense of light
> you divine the soul. (*PPC*, 119)

The dominating image in the poem is the eye in the face of the other, which announces the other's alterity and yet is obstructed in releasing a glance by the bars, the lattice, the mesh of language. The mesh (*Gitter*) has double significance here: first, it indicates that the other leaves only a trace in language, a "smoking splinter," and, as other, remains separate from language; but even more important, especially in the context of the question of whether the other can be described in terms of the otherness of Being, *Gitter* suggests a separation, a necessity of two types of otherness. In Heidegger's approach to language, otherness can be seen as either the invisible and inaudible mesh of paths or furrows, which bring language into being without themselves appearing in words, or as the shape (*Gestalt*) of friendship that listening to others gives to language. Celan's *Sprachgitter* makes clear that the alterity of the other should not be confused with the invisible mesh of language, which bars the other and obscures its distinctness.

"Sprachgitter," one of the key poems in Celan's own reflection upon his writing, intimates that indeed the difference between Being and the other marks language, that the other's mystery does not lie only in the mode of Being. Levinas therefore appears to be right when he observes that Celan's language functions also on a "pre-unveiling" level: "*le poèm se situe précisément à ce niveau pré-syntaxique et pré-logique . . . mais aussi pré-devoilant . . . [l]angage de la proximité pour la proximité, plus ancient que celui de la vérité de l'être*" (*NP*, 60) ("the poem situates itself precisely on this pre-syntactic and pre-logical level . . . but also pre-disclosing . . . language of the proximity for proximity, older than that of the *truth of Being*" [trans. mine]). The prefix *pre-* and the adjective *older* should not be taken here in the temporal sense, since the disclosure of Being itself marks the opening of temporality. Instead, Levinas attempts to manifest what cannot be in fact called a difference, since thought and difference do not apply to this distinction, the fold between Being and the other. This is why Levinas describes this economy in terms of both "more" and "less," since the direction toward the other means both more and less than Being ("*Plus et moins que l'être*" [*NP*, 66]).

Celan's poetry operates according to a similar economy: "*alles ist weniger, als / es ist, / alles ist mehr*" (*GW* II, 76). It inflects and often rejects the imagery, metaphors, and concepts used to describe what "is" and limits itself to virtually rendering the way in which language has been already directed to the other. Yet this reduction appears to matter "more" than Being, because it means "otherwise," in an attempt to detach the other from the meaning associated with Being. In fact "The Meridian" makes a distinction between the other understood in the context of Being and the absolutely other when, seeing poetry as paths (*Wege*), Celan asks: "And are these paths only detours (*Um-wege*), detours from you to you (*von dir zu dir*)? But they are, among how many others, the paths on which language becomes voice. They are encounters, paths from a voice to a listening You ("*Wege einer Stimme zu einem wahrnehmenden Du*") (*GW* III, 201/*P*, 53). This sentence marks a difference between poetry in which "you" can be compared to another "you" (*von dir zu dir*) and poetry for which the other remains absolutely other, *Du*. What makes possible the equivalency between "you" and another "you" is the detour of Being, where every other has a similar mode of Being. For Celan, however, this approach does not stress the autonomy of the other, and, due to its cognitive inclinations, it cannot turn into an encounter, an address to the listening *Du*.

The idea that it is possible, and perhaps even necessary, to read Celan through the chiasmus of otherness is suggested by his own description of the other as a face. In many among Celan's early poems, from *Mohn und Gedächtnis* to *Niemandsrose*, the other, *du*, is represented by the face, or by eyes, watchful, demanding, often filled with pain. In fact eyes seem to invade Celan's language, to watch the subject's words attempting to address the other, as, for example, in "An Eye, Open," where the eye becomes "no one's voice" (*PPC*, 133), the sign of the other's ("no one's" since the other cannot be named) influence upon language. The other's eye as the locus of alterity cannot be therefore identified with the physical eye, and to protect this distinction Celan writes in "Distances" about "eye in eye" (*Aug in Aug*) (*GW* I, 95). The "eye of alterity" is of course associated with the organ of sight; it in a sense appears through or in it. However, it itself is a nontransparent eye, which resists the subject's vision and thus veils the other. The frequency and intensity of such double or intersected images, and their relation to writing, leave no doubt that the other's face, his/her "dark eye" (*Dunkles Aug*), imprints itself upon language and directs it to the other. In this sense, this eye "watches" the lyrical subject; it becomes "visible" in language, as it "peers" from among words, images, and concepts.

The function of the eye in Celan's poetry suggests a parallel to Levinas's writings on the face. In Levinas, the other's face also is identified not with physical appearance but rather with the manner in which the other announces herself and yet covers her otherness and makes it inaccessible to the I. The parallel goes even further, since one can find instances in which Celan's poetry characterizes the other through what might be called the economy of the trace.

> Schliere im Aug:
> dass bewahrt sei
> ein durchs Dunkel getragenes Zeichen,
> . . . als stumm
> vibrierender Mitlaut gestimmt. (*GW* I, 159)
>
> Streak in the eye:
> to preserve
> a sign born through the dark

. . . as a mutely
quivering consonant. (*SG*, 98)

The cut in the eye is also a glass trace (*Glasspur*), which veils the
other at the same time that it signals him/her; that is, it traces by
its own erasure. This incision marks the eye of otherness in the
other's physical eye, a thin mark reminiscent of the "smoking
splinter" from "Sprachgitter." In language, such a sign functions
only as an indirect incision; it does not stand by itself but appears
as co-sounding with other signs/sounds—a consonant. However, it
can be paradoxically only a mute consonant, which vibrates
silently by the sounds of language, easily drowned in them and
forgotten, indistinguishable from words themselves. As in Levinas,
Celan's *Glasspur* cannot be identified with words; it is only a
scratch, a mark between words, a transparent, "glass" trace, a fur-
row pointing to the other. As the poem implies, the task of poetry
is to secure this frail trace, the other's sign, to make a place for it in
a fissure between words, images, concepts, all too familiar to let the
other remain other. This transparent incision characterizes Celan's
writings, to take Levinas's lead, as "poetics of non-indifference" to
the other. For as "The Meridian" demonstrates, Celan is not interested in approaching the other through the concepts of difference
or identity, through the similarity of genus, but instead in exploring the glass trace of the silent con-sonant, which indicates a readiness, an openness of language to the other. This openness should
not be read only in terms of Being but, as "Conversation in the
Mountains" implies, treated as an ethical dimension, not exactly,
as Lacoue-Labarthe convinces us, "different" from Being but one
toward which the saying of Being cannot remain "in-different."

"Conversation in the Mountains," which from the very
beginning concerns itself with the possibility of speaking, naming
("unpronounceable name"), and hearing the other, underscores
the fact that the other cannot be thought. Addressing the reader,
the I speaks about the other "whom you think you hear" (*P*, 17)
("*den du hörst, zu hören vermeinst*" [*GW* III, 169]). The verb *vermeinen* signals Celan's attitude toward language and its attempt to
think, or literally to mean (*meinen*), the other. *Meinen* refers to the
words pronouncing the other, words trying to address and think
the other within the confines of the matrix of signification. In
order to do so, they have to say, to "mean," the other, to make its
alterity conform to the standards of meaningfulness. However,
words do not live up to this expectation and inevitably distort the
other, as the prefix *ver* in *vermeinen* suggests a disfiguring, a false-

hood, literally a "mis-meaning." This dangerous, defacing turn characteristic of signification explains why the encounter in the mountains begins in silence: "There they stand, the cousins, on a road in the mountains, the stick silent, the stones silent, and the silence no silence at all (*und das Schweigen ist kein Schweigen*). No word has come to an end and no phrase, it is nothing but a pause, an empty space between the words, a blank—you see all the syllables stand around, waiting" (*P*, 19). However, the silence, the pause, the space between words is "no silence at all"; rather, it refers to an "unspoken" level of language, the openness to the other. The ending of "Conversation in the Mountains" indicates that Celan wants to differentiate between this silence and the silent call of Being. The voice referred to by Celan as "Klein" recalls that beforehand he loved only the burning candle and never loved others:

> 'I loved the candle which burned in the left corner, I loved it because it burned down . . . I did not love *it*, I loved its burning down (*ihr Herunterbrennen*) and, you know, I haven't loved anything since.
>
> 'No. Nothing. Or maybe whatever burned down like that candle.' (*P*, 21).

The burning candle becomes perhaps the single most charged image of this short text, figuring the tension between the ontological and the ethical stakes of language. On the one hand, the burning of the candle functions as a trope for the passing time, for the fascination with the very happening, with Being, as it indeed seems that "Klein"'s only concern was time, its passage, and the thinking of temporality. On the other, the candle signifies the memory of the dead and their annihilation by burning. The candle thus figures at the same time the "natural" passage of time and the "unnatural" incineration, natural death versus extermination. In a way, the tension Celan inscribes in the image of the burning candle continuously "refuels" this figure, making it into an emblematic trope for Celan's poetry.[38]

With the sign of the burning candle in mind, "Klein" has undertaken the journey through the mountains in order to distance himself from his early concerns, to arrive at a new understanding of self: "me with my burned candle, me with the day, me with the days, me here and there, me, maybe accompanied—now—by the love of those I didn't love, me on the way to myself, up here" (*P*, 22). Even though the passage is informed by a familiar rhetoric of self-discovery, a displacement ("here and there," "on the way"), this displacement is directed by the "love of those I didn't love," which suggests that it becomes ethical in its concern. "Klein" no longer deliberates only over time and Being; his new self arises in relation to others, in his first response to them. Similarly to "The Meridian," "Conversation in the Mountains" marks a fold between Being and the ethical, as it locates the ethical in language "otherwise" than in its origin in Being.

This "otherwise" figures prominently in Celan's most important and best volume, *Atemwende*, where one of the opening poems, "Vor dein spätes Gesicht," explicitly places the ethical apart from thought and thematization: *"kam etwas zu stehn, / das schon einmal bei uns war, un- / berührt von Gedanken"* (GW II, 15) ("something came to stand, / that already once was with us, un- / touched by thought"). If in the philosophical tradition the relation between the I and Being has been conceived in terms of perception, reflection, thought, for Celan the relation between the I and the other remains "untouched by thought," takes place "otherwise" than as thought. Even Heidegger, though he radicalizes both Being and thinking, and dissociates it from reflection and subjectivity in order to retain Being as otherness, places the emphasis on *Denken*. The human mode of Being, *Dasein*, means already a prereflexive thinking of Being, and the relation to the other is conceived within this primordial thinking. Celan insists, however, that this "relation" to the other takes place otherwise than thinking: while usually it is the subject that "thinks" the other, in Celan's poetry, conversely, it is the other who regards the I and challenges the subject through the other's face and eyes—a challenge that is never reversible to the categories of the subject. When Lacoue-Labarthe dismisses Levinas's reading of Celan's language as "otherwise than Being," he disregards the fact that the "beyond" (*au-delà*) does not necessarily, or not exclusively, refer to something that "is" beyond Being, to an other (transcendental?) order, but instead harbors the possibility of an other mode of "relating," which relates "otherwise" than thought does and yet is not reducible to the sensible or the empirical. In this other scenario, the other's eyes pierce the subject's vision; they disrupt thinking and define the I as being seen. As it tears thinking, this rupture indeed points not in the direction of Being but toward the other. It is in this sense that Levinas writes about "otherwise than Being," as a manner of "relating" not through differing or the original leap between Being and thinking, the way of language, but through non-indifference. In this context, non-indifference becomes the sign of the giving of sign (*"signe de cette donation de signe au point de se faire tout entier signe"* [*NP*, 59]) and, as such, is its own signified, for in a sense this giving of a sign precedes the difference between the signifier and the signified. In Levinas's eyes, this sign of the readiness to speak, to address the other, should not be read as the response and correspondence (Heideggerian *Entsprechung?*) to Being, for, even if this sign can be made only by a being who thinks Being, it happens not as a moment of thought itself but instead pre-disposes thought ethically. This is why Levinas insists upon the separateness of the ethical, upon its irreducibility to thinking and, subsequently, to reflection and knowledge. Here the address, the welcoming, of the other is not convertible to the thought of this welcome, and, as such, it retains an ethical significance that has already inflected the conceptualization of this encounter and rendered its subject non-indifferent.

In the context outlined here, Celan's poetics can be characterized as ethical in the Levinasian sense. As "Conversation in the Mountains" suggests, the burning of the candle, the passing of days, and the thought of Being are "accompanied" (*begleitet*) by the ethical, the welcoming of the other. Like "The Meridian," "Conversation in the Mountains" underscores precisely this chiasm of ontological otherness and ethical alterity, with its contingent difficulties and constant danger of collapsing its own distinctions. In spite of this thin line of separation, the welcome provides a direction (*Richtung*, corresponding perhaps to Levinas's *sens*) for language, mentioned so many times in "The Meridian," the direction that charges the opening for/of meaning that thought makes in Being with ethical significance. The ubiquity of the other (*Du*) in Celan's poems, frequent references to the other's eyes as the veil for alterity, and the emphasis upon twofold otherness manifest the distinctness of the ethical in language, its stubborn "otherwise," irreducible to the thinking of Being. The ethical here has no cognitive or normative sense but rather a linguistic one: it indicates a singular curve of language, a direction that inflects language toward the other. It produces a unique sense that language remains always dedicated to the other, notwithstanding the circumstances of its use or its explicit pronouncements. The fact that language is meaningful in the cognitive sense and can serve as a means of communication points to the ethical "envelope" of language, its ethical bent, untranslatable into words and "meaningless" within the cognitive framework.

↜ 6 ↝

CELAN'S POETIC MERIDIANS

In "The Meridian" Celan remarks that the ethical in language, the direction toward the other, continuously questions poetry and art: *"In-Frage-Stellung der Kunst, eine In-Frage-Stellung aus dieser* Richtung" (*GW* III, 193, emphasis mine). *Dichtung*, the primordial saying of Being, happens, as Heidegger claims, for the sake of Being, but, Celan adds, it ineluctably takes place also vis-à-vis the face of the other. Since Being is neither presence nor absence and cannot be said through words, poetry preserves and maintains this saying indirectly between words, in the invisible furrows, the interlacings (*Geflecht*), that let words mean. In its dialogue with Heidegger, Celan's poetics follows this model but at the same time modifies it: poetry is not only an infold of thinking into Being, a transpropriation (*Übereignung*), but also an address, a directing of language, as it comes into words, toward the other. In "To Stand" this turn takes place without language (*ohne Sprache*), that is, not by means of words themselves, and yet this volta is not quite empty or meaning-less, since the poem speaks about "all there is room for in that" direction, this bearing. Encoded in this turn is perhaps, to use Celan's idiom from "The Meridian," the signification of exposure to the other, the possibility of address and contact with otherness. In this characteristic move, Celan's poetry dissociates the ethical from the verbal content of the poem, from the meaning of words, and the structural properties of the text, leaving for it what perhaps signifies otherwise. This chapter follows these inflections of Celanian texts from their early themes and images of a poet(h)ic debt to others to the later, specifically linguistic figurations of the other's poetic trace. This development of Celan's work, its radicalization of the other's rupture of language, reflected in the increasingly short, halted, and self-silencing poetic idiom, will be read here in terms of poetic meridians marking the (im)possible encounter of language with the other.

Celan's early poems present this encounter mostly in thematic terms, as the invocations of others, memories of their faces, a painful remembrance of the Shoah. The ethical responsibility translates itself in this context into a task of meditating about others, the close ones and all the ones annihilated during the destruction of Jews in the Second World War. As Celan's specifically Jewish experience leads him to an acute sense of the need to recognize the significance of others for language, the ethical response of his poetry is marked here by the awareness of the death of others, which imposes the obligation of remembrance. Such remembering becomes a thematization of one's concern for others, the repetition in writing of the impossibility of escaping the ethical vocation. Thus the early poems inscribe in their imagery the others' faces, their eyes, the trace of their alterity that inescapably marks language. Their language still follows the conventional poetic precepts and is characterized by regular division into stanzas and the use of complete sentences, full lines, and words as semantic and graphic units:

> Du schlugst die Augen auf—ich seh mein Dunkel leben.
> Ich seh ihm auf den Grund:
> auch da ists mein und lebt. (*GW* I, 97)

> You opened your eyes—I saw my darkness live.
> I see through it down to the bed;
> there too it is mine and lives. (*PPC*, 79)

The other's eyes and the seeing of one's own darkness in them function here as a motif of otherness, in a poem that spells this theme in relatively long lines and regular syntax. Lines correspond to syntactic units, either full sentences ("*ich seh mein Dunkel leben, ich seh ihm auf den Grund*") or clauses ("*dass sich ein Ferge fand*"), with the poem focusing on the image of the other's eyes and their significance for the lyrical subject. The poem's semantics remains undisturbed: there are no coinings, no irregularities; the words preserve their usual, monosemic form.

In the later poetry, however, particularly in *Atemwende* and subsequent collections, the ethical announces itself not only thematically, or through a repeated address to the you, but by exposing the extra-verbal in language. It is no longer only a theme of writing or a conscious preoccupation with the other but an exploration of the ethical inflection of language. The disfigurations and discontinuities of those poems suggest that Celan tries to magnify there the impact this inflection has upon language, to bring it into the open by dislocating language and forcing it to acknowledge its ethicity. This is why a poem like "Sprinkle Ochre" seems to be written almost in a "different" language:

STREU OCKER in meine Augen:
du lebst nicht
mehr drin,

. . . .

mit ihrem Traum
streich über die
ausgemünzte
Schläfenbeinschuppe . . . (*GW* II, 322)

SPRINKLE OCHRE into my eyes:
no longer
you live in them,

. . . .

with their dream
graze the debased coinage,
the scale of
my temporal bone . . . (*PPC*, 311)

While the thematic remains similar—the other resists the subjective gaze and does not live in the subject's eyes—the language of the poem is dramatically different. The stanzaic units have no regularity; they seem to be coming out on a single breath, as short utterances, often not even complete sentences. Lines become very short, frequently only a single word, for example, an adjective *grossen*, or a verb *spar*, or an adverbial phrase: *mehr drin, an der*. These short irregular lines and breath-like stanzas signal the importance of typography in Celan's poetry, as they direct the reader toward the "whiteness" of the poem, its extra-verbal level. The severing and separating of sentences, phrases, or even words into two or three lines disrupts the semantic and syntactical layers of the poem, opens in them white spaces, which do not enter the domain of semantic or syntactic correlations. Analogical processes lead to coinings (*ausgemünzte*) or composite words: *Schläfenbeinschuppe*, a progressive straining and stretching of diction to indicate a withdrawal, a breaking away from words themselves. Unfortunately, Hamburger's translation does not retain the coinings and composites nor the two cases of word-severing in the original: *Grab-beigaben* and *er-zähl*. In the first case, Celan creates a composite and then exposes its creation by both breaking it with a hyphen and placing the word in two lines. A similar procedure opens a crack in one of the most important words for Celan: *erzählen*, to tell, where the hyphen exposes a fissure in the word but also in telling itself, an impossibility of ever saying the other, which grants the other the asylum of a pause. As Celan's poems repeatedly demonstrate, this extra-verbal interval can be made manifest only by cracking, fracturing, and hyphenating language, its syntax, semantics, or even words themselves.

With time, hyphenation and composite words begin to play an increasingly important role in Celan's poetry, even to the extent that they dominate the entire poem, as they do, for example, in "Schaltjahrhunderte":

> SCHALTJAHRHUNDERTE, Schalt-
> sekunden, Schalt-
> geburten, novembernd, Schalt-
> tode . . .
>
> . . . .
>
> (Unasyliert, un-
> archiviert, un-
> umfürsorgt? Am
> Leben?) (*GW* II, 324)
>
> LEAP-CENTURIES, leap-
> seconds, leap-
> births, novembering, leap-
> deaths . . .
>
> . . . .
>
> (Unasylumed, un-
> archived, un-
> welfare-attended? A-
> live?) (*PPC*, 313)

The hyphens not only point to the roots of the words or to semantic procedures that lead to establishing negation through the prefix *un* but expose the ending of lines, an interval at the end of each line. These intervals do not take place, however, at the end of a sentence, a clause, or even a unit of meaning; they are instead pauses inside words, which crack the uniform graphic and semantic shape of the words in order to establish what the poem calls "reading stations in the late word" (*Lesestationen im Spätwort*). The composite *Spätwort* indicates that words come in a sense too late; they can never therefore say what they themselves have missed. In the same move, the term *Spätwort* gives eminence to the unsaid, which signals itself only by making a fissure in the word, an opening that becomes a "reading station," a moment of pause, as if in the middle of the word, manifesting the other's unwordable alterity against the power of signification. In a similar context, Celan writes in "Kolon" about "the light of the word-eve" ("*Licht der Wort- / Vigilie*") (*GW* I, 265), where the hyphen in *Wort-Vigilie* separates the composite word into two lines, marking through silence that which precedes words, which has already passed, an-archically, as the eve of words. Another line from "Kolon" explicitly names the "word-eve" as the "location" of the other: "*Doch du, Erschlafene, immer / sprachwahr in jeder / der Pausen.*" The other is "language-true" only in "each of the pauses"; he/she remains other on the eve of words, on the narrow edges of meaning, as *die Enge* in "The Meridian" suggests.

Celan's poems often refer to these pauses inside words also as "word shadows" (*Wortschatten*). "Im Spätrot" from *Vom Schwelle zu Schwelle* speaks about "*schattenverheissendes Baumwort*" (a tree-word promising shadow) (*GW* I, 86), indicating that the other's name (*deiner Liebe Namen*) finds shelter precisely in these shadows and preserves itself on the edge of words. In *Atemwende*, for example, poetry becomes "*WEGE IM SCHATTEN-GEBRÄCH / deiner Hand*" (*GW* II, 18) (paths in the shadow-snout of your hand). This very short poem again manifests that poetry understood as "experience" (*Erfahrung*) finds itself in the other's shadow: on the one hand, it addresses its words to the other's shadow and looks there for blessing (*Segen*); on the other, the you can survive as the other, can retain its alterity, only in the words' shadow, never in words themselves. As Winfried Menninghaus has suggested, the word-shadows become an asylum from the light of words and thought; they balance the metaphoric of light in Celan's poetry. In "We Were Lying" from *Lichtzwang*, Celan suggests that the encounter with the other may become possible only through "darkening over" to the other (*hinüberdunkeln*), even though the reigning force of light (*Lichtzwang*), of words and their meaning, ultimately prevents the meeting: "*Doch kontenn wir nicht / hinüberdunkeln zu dir: / es herrschte / Lichtzwang*" (*GW* II, 239) ("But we could not / darken over to you: / light compulsion / reigned") (*PPC*, 289). "Darkening over" characterizes well this element in Celan's poetry that exposes the word shadows and their sheltering potential, as if against the ruling power of words, meaning, and images.

Only in these word shadows can the other preserve alterity and resist the appropriating tendencies of the poetic subject and its language, as the danger of appropriation from the final poem of *Atemwende* suggests:

> EINMAL,
> da hörte ich ihn,
>
> . . . .
>
> Eins und Unendlich,
> vernichtet,
> ichten. (*GW* II, 107)
>
> ONCE
> I heard him,
>
> . . . .
>
> One and Infinite,
> annihilated,
> ied. (*PPC*, 271)

Even though the poem refers to the other as "one," singular and "infinite," transgressing words and thought, the other can easily be reduced, appropriated, "annihilated" by language. This annihilation takes place when the other turns into a subject, when it becomes "ied." This double meaning is encoded, characteristically for Celan's playful or even violent disfiguration of words, in his "German" *ichten*, which coins a verb from the first-person-singular pronoun, *ich*, and/or at the same time transforms the verb *nichten*. Through its graphic proximity to *nichten*, *ichten* means therefore "to I," to change the other into the "I," into the subject and thus to destroy the other: *(n)ichten*. When "ied," the other becomes another subject or even merely a part of the poetic subject, an other negated, appropriated, erased. In other words, in this situation it is, then, the poetic subject that explains the other, that provides meaning, images, and words for her/him. In "Come," for example, this violent "iying" of the other gets represented in the image of the subject literally filling others with itself: "*lass mich euch zuschütten mit / allem Meinen*" (*GW* III, 102) ("let me bury you all with / everything of my own" [*LP*, 185]). This subjective projection upon others denies their autonomy and their otherness. They become like the subject, all the same, reducible to a common denominator and comprehensible, since all that belongs to the subject can be also attributed to the other. In its polysemy, *allem Meinen* identifies those possessions with meaning, since *meinen* also translates into English as "to mean." This perversely double sense of the German text, itself an ironic play on meaning, exposes, then, the dangers of the process of signification and poetic expression, equating it with the subject's strategy of saturating the other with its own meaning and hence interpreting the other in subjective terms. Meaning becomes equated with *ichten*, with annihilating the other by turning him/her into the I. "Come" indicates also that meaning inevitably remains related to subjectivity, and that even when the words attempt to "mean" the other, to be serious about marking the other's alterity, they inevitably "mean," signify, the other as the same and thus appropriate it.

It must be stressed, though, that, beyond the language-related connotations, Celan's use of the word *vernichten*, "to annihilate," points to the relation between language and writing, on the one hand, and death and destruction, on the other, a connection frequently highlighted, among others by Menninghaus and by Szondi in his analysis of *Engführung*.[1] An example of this analogy between writing/saying the other and destroying/burning the other can be found also in "Solve":

> vom winzig-lodernden, vom
> freien
> Satzzeichen der
> zu den unzähligen zu
> nennenden un-
> aussprechlichen
> Namen aus-
> einandergeflohenen, ge-
> borgenen
> Schrift. (*GW* II, 82).

This practically untranslatable poem opens with the image of the grave-tree (*Grabbaum*) split into burning logs (*Brandscheiten*), which associates death with burning, a strategy used again in the third stanza, where burning is explicitly linked to writing, with the written text flaring up (*lodern*). Through these multiple associations, the poem suggests that words consume the other, that meaning turns the other into "ash" and destroys her/his alterity. In the end, the other's unspeakable (*unaussprechlichen*) and uncountable (*unzähligen*) name signals itself only when the text draws apart, when it cracks open. It would seem, therefore, that the continuing images of the burning and annihilating text, tying Celan's poetry to the death of millions in concentration camps, also initiate attempts to "save" the other from words. This is why in "Solve" burning and destruction are countered by opening the text at the end of lines through hyphenation, as Celan consistently hyphenates all the key words in the poem: *zer-spaltener* indicates that the burning logs of the text can be cracked; this is also suggested by the hyphen and severing into two lines of *aus-einadergeflohenen* and *geborgenen*, two participles describing the text (*Schrift*); finally, the other's *un-aussprechlichen* name leaves its trace not in the adjective directly but instead in the hyphen separating the prefix. This excessive hyphenation, opening pauses inside words, becomes the characteristic feature of Celan's later poems, which disrupt and counter the appropriating tendencies of the poetic text, attempting to free the other from the domination of the subject and its *meinen*, its meaning and property.

This rupturing of words, creating *Lesestationen* in them, or exposing the intervals between the lines of the poem, constitutes part of the process by which Celan's work alters the word, as if against itself, into a *Gegenwort*. In "The Meridian," *Gegenwort* refers to Camille's words "Long live the king," which the text characterizes as "a word against the grain, the word which cuts the 'string,' which does not bow to the 'bystanders and old warhorses of history.' It is an act of freedom. It is a step (*Schritt*)" (*P*, 40). The "counter-word" describes a step away from the word and from the text (*Schrift—Schritt*), a step into its shadow. This coining indicates Celan's attempt to break language open, to wring from it a place for the other, an effort that finds its expression, for example, in "Deine Augen im Arm" from *Fadensonnen* when the text asks: "*Mach den Ort aus, machs Wort aus*" (*GW* II, 123). The paronomasia of *Wort* and *Ort*, "word" and "place," suggests that poetry should be written in a way that, by turning words against themselves, would make place for the other without translating the other's alterity into familiar images, concepts, or metaphors. Words should become *Lesestationen*, so they could point toward the other without resorting to naming. This sense of absence manifests itself best in *Gegenwort* itself, perhaps the single most important instance of paronomasia in all of Celan's writing. Although only an implicit paronomasia, it nevertheless becomes obvious in the context of Celan's concern for the other and its, to use Levinas's term, anarchic, linguistic trace, as visible in the single change of *o* into *a* which turns *Gegenwort* into *Gegenwart*, the present. This change in the semantic form of the "counter-word" both intimates its extreme closeness to and dissociates it from the present and presence enacted by words, implying that the other can never be present and that its alterity never enters words. *Gegenwort* suggests, therefore, a deviation from the word's presence into its shadow, into its hidden interval, where the other leaves its trace. Although she/he comes close to presence, merely a letter away, the other in effect disrupts the very paradigm of presence and absence that founds signification. Taken even more radically, *Gegenwort* implies a "paronomasia in Being," a slight change in the direction, an impossibility of containing the other within the same horizon.

This impossibility is signaled by a rupture in time, an indication that the other does not enter the flow of time but remains somehow "on the other side":[2] "*SCHAUFÄDEN, SINNFÄDEN, aus /* *Nachtgalle geknüpft / hinter der Zeit*" (*GW* II, 88) ("Threads of sight, threads of meaning / woven out of a night bile / on the other side of time" [trans. mine]). The fragments of vision and of meaning come together only on the other side of time, behind it, as, for Celan, both seeing and meaning direct language toward the other and in this turn point it beyond time. The movement of transgression surfaces again in the phrase "*wer / ist unsichtbar genug / euch zu sehn?*" (who is invisible enough to see you? [that is, the threads of sight and meaning?]). Although it is sight that points toward the other, in the last instance the other's alterity disrupts visibility and the spatio-temporal framework of thought and signification:

> in der Kalenderlücke
> wiegt ihn, wiegt ihn
> das neugeborene
> Nichts. (*GW* II, 321)

> in the gap of the calendar
> the newborn
> Nothing
> rocks him, rocks him. (*LP*, 99)

Several other poems by Celan link nothingness with the signification of alterity: in "An niemand geschmiegt" (*GW* I, 245), *niemand* (no one) becomes identified with the other, with *du*, as "*an nie-mand geschmiegt*" turns into "*an du geschmiegt.*" Similar implications arise in "Psalm" from *Niemandsrose* or in "Niedrigwasser" from *Sprachgitter*. In "Niedrigwasser," one finds an image of a word cut from the heart-wall by "no one": "*Niemand schnitt uns das Wort von der Herzwand*" (*GW* I, 193). All these poems identify a strategy by which in Celan's poems the other often becomes "no one" or "nothing," (in)accessible only through negative determination. For example, in "Leaflets-pain," the other becomes "the newborn Nothing," which announces itself through a gap in time. This time-caesura, accompanying the rupture of otherness in the poetic text, realizes the implications of *Gegenwort*, the inversion of words into "counter-words," and their withdrawal from the presence of meaning.

The frequency of *Gegenworte* in Celan's texts turns them into poetry about writing and language, a work addressing its own caesuras, *Lesestationen*, and time gaps, not only in the sense that these poems directly and openly reflect upon the poetic act and thematize it but primarily because Celan's texts are written as *Lesestationen*, that is, they fissure and dislocate language. In other words, they do not speak *about* otherness, the ethical in language, or the relation to the other—they themselves *are* this relation. As Szondi observes, for Celan the poem is not a representation of reality but reality itself;[3] that is, it happens as the reality of disclosing the world in and through language. Celan's poetry, then, does not represent, describe, or thematize but instead writes itself into that very disclosure, into the essential directions along which language unfolds, a strategy explicit, for example, in Celan's longest poem, "Engführung," which begins as an entrance into the "region of writing":

> VERBRACHT ins
> Gelände
> mit der untrüglichen Spur:
>
> Gras, auseinandergeschrieben. (*GW* I, 197)
>
> BROUGHT to
> the area
> with the unerring trail:
>
> grass, written apart. (*SG*, 157)

The very beginning of this poem becomes also the opening of a region of writing, where the reader is brought into the determining direction of language, the direction that—signaled by "grass," letters as Szondi suggests, "written apart"—marks a fissure of an "unmistakable trace" (*mit untrüglichen Spur*). As Szondi rightly observes, Celan does not build a comparison between landscape (*Gelände, Gras*) and writing but affirms that reality "is" only through and in language, that it is "written," a text.[4] Therefore the direction toward the other, the trace, is not simply a motif or a theme for poetry; rather, this ethical openness toward the other can take place only in language, where the other's alterity can be marked as that pre-established and pre-voluntary direction of thought, language, and writing toward the other.

Celan's poems continuously write themselves into this direction, into this narrow path of language: "Engführung" unmistakably points to *die Enge* in "The Meridian," as it indeed leads (*führen*) along the narrow, ethical path, opened in words written apart (*auseinandergeschrieben*). By lodging themselves in this narrowness, Celan's poems become, as Szondi, Menninghaus, and Sparr remark, "landscapes," which describe semiological or textual regions.[5] For example, in "Osterqualm," the smoke becomes severed with a keel trace similar to letters: "*OSTERQUALM, flutend, mit / der buchstabenähnlichen / Kielspur inmitten*" (*GW* II, 85) ("THICK EASTER SMOKE, flowing, with / the letter-like / wake in the midst" [*PPC*, 261]); the fishing net is woven out of the ends of thoughts: "*Das Netz darunter, geknüpft / aus Gedanken- / enden*"; and the boat is accompanied by three sand voices: "*Drei Sandstimmen.*" The elaborate image of a seaport in "Hafen" turns into a text when the letters on the large crane write an "unname": "*die / Buchstaben der / Grosskräne einen / Unnamen schreiben*" (*GW* II, 52), referring here to a name written apart, its fissure, unvoiced, without word—the other. In a parallel move, even the body in Celan's poems becomes a scene of writing. In "Niedrigwasser," the other carves her/his name upon the wall of the heart, and in "Unter die Haut" the other's name is implanted under the skin of the subject's hand: "*UNTER DIE HAUT meiner Hände genäht: / dein mit Händen / getrösteter Name*" ("SEWN UNDER THE SKIN of my hands: / your name / that hands comforted") and the shimmer of letters pours out of the pores: "*der / Buchstabenschimmer aus / der wahnwitzig-offenen / Pore*" ("the letter effulgence from / the dementedly open / pore") (*GW* II, 49/*PPC*, 239). The merger of writing and landscape or physical objects and bodies signaled here only by several examples has double significance for Celan's language: on the one hand, the objects "are" language, in the sense that they cannot exist outside of language and meaning, and, on the other, the poems themselves probe the regions of writing, or indeed their shadows, the unwritten *Unname* of the other.

Celan's writing on writing is characterized by the fact that, through composite words, paronomasia, parallel structures, and juxtaposition, the key words and images in his poetry become interlaced, form chains and clusters. For example, in "Tabernacle Window," the name is identified with breath: "*ein Atem? ein Name?*" (*GW* I, 278). "An niemand geschmiegt" equates "no one" with the you, the other, while in "There was earth inside them" "no one" and "you" become part of a chain of names: *"o einer, o keiner, o niemand, o du"* (*GW* I, 211) ("o one, o none, o no one, o you" [*PPC*, 153]). Thanks to those various poetic devices, Celan's language achieves a particular degree of interrelation between important themes, motifs, images, and ideas, connections that not only build a network of references within Celan's poetry that would enable its reading in terms of thematic or conceptual clusters but also unmistakably point them toward the other: either by opening a caesura inside words, by severing and separating them into two different lines, or by directly relating it to one of the "names" indicating the other: *du, Name* or *Unname, Schatten, Richtung, Atem.*

The connections between motifs, metaphors, and images and their tracing of the other's "names" have been extensively illustrated by Menninghaus in the second part of *Magie der Form, "Intention auf den 'Namen' als organisierendes Kraftfeld der Semantik elementarer Motive und Metaphern,"* which presents the textual operations that produce clusters of images in Celan's poems: time, daynight, anthropological images (eye, mouth, hand, heart), geological and chemical (sea, water, earth, sand, mountains, glacier, ice, snow, crystal, stone), astrological (star, moon, sun, sky), botanical (rose, flower), optical (light, evening, shadow).[6] Illustrating an immediate relation between these groups of images and the fact that Celan's language turns upon itself in its intention of names, Menninghaus presents a compelling argument that the link between the image clusters and the turn toward the other create a second or double semantic within Celan's poetry: *"Die 'zweite' Semantik, der ihrer Form eigene Gehalt von Celans Metaphern beruht nämlich auf einer Assimilation der 'primären' semantischen Determinationswerte an ihr formales 'Schwimmen'"* (*MF*, 172) ("The 'second' semantic, the contents of Celan's metaphors particular to its [the semantic] form, depends namely upon an assimilation of the 'primary' semantic determinations into its formal 'swimming'" [trans. mine]). The "swimming" refers to "the swimming word" (*schwimmende Wort*) from *Lichtzwang* (*GW* II, 268), which for Menninghaus indicates the semantic instability of Celan's poetry, its tendency to swing away from the verbal content in the direction of *Name*. This linguistic "swimming" indeed opens a double semantic, in which the semantic content of the text becomes often of secondary importance and takes on another, "essential," function, which consists in pointing in the direction of the second semantic. Indeed, in "Kleide die Worthöhlen aus" Celan postulates overhearing the second tone of words: *"und lausch ihrem zweiten / und jeweils zweiten und zweiten / Ton"* (*GW* II, 198). The second tone of words, distinguishable from their phonetic and semantic form, creates a sequence of silences that runs invisibly through the poem. A similar approach to Celan's poetry has been suggested by Levinas, who in "De l'être à l'autre" uses his differentiation between *signification* and *signifyingness*, with the latter term indeed describing a second semantic, the very moment of giving the sign, the signifyingness of this giving and openness, which precedes the meaning of the given sign.[7] This gift of the sign cannot be described in semantic terms *sensu stricto*, since it does not enter words and cannot be reduced to semantic and syntactical relationships between them but is instead preserved in the word-shadows, as a direction or an inflection of language that opens the very possibility of producing words.

Since the second semantic or signifyingness precedes words, it functions as the very formation of poetry's "narrowness," or, as Menninghaus calls it, "the inner language-curves of poems" (*"die innerem (Sprach-)Kurven der Gedichte"* (*MF*, 211), or, in short, *Gedichtkurven*. In their turn toward *Name*, these curves of language link all the poetic strategies—metaphorizing, the "swinging" of the semantic, predication, composite words, parallelism, paronomasia, etc.—and, by silently weaving through the text, "magnetize" and direct them in an address to the other. These gathering curves should not be mistaken for a latent structure of the poetic text; they do not provide a basis for the poem's form or structure but instead function as just an indication of the unspoken direction of language, as an inflection of its semantics into an other (ethical?) "meaning." As "The Meridian" suggests, such curves can therefore be named the "curve of breath": *"Atem, das heisst Richtung"* (*GW* III, 188) ("breath, that is, direction" [*P*, 39]). In "The Meridian," the direction in which the poem addresses or sends itself becomes that of a breath, of an interval between words, where the moment of taking in another breath provides a pause in which the other can signal its separateness and alterity, its own breath, apart from words, meaning, and thought. Indeed, the text of Celan's speech defines poetry in terms of breath: *"Dichtung: das kann eine Atemwende bedeuten"* (*GW* III, 195) ["Poetry is perhaps this: an *Atemwende*, a turning of breath" [*P*, 47, slightly modified]). On the one hand, *Atemwende* indicates a turn from one word to another, an interval of silence or the whiteness of the page, which provides the "shadow" for the other, and, on the other hand, it effects a turn of the text toward the other, performing the function of an ethical rupture of language.

Such rupture of language indicates best what this study calls the "ethicity" of language, that is, a linguistic inflection, a displacement from its semantic and cognitive functions toward the acknowledgment and silent respect for the other. The sense of such ethicity eludes words for the simple reason that all words find themselves already inflected and affected by it; they all "sense" their exposure and direction to the other. Celanian disfigurations of language provide an excellent illustration of how poetry can almost force this unwritten ethicity into the open or at least call attention to its inflection and silent erasure from words. The ensuing difficulty of speaking about this ethicity manifests itself in showing how, despite its erasure continuously performed by words, the ethical nevertheless inflects language and bends it into a curve "magnetically" drawn toward the other.

As "The Meridian" explains, this curve, marked as the turn of breath, allows one to discern the twofold otherness: "it is perhaps this turn, this *Atemwende*, which can sort out the strange from the strange?" (*P*, 47). The turn of breath, or, as Celan calls it a moment later, *Atempause* (*GW* III, 197), makes possible the differentiation between two kinds of otherness; it marks the alterity of the other against the otherness of Being. It can perhaps achieve it only as a breath, an indication of a breathing human being, a pause in which that breath can be heard unnamed.

In accordance with this general trend of Celan's imagery, in "Schieferäugige" the other is enlivened by breath (*verlebendigt vom Hauch*) and remains upon the vocal cords: "*Mit dir, / auf der Stimmbänderbrücke, im / Grossen Dazwischen*" (*GW* II, 98) (With you, upon the arch of the vocal cords, in the great in-between). Poetry, in the sense with which both Celan and Heidegger invest *Dichtung*, remains with the other on the vocal cords, before the words are voiced, as *Dazwischen* refers not only to the opening between the cords but also to the caesura in words, the severing that forces a taking of breath in the middle of a word. "Lichtenbergs zwölf" presents the necessity of securing and preserving the vocal cords: "*Eine Stimmritze, ihn / zu bewahren, / im All*" (*GW* II, 91), a demand indicating that the aim of the poetic text is to preserve the opening of the cords without producing voice, with the very issuing of breath signifying a turn toward the other. This image returns again in "Offene Glottis," where the opened glottis and the stream of air (*Luftstrom*) are opposed to the "overtruthed eye-signs" ("*überwahr- / heited / das augen-, . . . zeichen*" [*GW* II, 388]). In a move that implicitly questions the dominion of intelligibility and knowledge over the other, their tropes, eyes, are said to possess too much truth, or, as "Tübingen, Jänner" also puts it, they are "overtalked to blindness" ("*Zur Blindheit über- / redete Augen*" (*GW* I, 226). Predictably, both coinings (*überwahrheited* and *überredete*) are severed with a hyphen, as if opened by a breath that disrupts vision, thought, and meaning.

It is possible, in fact, to claim that these and other *Gegenworte* characteristic of Celan's poetry result indeed from the turning of breath, as they mark the fissure that *Atemwende* opens in the text. A paradigmatic poem in this context is "Weggebeizt," which brings together the issues of language, otherness, breath, and meaning:

WEGGEBEIZT vom
Strahlenwind deiner Sprache
das bunte Gerede des An-
erlebten—das hundert-
züngige Mein-
gedicht, das Genicht.

Aus-
gewirbelt,
frei
der Weg durch den menschen-
gestaltigen Schnee,
den Büsserschnee, zu
den gastlichen
Gletscherstuben und -tischen.

Tief
in der Zeitenschrunde,
beim
Wabeneis
wartet, ein Atemkristall,
dein unumstössliches
Zeugnis. (*GW* II, 31)

Cauterized by the
radiant wind of your language
the palaver of in-stilled
ex-perience—the hundred-
tongued perjury-
poem, the no-em.

Whirled
out,

free,
the road through the human-
shaped snow
the penitent snow, to
the cordial
glacier-rooms and -tables.

Deep
in the time-crevasse,
by the
honeycomb-ice,
there waits, as a breath-crystal,
your unimpeachable
testimony. (*SG*, 227)

This poem contains all the essential elements of Celan's poetics: it opens with the opposition between the language of the subject and its experience, its palaver (*Gerede*), which as "Tübingen, Jänner" implies becomes blind to the other, and its result, "the hundred-tongued poem," becomes the dominion of the subject and is always "my-poem" (*Mein-gedicht*). *Mein*, however, suggests also a falsehood, a perjury, indicating that the subject's text is only a false poem, a pseudo-poem. This ambiguity encoded into *Mein-gedicht* indicates Celan's point that the other cannot be thought or "meant," that she/he escapes meaning. This is why the poem, always the subject's possession, becomes *das Genicht*, a "no poem," which instead of poetizing (*dichten*) annihilates (*nichten*) the other, or, to put it differently, which, in order to poetize the other, has to nihilate her/his alterity. However, *das Genicht* itself becomes in turn ambiguous, as *nicht* refers both to the destruction of the other's alterity by words and also to the other's trace, preserved as nothing, "no one," an *Unname*.

This trace, "the radiant wind of your language," ruptures the subject's speech and opens a fissure in it, reinforced by the abrupt ending of the line after "*WEGGEBEIZT vom*." This rupture turns into a road (*Weg*), a direction, which leads through "the human-shaped snow," where the transformation, as Gerhard Buhr suggests, indicates, through the abrupt ending of the line after *zu*, a pure, "unworded" direction of the poem[8]—its ethicity, since *menschen-gestaltig* implies that this direction concerns itself with others. The road leads through the snow, the word that in Celan's poetry refers to the whiteness of the page or the coldness and indifference of words. Here, though, this "freed" direction turns the snow into "penitent-snow" (*Büsserschnee*), an image revealing the ethical significance of the poem, an attempt to "atone"(?) for the indifference of words and their semantic involvements. As Celan makes clear, only in this ethical direction can the other find hospitable "glacier-rooms and -tables," reminiscent of the shadowing nature of pauses and wordless moments in Celan's poetry.[9] These sheltering ruptures can be found in the "time-crevasse" where the "breath-crystal" lies—the testimony and trace of the other. *Zeugnis* suggests that the breath-crystal must be recognized as the other's sign, a sign of breathing that has not yet entered language. This breath indicates that the gaps and pauses of the poem are not empty but instead signal the other's alterity,[10] as "Weggebeizt" explicitly links breath and *Atemwende* with the trace of the other, which assumes here the shape of an invisible breath-curve, rupturing both the poem (the hyphen suspends "the hundred-tongued perjury-poem" twice) and time. *Zeitenschrunde* further manifests that the other's trace signifies beyond the linear movement of time and cannot be linked with any particular moment, whether past, present, or future. All these images of dislocation mark a breath-curve that runs through and fissures the text, depolarizing language and rupturing its oppositional schemes in order to find a room without language (*"ohne Sprache"*) where the other could be free from words.

Such fissure through the poem, through its words and blank spaces as well as its semantic and syntactical interconnections, becomes the most frequent image in Celan's poetry, recurring most regularly in the collection *Atemwende*, where, as the title suggests, the breath-curve repeatedly ruptures and reverses the flow of language. For example, "Der mit Himmeln geheizte" speaks about a fiery rift through the world: *"Feuerriss durch die Welt,"* from which comes a call: *"Die Wer da?-Rufe / in seinem Innern"* (*GW* II, 101). In "Bei den zusammengetretenen" the other appears by the words and signs (*Zeichen*), without sound (*"ohne Laut"*) (*GW* II, 69). "On the white prayer-thong" mentions *Spaltworte*, the "rift-words,"[11] a Celanian synonym for *Gegenwort*, a word with a gap in it, with a *Lesestation* for the other, while "Die fleissigen" from *Fadensonnen* writes about *"die geheizte Synkope"* (the heated syncope), *"die Zwischenlaute,"* and *"die Schattenpalaver"* (the shadow-palaver), all indicating a departure from words, an interval, a shadow, or a between of a syncope. Similar fissures in names appear in "the names spoken backward" (*"Die rückwärtsgesprochenen Namen"*) (*GW* II, 312), while in "World to be stuttered by heart" a name is sweated out of a wound in the wall (*GW* II, 349).[12] In "Der überkübelte Zuruf," even though the other signals him/ herself on the edge of the book

(*Buchrand*), the shimmner of words functions as a barricade: *"komm mit dem Leseschimmer, / es ist / die Barrikade"* (*GW* II, 366).

Celan's poetics illustrates that the "barricade of words" can be broken only by invisible and unvoiced traces of the other, the breath-curve, which "unwords" (*entworten*) the poem (*GW* II, 123). The turn of breath in Celan's poetry, its *Atemwende*, moves in "the movement of silence toward you" (*der Schweigestoss gegen dich*) from word toward silence (*unbefahrbares Schweigen*) (*GW* I, 193), through a distance that cannot be traveled by any words. The workings of this poetics of silence and unwording become conspicuous in "At Brancussi's, the Two of Us" (*GW* II, 252/*PPC*, 291), where art attempts to make audible (*verlauten*) what remains silent; it turns itself toward the wound of language,[13] in which the you abides lonely, safe from both "my scream" and the powerful words of the subject, already modeled and complete ("chiselled already, white"). These unworded curves of the poem become therefore a pre-script, a pre-writing (*Vor-Schrift*) in the idiom employed by Celan in "Wirk nicht voraus." Although the other announces him/herself only as a *Vor-Schrift*, a pre-scription in the form of an unworded space, his/her trace can nevertheless be preserved in language; it is "singable":

> SINGBARER REST—der Umriss
> dessen, der durch
> die Sichelschrift lautlos hindurchbrach,
> abseits, am Schneeort. (*GW* II, 36)

> Singable remainder—the outline
> of him who mutely
> broke through the sickle-script,
> aside, at the snow-place. (*SG*, 231)

The "snow-place" again refers to the semantic space of the poetic text, which the other breaks apart with his/her outline, his/her trace, with the rupture of alterity drawing the poem aside, apart from words, to its "singable remainder."

In this poem from *Atemwende*, Celan's poetry comes in a certain sense its full circle, writes its meridian, for "the sickle-script" functions here as the figure for the poetic curve, the indication of the meridian as the road of the encounter with the other. Toward the end of "The Meridian," Celan describes precisely the moment of finding such a meridian:

> I find the connective which, like the poem, leads to encounters.

> I find something as immaterial as language, yet earthly, ter-
> restrial, in the shape of a circle which, via both poles, rejoins
> itself and on the way serenely crosses even the tropics: I
> find . . . a *meridian*. (P, 55)[14]

The speech leaves no doubt that it is precisely the instances of
Atemwende that function in Celan's poetry as meridians: an invisible, immaterial, and yet real, "earthly" as Celan puts it, direction.
The invisible meridian becomes a connective which links
(*verbinden*) all the motifs, themes, metaphors, and images, and
leads (*führen*) them toward the other. As the use of *die Tropen* suggests, the poetic meridian crosses all poetic tropes and leaves its
breath-like trace, an *Atemkristall*, upon language. As a result,
Celan's texts become invisibly and silently cracked or fissured by
poetic lines, which run apart from words, "etched away" from the
formal or semantic levels of the poem.

The ethical significance of the Celanian meridian becomes
visible specifically in its inflection of the poem into an encounter
with the other, where the other, no longer even a face or an eye,
appears merely as a short pronoun, "you," a word that names, or
rather unnames, "no one," as it "unwords" (*entworten*) language.
The other can therefore leave its "unname" only in the language
cracks, folds, silences, in blank spaces or dashes. To the extent that
all figures in Celan's language direct themselves toward this
Unname, they no longer function simply or only as metaphors but
in fact disavow or, better, inflect their own figural nature: they
have neither literal nor metaphorical status, since they manifest an
ethical direction irreducible to linguistic terms. Since, in addition,
Celan's poetry no longer concerns itself with the issues of referen-
tiality or representationality, his poems do not represent the relation to the other but rather *happen* or take place as this interrupted
relation, an address to the other. This is why the silencing of language so pervasive in late poems cannot be mistaken for a profes-
sion of the representational inadequacy of language with respect to
the other. Instead this strategy exposes and foregrounds the poetic
curves of language, the meridians, through which Celan wants to
lead language toward an encounter with the other. In this reading,
Celan's poetics becomes an attempt to reveal the invisible cracks of
language, the fissures in the "language of Being" caused by the
other's alterity. The peculiarities and difficulties of his late poetry
lie perhaps in this very "ethicity," in this specific "magnetization"
of language by and toward the other. These short texts, full of
Gegenworte and *Spaltworte*, extend language, reshape and bend it

into a meridian, in order to reveal a rift, otherwise unseen and meaningless, hidden under the pile of words. Their ethical concern is an all-directing, wordless line that dislocates language and dispatches the poem to the other.

✧ CODA ✦
Semiosis of Listening or an Other Meeting between Heidegger and Celan

Nur Gebilt wahrt Gesicht
Doch Gesicht ruht im Gedicht
—Martin Heidegger[1]

There have been various readings proposed of the encounter, both actual and intellectual, of Celan and Heidegger: Celan's own poem "Todtnauberg," the studies by Gadamer, Lacoue-Labarthe, and Pöggeler, essays by Schmidt and Fynsk,[2] Levinas's short piece from *Noms propres*, whose title "From Being to the Other" indicates the change of emphasis that Levinas sees in moving from Heidegger to Celan, or, most recently, Fóti's *Heidegger and the Poets*, which brings Celan to bear upon the question of ethics in Heidegger's work.[3] The frequency with which this "encounter" is replayed in various critical responses testifies to the need to bring into a dialogical situation perhaps the most important and influential thinker of the twentieth century and the poet whose work is most "contemporary" in its poetic, historical, and linguistic explorations, the need made all the more acute and concrete by Heidegger's engagement with Nazism in 1933 and Celan's survival of the Holocaust. Celan's own interest in Heidegger's work,[4] especially in his conception of language and poetry (in the sense of *Dichtung*, not *Poesie*), prompting his visits to Todtnauberg, as well as some of his poems and "The Meridian," is amply documented. What will continue to spark debates, however, is the question of what brings Celan and Heidegger close, what, bearing in mind their differences and the historical circumstances of their encounter, Celan finds significant in Heidegger's thought for his own concern with the other.

The reading offered here as the coda, partly an outcome of this book, partly an opening onto another problematic, stages yet another meeting between Heidegger and Celan, one made possible in the context of Celan's tropism toward the other and arranged with a view to articulating the implicit chiasmic crossing of "onto-logical" and "ethical" alterity in Heidegger's own thought. Among different discussions of Celan and Heidegger, Dennis Schmidt's essay "Between Meridian and Other Lines: Between Heidegger and Celan" reads both their proximity and difference through the issue of pain, through the link between language and pain, words and the unspeakable, explored by Heidegger in his essay on Trakl: "That experience, the painful experience of the poem, an experience of departure, of being on an edge, a threshold, is, for both Heidegger and Celan, the defining human experience."[5] Schmidt underscores pain, death, and departure as the issues that disclose a link between Heidegger's conception of language and Celan's poetic work—in other words, the liminal experiences that bear on the question of otherness. Keeping in mind that for Celan death and the other have a distinctly transformed face, "defined by the possibility of mass death, of the technologization of death, of the Holocaust and Hiroshima" (35), my reading explores the limits of language in otherness, pivoting specifically on the question of listening as the threshold of alterity, as it is marked in the work of Celan and Heidegger. This meeting is orchestrated here in the shadow of Levinas's conception of ethical alterity in a way that would account, against the backdrop of Celan's explicit concern with the other, for Heidegger's notion of otherness and its dependence on the concept of listening developed in his later writings on poetry and pre-Socratic fragments. In this way, the emphasis that Celan's engagement with Heidegger's thought gives to the other may allow us to discern better the possibility of an "ethical" reading in Heidegger's own work. To that effect, even though the chapter brings face to face Heidegger and Celan, it also implicitly confronts the Levinasian reading of Heidegger, rearranging this other significant meeting so that it could possibly take place otherwise than it is staged by Levinas's texts themselves.

These complicated mediations among Heidegger, Celan, and Levinas can also help us appreciate the often unacknowledged extent to which Levinas's thought is involved with Celan, borrowing his tropology of breath, its turns and inversions, gathered in the figure of *Atemwende*, to foreground better its own equivocal modality of "otherwise than being." Even though Levinas wrote only one brief text explicitly dedicated to Celan's work, the echoes of Celan's idiosyncratic vocabulary and poetic figures seem to reverberate ever stronger in Levinas's later texts, culminating in the focal trope of *Otherwise than Being or Beyond Essence*—substitution. Not only does the chapter entitled "Substitution" have an epigraph from Celan, the line that probably suggested to Levinas the very idea of substitution as the figure for the openness and vulnerability to the other, but the entire book may have found the "inspiration" for its language of held, interrupted, or inverted breathing in Celan's poetry of *Atemwende*.[6] Already the beginning of *Otherwise than Being* speaks about the *"breathlessness of the spirit*, or the spirit holding its breath, in which since Plato what is beyond the essence is conceived and expressed" (*OBBE*, 5/*AEAE*, 5). The whole book continues to employ the rhetoric of respiration reminiscent of the idiom of Celan's verses, culminating in the explicit connection that the ending makes between the passivity of exposition to the other and the figure of inverted breath: "[i]t is exposure to the openness of a face, which is the 'further still' of the undergoing of the closure of the oneself, the opening up which is not being-in-the-world. A further deep breathing even in the breath cut short by the wind of alterity" (*OBBE*, 180).[7] What is most significant, however, is the fact that Levinas employs this idiom of respiration to specifically foreground his critique of ontology and mark the precarious otherwise of the exposition to the other. For Levinas's language, implicitly ("being-in-the-world") and explicitly invoking Heidegger in these concluding pages (for example, p. 182), leaves little doubt that at stake in Levinas's "inspiration" by Celan is the fold between the ontological and the ethical, the "perhaps otherwise" with which both Celan and Levinas confront and inflect Heidegger's thought.

Language "speaks"; to paraphrase Heidegger, it breaks open into words and names beings. Such a statement seems to corroborate not only the phonocentrism of the Western intellectual tradition but also its broader, often understated, approach to language, with its focus and emphasis on the active aspects of language, usually speech but also, more recently, writing. For, notwithstanding the recent inversion of "priority" between speech and writing and even the implied resistance of writing to categorization in terms of passivity or activity, this entire opposition remains invested with a sense of activity, especially when considered against the backdrop of listening, with its standard connotations of passivity or receptivity. In such contexts, listening comes into play only secondarily, to the extent to which language as speech addresses those who listen, and as such demands, calls for listening. This secondariness means above all that listening comes to be defined in relation to speaking, often simply as a reception of speech, a readiness to understand, to accept, and, perhaps, to respond. In the end, the secondary function of listening renders it even "less" than a supplement of speech, the role reserved usually for writing, and hence an addition, an "afterthought," to the "proper" unfolding of language. However, both Heidegger's conception of language and Celan's work readily question such notions of speaking and listening, and complicate the schema by claiming not only that speech involves listening but that, in fact, language as such takes place in listening, that is, to the extent that one already "listens." Perhaps this revision of the secondariness of listening carries as far as to imply that not simply speech but also what we have recently come to understand as "writing" find themselves predisposed, influenced, or inflected by what we still try to envision as "listening."

In the context of Heidegger's numerous essays that present language in terms of speaking (*sprechen*) or saying (*sagen*), it becomes necessary to ask whether the modalities of such "speaking" can be exhaustively described only as those of laying open, unconcealing, or letting be by way of words. In these writings, Heidegger implicitly relies on the etymological proximity of *Sprache* (language) and *sprechen* (speaking), which becomes most visible in his famous statement *Die Sprache spricht,*[8] usually translated as "Language speaks." Taking into consideration the lexical closeness of *Sprache* and *sprechen* and the multiplicity of connotations with which Heidegger's texts invest this relation, one would need to render this apparently tautological formulation into English by turning "language" into a verb, *to language,* and write, after a well-known Heideggerian fashion, "language languages." This destabilization of the boundary between the nominal and the verbal foregrounds the fact that the lexical bond between *Sprache* and *sprechen* does not necessarily mean that *Sprache* should be read in this context as speech, in accordance with phono- and logocentric hierarchies, but rather that what Heidegger calls *sprechen* happens as more or otherwise than just mere speaking. Even more important, though, *sprechen* cannot be read simply as speaking, because it, in an "essential" (*wesentlich*) way, involves listening. The inadequacy of the logocentric categories becomes manifest when we realize that this Heideggerian sense of listening, tracing upon *sprechen,* understood here not just as speaking but instead as the happening, the "languaging," of language, leaves language exposed, near, fundamentally open to otherness.

It is indeed the question of otherness, the importance of others, that makes the pairing of Celan and Heidegger both necessary and problematic, especially in view of the widely shared opinion about the depopulated and neutral landscape of Heidegger's thought. By contrast, the urgency of listening and addressing the other is explicitly at the center of Celan's poetics, even though such otherness does not mark the simple sense of the presence of others in his texts but rather points to a "strange" linguistic trace. Heidegger's case, however, to use his own words, calls for thinking, and not least because the question of relating to others is perhaps the most provoking, that is, most thought-provoking, aspect of his work.

In the broad context of the resurfacing controversy surrounding Heidegger's thought and his engagement with National Socialism during the rectorship in 1933, the notion of a listening exposure of language and its significance may not only become helpful in refiguring the proximity to Heidegger's texts on language and poetry evidenced by Celan's "The Meridian" but also provide an inroad into the problem of otherness and ethics raised with regard to the German thinker. At the least, the lexical closeness of *Sprache* and *sprechen* and the sense of the listening of language that it carries for Heidegger can perhaps allow for a more complex mapping of Celan's encounter with Heidegger's meditation on language. This meeting becomes especially interesting because both Celan's poetry and prose, as critics have pointed out, proffer what might be called a poetics of otherness. By stripping language of any pretenses to knowing or troping others and yet maintaining the historical specificity of post-Holocaust writing, Celan's poetry becomes an address to the other, a discourse of "listening." As a brief example of this idiom, let us take the first stanza of "Ich kann dich noch sehn":

> ICH KANN DICH NOCH SEHN: ein Echo,
> ertastbar mit Fühl-
> wörtern, am Abschieds-
> grat.

> I CAN STILL SEE YOU: an echo
> that can be groped toward with antenna
> words, on the ridge of
> parting.[9]

This fragment indicates how profoundly Celan's language is marked by the other and yet how reticent it remains about it. The other can be traced only as an echo of one's own words as they separate themselves from their "origin," a reverberation not very well received by one's own antenna-like words. I want to suggest that this turn toward the other in an attitude of attentiveness is what in effect envelops Celan's language in the sense of exposure or exposition to the other. Furthermore, this turn is less a meaning *of* otherness itself than a semiosis of listening, that is, a sense no longer "meaningful" or thematizable under the rubric of otherness but also not reducible to simple passiveness or receptivity. This shift of emphasis comes as a result of the displacement of the other's radical alterity beyond the notion of otherness, for it is so "other" that its sole mark becomes the listening evidenced by one's own words.

Such approach to poetic language directs us, via Levinas's writings on alterity, to Heidegger's essays on poetry and their emphasis on the importance of listening in the way language speaks. What then provokes questioning in this encounter of a poet and a thinker is the proximity of Celan's poetics, as discussed here in reference to "The Meridian," to Heidegger, its closeness to his thought, be it as a challenge or a critique, even a debt, or perhaps both. It is not, however, a question of simply illustrating how Heidegger's thinking informs Celan's work or provokes it but rather one of seeing how close the two come, and of reading in this proximity not only Celan or Heidegger but, primarily, language's involvement with the other. For at stake is not only a historical proximity but also the neighborhood of poetry and thinking, that nearness of poetry and thought, which, as Heidegger posits, becomes indispensable for an experience of language (*Erfahrung*), for thinking the way of language.

Since Celan's proximity to Heidegger becomes visible nowhere better than in "The Meridian,"[10] this essay will serve here as the illustration of Celan's poetics. "The Meridian" reads indeed in the neighborhood of Heidegger's thinking, perhaps just as Heidegger should be approached in his closeness to another poet, Hölderlin. In fact, it is only amidst these multiple proximities that one can read the closeness between Celan and Heidegger and the role that listening to others assumes in their writings. We have already proposed engaging this difficult sense of otherness in Heidegger, and Celan's proximity to it, through two apparently very different readings: one suggested in a short and oblique essay by Emmanuel Levinas in *Noms propres*, and the other, proposed by Philippe Lacoue-Labarthe in his book *La poésie comme expérience*,[11] formulated, to some extent at least, as a response to Levinas. Those two readings could be briefly summarized as arguing for seeing the alterity of the other person traced upon Celan's poetry either in terms of the other's being or "otherwise than being." Thus both of them situate Celan in proximity to Heidegger: Levinas by turning

Celan against Heidegger and reading otherwise than through being, and Lacoue-Labarthe, without deemphasizing his concern for the limited significance of others in Heidegger's work, by arguing in manifestly Heideggerian terms.

In "De l'être à l'autre" ("From Being to the Other"), Levinas approaches Celan openly in terms of his own philosophy, in the context of language marked by its exposure to the other. In this view, Celan's poetry becomes "utopic," as "The Meridian" itself suggests, but utopia here indicates the absence of any place from which language could know, fix, still, or place the other. The other becomes significant, or signifying, for language only as a trace under its own erasure, only as a disappearing incision left by the other's trace. There is no other, but as trace(d). Most important, however, Levinas explicitly reads this utopic trace against Heidegger, against the question of Being. "The absolute poem does not say the meaning of being, it is not a variation on *dichterisch wohnet der Mensch auf dieser Erde* of Hölderlin."[12] In other words, what signifies in the trace is not the other's being but "otherwise than being," the specifically ethical responsibility before the other, which cannot be explained simply by the fact that the other is (exists). The emphasis thus shifts, as the title suggests, from Being to the other, who traces upon language otherwise than through Being. The significance of this tracing is ethical, as opposed to what inexactly may be termed the ontological sense of Being, bearing in mind, however, the fact that Heidegger makes clear that his own questioning can no longer be contained within the limits of ontological thought. The other in Celan's poetry is then "otherwise than being,"[13] set against Heidegger, especially, as Levinas implies, against the neutral, impersonal sense of Being, which leaves no ethical space, in the specifically Levinasian sense of ethics, for the other. The neutralizing, impersonal Being turns the other into an other being, present among many entities; it muffles the force of the ethical exposure.

Lacoue-Labarthe also presents Celan's poetry as a question posed to Heidegger, perhaps even a rebuke for the absence of others in his work. This question, no matter how reproachful, plays itself nevertheless within the horizon of Heidegger's thinking. In that sense, Lacoue-Labarthe's reading can be said to be much more Heideggerian. First of all, he argues that the alterity of the other in Celan's poetry can be explained only as the otherness of his/her being and, even though poetry marks an openness to the other, an acceptance of the gift of alterity, addressing the other becomes tantamount to responding to Being. The difference between Celan's

address to the you and Heidegger's saying (*Sage*) would lie then in
the difference of thinking and poetry, not in a turn of "otherwise
than Being," which Levinas claims for Celan's poetry. Celan's question to Heidegger would be, then, posed within the perimeter of
Heideggerian thinking; it would constitute another mode of "saying Being," though evidently better tuned to others and their difference than Heidegger's own thought.

The two readings of the proximity between Celan and Heidegger diverge at moments so dramatically that they ultimately
seem to cancel each other out, without any room for mediation, or
better, without any indication of their own possible closeness. Yet
precisely what characterizes the position of Celan's poetics in "The
Meridian" is a chiasmic proximity between "ontological" and "ethical" otherness: "*Aber es gibt vielleicht, und in einer und derselben
Richtung, zweierlei Fremde - dicht beieinander*" (*GW* III, 195)/"But
there may be, in one and the same direction, two kinds of strangeness next to each other" (*P*, 47). Celan writes *dicht beieinander*, for
"next to each other," and *dicht* implies not only the extreme closeness of those two kinds of strangeness, the "thickness" of their relation, but also suggests that this closeness is itself poetic; it is a matter of the poetic unfolding of language. This sentence becomes
pivotal to our project here: not only because it suggests Celan's
interest in Heidegger's thought but because it underscores through
the word *dicht* the importance of Heidegger's own proximity to
poetry, specifically the connection between his articulation of otherness in terms of nearness and the poetic (*Dichtung*) in language.
Furthermore, it opens the possibility of a dialogue between Levinas
and Heidegger, with a view to the problem of "ethical" saying in
Levinas and listening in Heidegger. Implying a twofold otherness,
two kinds of otherness, close, poetically near each other, "The
Meridian" describes a fracture, a narrow crack, that runs through
and binds Celan's poems. It is perhaps this thin line separating the
"ethical" and the "ontological" that Celan's poetry invites us to
think, for, as "The Meridian" maintains, Celan has no wish to
enlarge art but rather proposes to "take art with you into your
innermost narrowness" (*P*, 52).

What is most interesting to us, though, is that Celan talks
about this meridian in proximity to Heidegger, since the speech
locates Celan's poetry against the backdrop of Heidegger's thought.
The text takes us on a journey through a Heideggerian landscape,
and, even though we travel with Büchner and Lenz, or rather, as
the end of the journey reveals, with Celan himself, we traverse a
path through a Heideggerian territory. It is enough to merely flip

through the pages of the speech to realize how distinctly Heideggerian its terminology becomes: strangeness and otherness come immediately to mind, but also *Dasein*, being-there, the Heideggerian word for the human mode of being, *Geheimnis* (mystery), *Begegnung* (encounter), the mystery of the encounter, *Heimkehr* (homecoming), *Entsprechung* (corresponding), *Nähe* (nearness), *Gespräch* (conversation), and finally *der Weg*, the way, the key term in Heidegger's *On the Way to Language*[14] in his scenario of undergoing an experience (*erfahren*) with language and its way to words. All those words play a crucial role in Heidegger's "experiences" with language; they direct us toward the very being of language (*Sein* or better *Seyn*), toward its "languaging." The inflections Celan gives to these terms in the context of his struggles with "the thousand darknesses of murderous speech" cannot help but evoke Levinas's own strategic dislocation of Heideggerian terms, which brings them into an "ethical" perspective: the trace of the other, the saying differentiated from the said, the proximity or nearness to the other.

To the extent that "The Meridian" sketches Celan's poetics and guides us through its exposure of language to the other, it is important to emphasize the fact that it does so in proximity to Heidegger's thinking. Can we say, then, after Levinas that Celan inverts Heidegger's terminology, bends it and deflects it toward another course, away from Being and toward the other, or that this change is only a change in the mode of saying, but yet that it still bespeaks Being, the being of the other, as Lacoue-Labarthe suggests? How are we to conceive this Celanian ethics, or better, the ethicity that marks his poetic language? How can we read the closeness, the poetry (*Dicht-ung*) of the two kinds of otherness? I will follow Celan's hint in "The Meridian," borrowed in turn from Heidegger, to listen to this poetics of otherness in its proximity to thinking, thus in this case in its closeness to Heidegger and the Levinasian polemics. Such neighborhood of poetry and thinking returns us in its own way to Heidegger's thought, only to send us back again toward Celan's poems. It necessitates a rereading of Heidegger, of the proto-ethical concern of thinking that he uncovers and its openness to others in light of Levinas's ethics and Celan's poetic encounters with the other.

Obviously the problem of *ēthos* in Heidegger, and its relation to both thinking and poetry, particularly in the writings on Hölderlin, merit a much longer study, especially in view of so much confusion and contention about its importance for the Heideggerian project. However, here it is only possible to indicate the direction in which one would have to take this questioning, and merely to the extent to which such inquiry has been provoked by Celan's proximity to Heidegger. It has become almost a custom by now to refer to "Letter on Humanism" as soon as the question of ethics is raised in relation to Heidegger's thought. This is indeed where this encounter with Heidegger will begin, but with the awareness that focusing such a discussion exclusively or primarily on "Letter on Humanism" leads to a widespread underrating of the ethical concern of Heidegger's thinking as such. One has to bear in mind all the time that Heidegger is very cautious about using the word *ethics,* since its inception coincides with the rise of metaphysical thought and the forgetting of the question of Being. Therefore, in "Letter on Humanism," Heidegger initiates a rethinking of the word *ēthos,* in order to reveal the roots of ethical thought. He suggests that *ēthos* describes first of all the abode of thinking (*Aufenthalt des Denkens*); it pertains to the very manner in which human beings think. Thus the originary ethics (*ursprüngliche Ethik*)[15] lies in the truth of Being, in the thinking directed toward Being, which as such constitutes the human element, that is, the human mode of being. In other words, "Letter on Humanism" proposes to understand the very mode of being characteristic of human beings as ethical in an originary sense. Even though such thinking obviously does not constitute ethics as yet or have any such objectives, it nonetheless opens the possibility of ethics in the first place.

Heidegger describes this originary sense of thinking as concernful, as concerned for what it encounters and thinks. Thinking becomes tantamount to concern as Heidegger plays on the sense of *Sorge,* care, and *Besorgen,* which might be paraphrased as holding oneself in a caring and concernful manner toward what one thinks. Yet what is it that thinking cares for; where does its concern lie? From the beginning of *Being and Time,* Heidegger makes manifest that the concern of thinking lies in attending to Being, in taking care of the "house of Being." Such approach to thinking allows Heidegger to refer repeatedly to thinking as letting-be (*Sein-lassen*), which makes evident that in this context to think means to let be, to allow something, or someone, to be in such a way that it is its own (*eigen*), that it is as what it is in its being. In other words, thinking lets beings or entities be in what constitutes the particularity of their own being, their otherness. In this sense, one may claim that this kind of thinking is "ethical," or better yet, one can say that thinking occurs ethically, in a continuous attempt to refrain from its own violence of intelligibility. Just like Heidegger, I hesitate here to use the word *ethics* to avoid an easy misunderstanding, and I do it only in the context of what Levinas has written about ethics as the trace of the other, that is ethics that operates without rules or laws and instead marks thought and language with a sense of responsibility toward others that cannot be translated into verbal commandments.[16] It is indeed the Levinasian conception of language as the site of what could be called the "radical" ethical relation to the other that can allow us to see the ethical dimension of Heidegger's discussion of *ethos* and listening.

Obviously the thinking that Heidegger has in mind does not result immediately in a formulation of ethical norms and moral prescriptions. Instead, it indicates where ethical thought, whether prescriptive or normative, originates. Heidegger attempts to elucidate in "Letter on Humanism" that what the metaphysical tradition has identified as ethics—as distinguished, for instance, from ontology, epistemology, or logic—arises from what he calls thinking understood as letting otherness be. In other words, Heidegger's thought implies that there is ethics, or that there are many different ethics, only because thinking lets or can let be. In this context, it becomes possible to say that thinking as such becomes proto-ethical in Heidegger, since this thinking, *das andere Denken*, gets underway only insofar as it lets be. Therefore, such thinking qua thinking is respectful of otherness, on all its levels, whether pertaining to human beings, animals, or any other kinds of entities, including the non-organic ones. Furthermore, following this Heideggerian lead, it is possible to say that our everyday thought, always inevitably forgetful of thinking that lets be, can become unethical only because it is ethical in the first place.

In his admirable recent book *The Middle Voice of Ecological Conscience*, John Llewelyn calls this ethical sense of thinking and/or poetry "ontological responsibility," which arises from the very way human beings are: "following the account of belonging within the fourfold that Heidegger derives from Hölderlin, we can derive or forge an account of responsibility broad enough to accommodate direct responsibility toward nonhuman beings."[17] The human mode of being makes manifest this broad sense of ontological responsibility for the way other beings are, not only other human beings but anything that is. Underscoring Heidegger's proximity to poetry, Llewelyn suggests that this sense of responsibility emerges from thinking and poetry attending to beings in a way that lets them be in their otherness. Within the scope of thinking that lets be, there is clearly room for responsibility toward other human beings, a concern that manifests itself in caring for the way they are, in letting them be in their otherness.

The respectfulness toward any being necessarily embraces the sense of respect and responsibility toward other human beings, and even in *Being and Time* Heidegger indicates that this mode of responsibility has its own particular character, namely that of caring for—*Fürsorge*—as opposed to *Besorgen*, which in turn describes the manner in which thinking approaches non-human beings.[18] However, in the context of Levinas's position on ethics and responsibility and especially in view of Celan's concern with Heidegger's thought, one has to pose a question precisely about the distinctness of responsibility to other human beings. For the crux of Levinas's argument, to put it very briefly, lies in positing that inclusion of the responsibility toward others within the concern for all kinds of beings suppresses the unique sense of our exposure to others, our vulnerability before them. Levinas, then, detects a crack in otherness, a double fold, a chiasm, which brings us immediately into the region through which Celan traces a way toward the poetics of the other. Still, that region for Celan is manifestly Heideggerian; it opens itself only through proximity to Heidegger's thought. What remains to be asked, then, is the Levinasian question: whether a chiasmic or twofold otherness, a fold that gives distinctness to other human beings, and that guides Celan's journey, runs also through Heidegger's writings. One must inquire in this context, therefore, if Heidegger turns thinking toward others in a way that cannot be accounted for within the play of the fourfold—a turn that, to use Levinasian terms, cannot be simply explained as a respect for the other to the extent that he/she is *a being*, that is, as letting him/her be in his/her alterity as *an other (human being)*.

An indication that Heidegger indeed may think the relation of *Dasein* toward others in a twofold way comes already in *Being and Time* and becomes more prominent in the later writings, especially in the essays and lectures on Hölderlin's poetry. In *Being and Time*, the ek-static mode of being characteristic of *Dasein* is described as a double structure of "being-in-the-world" (*In-der-Welt-sein*) and being-with (*Mitsein*).[19] It can be argued that, although within this double structure both parts are said to be equiprimordial, *Mitsein* carries with it more emphasis, not in terms of detailed analysis, which in fact the book provides mostly for "being-in-the-world," but rather because of some remarks that suggest that the understanding or thinking of the world takes place only to the extent that the world is thought "with others." In fact, in the context of the later writings it becomes clear that already in *Being and Time* Heidegger provides an opening for a sense of thinking that, as its pre-condition, brings with it the others. In other words, *Mitsein*, "being-with," implies also a thinking-with, that is, a thinking with others that becomes at the same time turned toward others, a *Mitdenken*.

As Llewelyn has shown, thinking in Heidegger bears with it a sense of broad ontological responsibility for anything that is—the responsibility that lies in letting everything be as what it is, and as such underscores the possibility of thinking that would not violate the otherness of beings. Conceived this way, ontological responsibility is already tiered: in its broad ecological scope, it differentiates among at least three domains, which Heidegger's work holds as distinct—thingness, animality, and *Dasein*. Such sense of the ontologically responsible thinking, if approached within the context of *Mitdenken*, however, reveals possibly another fold in itself—a direction toward others, which cannot be explained simply in terms of thinking others as beings, that is, as other human beings. Does the ethical already double itself here, overlaying *Gelassenheit* with an other sense, one that gives meaning to letting-be, that allows it to "make" sense by holding it open to others?[20] The pivotal thirty-fourth chapter of *Being and Time*, "Being-there and Discourse. Language" (160–167), intimates that it becomes possible to think other entities as beings, including other human beings, only because thinking as such listens to others. In other words, thinking is a thinking-with, and it thinks to the extent that it also listens, or better yet, has always already listened to others. In this chapter Heidegger remarks that *Dasein* listens as if to "the voice of the friend whom every *Dasein* carries with it."[21] To put it differently, *Dasein*, that is, the way in which every human being is, is determined in its structure by an already accomplished, an-archic(?), to allude to Levinas, turn toward its friend, which "tunes" (*stimmen*) it to others. What interests us here, still pursuing a Levinasian lead, is whether this listening becomes equivalent to thinking the other, that is, to letting the other be an other human being, or whether it harbors a displacement of even this mode of thought. To put it more precisely, it becomes necessary to inquire whether the fact that *Dasein* carries a friend with it indicates that listening to others implies only a concern with the other as a being, qua Being, or that it perhaps maintains a sense beyond, or otherwise than, the thought, representation, or understanding of the other. In other words, does Heidegger's thought allow for a sense of listening that exceeds the ontological responsibility of letting each thing be?

The chapter on language from *Being and Time* maintains that listening to others marks the way in which *Dasein* turns and opens itself to the world: "listening to . . . is *Dasein*'s existential way of

Being-open as Being-with for Others."[22] The last phrase reads in German *für den Anderen* and demonstrates that listening does not simply belong to *Mitsein* as a mode of being-with (others). As Heidegger remarks a little later, listening to others in fact develops being-with, however, not only as being with others but rather as being-with for others. The flip from "with" to "for" can be read as indicative that here listening to others does not inscribe itself within being-with or simply mark the perimeter within which *Dasein* recognizes itself as being with others. Instead, listening can be said to introduce a turn or a fold into *Mitsein*, to such an extent that being-with happens no longer simply as being with others but becomes being for others. This sense of listening, which exposes to and for others, accompanies Heidegger's reflection on thinking and poetry, showing that such listening turns thinking into *Mitdenken*, into thinking-with, which thinks to the extent that it has already been listening. Heidegger's later writings maintain this distinct sense of a "listening thinking," of thinking that has already been predisposed toward others. Even though this listening to others comes confusingly close to listening to the call, the claim, or the demand of Being itself (*Anspruch, Zuspruch*),[23] it does not merge with what Heidegger, especially in his essays on Heraclitus and *logos*, describes as a belonging hearing, namely, a hearing (*hören*) that belongs (*gehören*) to Being, which, in other words, listens to the way Being (mis)says itself.[24] Even within this context, the exposure of listening to others remains distinct, since Heidegger implies that thinking belongs to Being and thus hears its saying *as* it already listens to others. Listening is thus twofold, and one can think beings, one can think the other as a being, only because one already listens to the other, because one's thinking unfolds for the other. This particular turn of thinking not only allows Heidegger to approach thinking pre-subjectively but also indicates how such thinking, to the extent that it takes place for others, namely, as it listens to them, has the validity of listening to the unfolding of Being, never to be mistaken as occurring simply within the confines of a particular, individual subject.

When we realize that for Heidegger both thinking and poetry can occur only to the extent that they "hear" others, that they are a mode of listening, the conversation between Heidegger's idea of language and Celan's poetics of otherness in "The Meridian" becomes easier to follow. In the middle of the speech, Celan in fact defines poetry in terms that can be related to Heidegger's insistence on listening: "poetry is perhaps this: an *Atemwende*, a turning of our breath. Who knows, perhaps poetry goes its way—the way of art—for the sake of just such a turn?" (*P*, 47/*GW* III, 195). Celan indicates here that poetry may be constituted primarily by its turn toward the other, by the turn of its breath. The beginning of the speech identifies such a turn with a distance from the poetic subject: "The man whose eyes and mind are occupied with art—I am still with *Lenz*—forgets about himself. Art makes for distance from the I (*Kunst schafft Ich-Ferne*). Art requires that we travel a certain space in a certain direction, on a certain road" (*P*, 44/*GW* III, 193). *Atemwende*, the turning of breath, is a breath-turning, breath-taking reversal of the poetic paradigm, within which the subject becomes muted, loses its breath. In other words, the subject can no longer be defined in terms of self-expression and speaking, as the turning of breath leaves the I, thought, poetry, and language— breathless. The poem no longer just speaks; rather, it speaks to the extent that it remains silent and listens to the other. As Celan puts it, *Atemwende* takes the breath away from speaking; it takes "breath and words away" (*P*, 47); it silences into a listening. Thus it is no longer the breath of the I, the breath of the poem, that matters but rather the breath of the other. To the extent that *Atemwende* describes a turning of breath toward the other, in an attempt to let the other's breath mark language, Celan's poetic language exposes itself to the other, even if the other's breath cannot as such be inscribed in the poem, and the other should not be thought or thematized. It is at this point that Celan's poetry can be said to share Levinas's sense of language, with its emphasis on the rupture of the said by the saying and on the exposure of the "me" toward the other. As an index of alterity, then, Celan's *Atemwende* marks a readiness, a pause in one's breath, an opening, or a point where language is exposed, attentive, listening to the other, and, in that specific sense, responsible to her or him.

Celan makes it explicit that such a turn of breath allows poetry to be itself: "after this, the poem can be itself . . . can in this now art-less, art-free manner go other ways" (*P*, 47). Poetry is itself only as art-less, as art-free, as opening a distance from aesthetics, as free from its concerns. This "art-less" (*kunst-lose*) view of poetry lets it become precisely breath-turning, as it brings to light the marks of its exposure and listening to others. As Celan indicates, such turn of breath may also allow us a glimpse of the fold in otherness: "it is perhaps this turn, this *Atemwende*, which can sort out the strange from the strange" (*P*, 47/*GW* III, 196). The listening in poetry, in language as such, turns us into the direction of the other's alterity that cannot be described simply as the other's mode of being, if only because this direction is not so much the mark of the other, the index of its alterity, as an incision in language itself, the I's openness to the other, an *Ich-Ferne*.

In Heidegger's thought, such a direction breaks open in his writings on poetry, in particular on Hölderlin. In fact, most of his essays and lectures on Hölderlin—beginning already with *Erläuterungen zu Hölderlins Dichtung*,[25] though this becomes most obvious in the Hölderlin lectures during the war and in late essays—show some interest in the listening in poetic language, in its openness to others. As I indicate elsewhere,[26] in his essays on poetic language Heidegger is not as much interested in interpreting the poetry as in clearing the room for recognizing the poetics that animates language. Thus his primary concern in Hölderlin's case lies with elucidating the sense of language within which his poetry operates, namely, its openness to others in "conversation."

In an early essay, "Hölderlin and the Essence of Poetry," Heidegger quotes as one of the five pointers for the thinking of the essence of poetry the following excerpt from Hölderlin:

> Viel hat erfahren der Mensch.
> Der Himmlischen viele genannt,
> Seit ein Gespräch wir sind
> Und hören können voneinander.[27]

> Much has man learnt.
> Many of the heavenly ones has he named,
> Since we have been a conversation
> And have been able to hear from one another.[28]

Part of the essay then elaborates this Hölderlinian sense of conversation (*Gespräch*), which as Heidegger makes clear does not refer to an everyday talk but rather has an ontological significance. In other words, such conversation describes language in its unfolding, its *Wesen*, and indicates that language, although it is a saying, a speaking, speaks to the extent that it listens. Thinking and speaking are not somehow inside us, isolated and separated from others, with conversation as a way of externalizing and communicating our ideas and experiences. Instead we experience and think through a conversation, or better yet, in a conversation, which implies nothing short of the idea that our thinking and speaking have always already been opened toward others. As Heidegger remarks in this context, the "essential being" of poetry can be determined only through conversation, as Hölderlin expressly links with conversation the possibility of knowing and naming the heavenly ones and the holy, the most important aspects of what

Heidegger identifies as the task of the poet. In other words, to the extent that language has been a conversation, poetry is in its "essential being" open toward others. In effect, poetry unfolds into poems (*dichten*) insofar as it listens to others, with this listening understood in a modality of a linguistic pre-scription, bearing upon what the poems say, upon their "said," or as an index of its exposure to others.[29]

That such dependence of language and poetry on listening has an ethical sense becomes evident in another of Heidegger's essays on Hölderlin, " . . . Poetically Man Dwells. . . . " Engaged again in thinking what poetic language discloses to us, Heidegger describes poetry as a sense of measure, which gauges the human dwelling; that is, it situates human beings in their relations within the fourfold—the world—and thus allows them a sense of familiarity, a foreknowledge of the place in which they dwell. Heidegger claims that poetry is most its own—that is, as what it is in its *Wesen*, its "essencing" one might say—when it measures and gives human beings a sense of their dwelling. Yet, quoting Hölderlin's poem "In Lovely Blue," Heidegger makes manifest a surprising dependence of poetry's coming into its own (*er-eignen*) on kindness (*Freundlichkeit*):

> . . . So lange die Freundlichkeit noch
> Am Herzen, die Reine, dauert, misset
> Nicht unglüklich der Mensch sich
> Mit der Gottheit . . . [30]

> . . . As long as Kindness,
> The Pure, still stays with his heart, man
> Not unhappily measures himself
> Against the Godhead . . . [31]

Poetry is poetic, that is, it measures *Dasein* as dwelling in what remains other only as long as there is kindness, only as long as language is turned breath-takingly, to use the Celanian idiom, toward others. The prominence Heidegger accords to the word *Freundlichkeit* in this fragment of the poem refers implicitly to that fragment of *Being and Time* that talks about the friend, whose voice *Dasein* always carries with itself. *Freundlichkeit* thus underscores again that language always carries the other with it; it bears the burden of exposure. For Heidegger, therefore, poetry is its own only when there is kindness and friendship, only when poetry is, we might cautiously say, "ethical." In other words, it is only when kindness underwrites language that one "creates poetry from the very nature of the poetic."[32] When seen against the background of the Heideggerian "hermeneutics of nearness," those comments coming at the end of one of Heidegger's most interesting engagements with poetry make clear that poetic language becomes for Heidegger indissociably linked to others. The others become important for poetry not only as part of what it deals with, represents, or describes but rather in a fundamental sense, as a moment of turning toward others, which pre-scribes language to them.

The importance of this linguistic pre-scription comes best into view in the fourth part of Heidegger's lecture course on Hölderlin's hymn "Andenken" from the winter semester 1941–42.[33] In this closing part of the lectures, Heidegger again underscores the listening character of poetry, its unfolding (*Wesen*) as a "conversation with friends" (*das Gespräch mit den Freunden*). The entire lecture series elaborates the sense of poetry as the naming of the holy (*das Heilige*), with the holy taken as that which gathers everything together and allows it to reach its Being (*Wesen*). However, as in " . . . Poetically Man Dwells . . . ," poetry names the holy only to the extent that it itself is a conversation. On the one hand, poetry listens to what Heidegger calls the saying of language itself, that is, to the manner in which anything that comes into being shows itself in its relation to the fourfold. On account of this proximity, human beings are the listeners and the speakers of language, and, as practically all of Heidegger's essays on language manifest, they speak to the extent that they "correspond" (*entsprechen*) to the saying of language and resay it (*nachsagen*). Such speaking comes thus as the saying after the saying (*Sage*) of language, a *nachsagen*, an "after-saying," which is not simply an effect but rather a "translation" into words of what says itself only as the unsaid. It would be a mistake, however, to claim that the "essential nature" (*Wesen*) of poetry exhausts and explains itself in this relation of hearing and responding to the saying of language. Instead, what overlays and influences this "response" (*Entsprechung*) to the saying of language that constitutes *Dasein*, what perhaps even inflects it beyond re-cognition and revealing, is the openness and listening to others, to "friends."

The lectures on the hymn "Andenken" make prominent the fact that all that is thought poetically in poetry can be thought as such only in conversation: "*Vielmehr wird das Gedachte im Gespräch erst gedacht*" (Rather what is thought is thought first in conversation).[34] In other words, poetic thinking transpires only in a conversation, in an exchange or a turn toward the other, that does not come post facto, as an exteriorization or communication of a subjective content; rather, such communication receives its possibility from the "conversational" nature of language. One should not underappreciate here the significance of this Heideggerian implication, for it means nothing short of postulating that *das andere Denken*, and possibly *das andere Dichten* on the order of Celan's poetic meridians, becomes thinkable only through an exposure of language, an ex-positing of the said of language toward the other. Differently put, thinking and poetry, as ontologically responsible in that they let every thing show itself as what it is in its alterity, unfold already as a conversation: they take place as pre-scribed to or for others. Most important, what I call here openness, exposure, or index of alterity, do not simply mark a feature of thinking and/or poetry but instead illustrate how thinking qua thinking and poetry qua poetry unfold as listening.

In fact, Heidegger claims in the lectures on "Andenken" that the image, the figure, in which truth can, if at all, be thought by thinking or poetry is precisely friendship: *"Die Gestalt dieser Wahrheit ist die Freundschaft."*[35] As a linguistic pre-scription, friendship delineates the figure (*Gestalt*) of what Heidegger at this point still calls the truth of Being. It is therefore impossible to maintain that the truth of Being takes place exclusively for the sake of Being, that it is absolutely neutral and impersonal in its happening. For what Heidegger suggests is that the activity of thinking itself is indelibly marked by others, that it "makes sense" only when it transpires as friendship. On this account, the truth of Being occurs for others: that is, we think and come near it for the sake of friendship, for others, or, at least, we come near the truth of Being already in friendship, already listening to others, bearing their mark with us. Extrapolating from this, we can say that as we turn toward the language (of Being) we are already turned toward others, or that when we listen to the saying of language we have already been listening to others. In other words, the occurring of Being, which lets every being come into its own, *das Ereignis*, bears the stamp of friendship. To say as Heidegger does that the historical occurring of truth arranges itself into the shape of friendship means that all that happens bears the mark of the turn of thinking toward others. This turn does not simply come after a reflection, as an acknowledgment of the binding power of the rules for ethical behavior, but instead makes possible and affects any such articulations. Language, poetry, and thinking are always turned toward others; they can approach and think the world, things, and the other (human beings), only as they listen to others. To that extent, it is possible to claim that, in the last count, Heidegger's view of language is determined by his notion of friendship: it is the openness to others, a linguistic listening figured as friendship, that allows language, thinking, writing, to be in any sense ethical.

Redescribing Heidegger's readings in the neighborhood of Hölderlin's poetry discloses a conception of "language in friendship," language whose shape is decided neither arbitrarily nor by fate but rather, in Heidegger's sense of the historial, by its openness toward others. Such an approach to language and otherness might be said to explain itself, in addition to a broad ontological responsibility for letting everything be what it is, also in terms of a possible fold in otherness.[36] Since for Heidegger language unfolds as a conversation, in which truth reveals itself only in the shape of friendship, the sense of responsibility for the disclosure of any being is already affected by the openness of language toward others. As language lets everything emerge, it also already turns itself toward and listens to others, as if following the prescription articulated with such force by Levinas. In other words, language is here seen as always indexed by ethical alterity. Such understanding of language implies that the others are present in Heidegger's writings not only as beings, that is, to the extent that they are thought as other human beings, other *Dasein*, but also as marked, figured, by listening, which pervades both thinking and poetry. Putting it differently, the thought of others is predicated here upon a prior, *ursprünglich*, listening that pre-dates and pre-dict(ate)s the rules of cognitive engagement.

It is possible to see Celan's poetics in "The Meridian" as defining itself in proximity to this approach to language and poetry, for the two kinds of strangeness, the twofold otherness, that the text locates in poetic language can be said to be already to some extent at play in Heidegger. In fact, a reading of Heidegger in the context of Levinas's work on alterity, of Heidegger's understanding of poetry and, especially, the usually undervalued role that others exercise in his idea of poetic language, can allow us to come closer to Celan's own poetry, often too quickly labeled as hermetic or extremely personal. In proximity to Heidegger and Levinas, the strangeness and impalpability of many of Celan's poems can be seen as resulting from his attempt to sound in poetry the sense of listening, to index, by means of folds and fractures in words (*Gegenworte* or *Spaltworte*), the ethical in language. As for Hölderlin and Heidegger, for Celan poetry in a turn of breath becomes a listening conversation: "[t]he poem becomes conversation" (*P*, 50). This sense of listening never becomes simply a theme in Celan's poetry or one among its concerns, since Celan writes his texts in such a way that all their themes, images, and allusions, even the most enigmatic and personal ones, already "listen" to the other: "For the poem, everything and everybody is a figure of this other toward which it is heading" (*P*, 49).[37] The enigma of Celan's poetry often does not lie directly in his texts, their form or their content or even their metaphoric, but rather in the way in which they have come to be marked by listening to the other: an instance of a double semantics or an inflection of the semantic field per se.

As Celan's poetry listens to the other in its "turn of breath," its *Atemwende*, it projects the sense of poetry as produced not through the expiration of the breath of its subject but rather with this breath restrained, involuted, turned back and withdrawn. If through this turn of breath Celan's poetry clears a space for the other, then such opening does not mean that this space is ever filled, that the other appears within it in a phenomenal or linguistic sense and that language comes to know, think, and thematize the other. Instead, the openness, the slight emptiness, of this space itself becomes the mark, strictly speaking not of the other but rather of a direction, a listening turn to the other on the order of the Levinasian injunction about the saying. In its turn of breath, the poem finds itself on the way, toward an encounter (*Begegnung*) with the other, and its text remains steeped in the mystery of that encounter: "The poem is lonely. It is lonely and *en route* (*unterwegs*). . . . Does this very fact not place the poem already here, at its inception, in the encounter, *in the mystery of encounter?*" (*P*, 49). For Celan poetry is always on the way; it itself is a way, extending language, beyond just a textual gift, toward the other. This extension stretches the poem into a meridian, a mark of coming close to the other in listening, through holding one's breath—*Atemwende*.

This turn of breath never inscribes itself positively into the poem, as it cannot signify in the way words do. To underscore its unusual semantics, Celan uses the rhetoric of "perhaps" (*vielleicht*), and all his statements in "The Meridian" about the twofold otherness are cast in it (*P*, 47). However, as is also the case with Levinas's use of *peut-être*, such language does not imply a tentativeness on Celan's part but instead points to a peculiar mode in which the turn of breath envelops his texts. In other words, it is a way of indicating the difficulty with which language refrains from thinking the other and thinking about the other, a gesture of "desperate conversation" that would think *toward* the other. Through this gesture, Celan's poetry finds itself always on the way, without ever bringing the other within its view, into its words. The other, then, never comes into words; on the contrary, the words, in a turn of breath, extend toward the other.

Celan's "breath-turning" poetics situates itself in the neighborhood of poetry and thinking and, specifically, in proximity to Heidegger's thought on language and poetry. It traverses Heidegger's thinking in order to relocate the emphasis onto approaching language through its openness toward others, for Celan a historical necessity in view of this century's mass annihilation of "others" and the Holocaust. Obviously, in Heidegger's own writings, the others are not as often explicitly mentioned as they are in Celan's poetry, nor are they given the same set of connotations and images—death, ashes, the need to bear witness. Furthermore, vis-à-vis Levinas's repeated emphasis on the exposition to the other, this problem appears "unthought," almost downplayed in Heidegger's work. Heidegger indeed focuses his analyses mostly on "responding" (*Entsprechung*) to the saying (*Sage*) of language, and he foregrounds the fact that it is the fourfold, that is, the interplay and the happening of the world as letting beings, and among them mortals, be by way of words, that language "says," and we resay in(to) words. Yet the way Heidegger writes about poetic language suggests that, even when the others are not named in words, what is being said or written bears a stamp of friendship. The human responding to the saying of language carries a pre-scription of listening to others, an index, a reminder, which, although not written into words, and often not directly acknowledged in Heidegger's work on language, pre-scribes both poetry and thinking. Thus as the fourfold is brought to stand in words, the very movement of language into words takes place as a conversation; it is minimally marked by its listening to others.

The uncovering of the importance of listening to others in Heidegger's work could affect our understanding of a number of its key issues and concepts. It obviously modifies our sense of how Heidegger envisions language, which can no longer be interpreted only as a matter of response to the call of Being. Furthermore, one would have to reassess in this context the two fundamental notions Being and *Ereignis*, as it is precisely in the context of *Ereignis* that all of Heidegger's later works discuss language. Such questioning could shed light on the ethical aspects of the various modulations of the sense of "giving," as they are implied in the phrase *Es gibt* toward which Heidegger's later texts gravitate, and, finally, recast the ethical questions addressed by and to Heidegger. Just to intimate the possible consequences of such a reading: the question of Being or of event (*Ereignis*) would have to be approached from the point of view of listening and "friendship" with others rather than through the conjunction—the Same (*das Selbe*)—of Being and thinking. Thus Heidegger's notion of thinking (*Denken*) becomes increasingly complicated, as it accounts not only for bringing into words and concepts the unfolding world but also indicates an always already "present" attentiveness to others—an "ethical" turn of thinking. Thought and language, then, are perhaps more than a response (*Entsprechung*) to Being, for, as thought answers and brings into words (*Antwort*), its response "makes sense" because it already involves others. What enters and complicates the picture is the implicit idea that thought operates pre-subjectively in a way that reflects its "sensitivity" to others. Even more radical, perhaps, is the implication that it is thanks to this openness to others that thinking can at all function as thinking, that it becomes of cognitive value, here in the Heideggerian sense of re-cognizing the complex, the interlacing (*Geflecht*), of relations that gathers the world. In other words, thinking gets its critical momentum, and its validity, not from self-legitimating consciousness, the *cogito me cogitare*, maybe not even from the discursive practices that shape and intersect in it, but through its underlying "ethicity." At the least, this ethical dimension figures in the power play of discourse, disrupting and inflecting its politics. Although this exposure to others refuses itself to the matrix of signification, it nevertheless affects it, endowing it both with the possibility of signifying, of making sense as such, and with an ethical import. For what underlies Heidegger's statements about language from his 1940s lectures and subsequent essays on Hölderlin to *On the Way to Language* is the thought that the signifying mechanism of language weaves its web of relations in view of listening to others and its wordless semiosis.

It is possible, then, to see Celan's interest in Heidegger as a way of engaging the problematic of the listening of language, which, to use Heidegger's own term, remains "unthought." "Unthought" here does not mean that Heidegger is not aware of it or does not think it; rather, "unthought" refers to that which, through its minimality, its pre-scriptural/vocal character, calls for thinking, and as such remains in need of thinking and questioning. In the context of Heidegger and his "hermeneutics of nearness," it is the place of the others in his thought, their importance for language and for the question of Being, that remains most unthought, that most calls for our inquiry, in particular in view of recent debates on Heidegger's political involvements and his support for National Socialism. Such inquiry, bearing in mind the pertinent arguments raised in the context of Heidegger's thought and its engagement with Nazism, technology, and modern culture, may provide an inroad into the sense of the ethical and perhaps also the political in Heidegger, and the manner in which listening to others pre-scribed upon language "figures" (in the sense of *Gestalt*) those concerns.

Are we giving here too much credit to Heidegger? Perhaps so, but in the context of Celan's response to Heidegger this credit only brings into sharper focus the accusations of complicity of Heidegger's thought with National Socialism. The difficult interlocution between Celan and Heidegger accentuates precisely the disparity between the radical implications of Heidegger's work on difference and alterity and his failure to openly address specific differences, conflicts, and inequities that emerge from history. When Celan engages the critical opening made by Heidegger's work, his poetry not only remains mindful of its theoretical potential but in fact makes this opening crucial to articulating the political and ethical demands of his time. In this way, Celan's work becomes a question posed to Heidegger's thought, a question that demands exploring why the insights into ethics and politics that Heidegger gains by rethinking relationship to otherness do not compel his writings to respond to the horror of the Holocaust and the atriocities of the war. Why does Heidegger fail to use the radical opening offered by his work to explicitly critique its own entanglements with Nazism in the 1930s? As Levinas's inscription to *Otherwise than Being or Beyond Essence* makes clear, attempts to rethink the problems of ethics, language, and difference today are intertwined with the remembrance of the victims of the Holocaust, of anti-Semitism, of the hatred of the other. In a similar vein, Celan's reproach to Heidegger indicates that the unthought to which Heidegger's texts point cannot be confused with silence or indifference. On the contrary, this unthought requires a new degree of attentiveness to others and a rethinking of the work of memory, both of which become manifest in the special linguistic rigor so characteristic of Celan's work.

By way of ending, let me here draw attention again to the fact that what is at stake in my questioning of listening with Heidegger, Celan, and Levinas is an attempt to rethink it otherwise than in metaphysical terms, on the order of Derrida's writing about listening, philosophy, and its other in "Tympan."[38] To put it simply, here listening is no longer at the subject's discretion. Thus it is no more a trope for the subject's comfortable relation to the outside, to the other, a relation where the tympanum regulates the subject's openness to the other, monitors and controls, so to speak, the amount of otherness that it lets in, as it also shelters the subject and separates it from the "real" outside, from what Levinas calls absolute exteriority. Here listening, if it is still the right term to use, has a changed valency: it is a radical ex-positing, a displacement of the subject. The other is no longer an outside, already turned into the comfort and familiarity of the interior, but instead marks the impossibility of closure, of covering one's ears. In this context, it is not the subject, already constituted as itself, already speaking itself, that decides to listen. Rather, the subject, before it can speak, is already "all ears."

⟡ NOTES ⟡

Introduction

1. Gerald Bruns's important study *Heidegger's Estrangements: Language, Truth, and Poetry in the Later Writings* (New Haven: Yale University Press, 1989) eloquently argues for the central role of language in Heidegger's project of overcoming metaphysics and shows the pivotal role that poetry and literary idiom play in shaping Heidegger's late works. It is the first book to provide extensive argumentation for the indispensability of Heidegger's engagement with poetic language to the understanding of the development of his thought.

2. See Thomas McCarthy's "Introduction" to Jürgen Habermas, *The Philosophical Discourse of Modernity*, trans. Frederick G. Lawrence (Cambridge, Mass.: MIT Press), xii.

3. Jacques Derrida, *Margins of Philosophy*, trans. Alan Bass (Chicago: University of Chicago Press, 1972), 27.

4. In my reading I focus on the "strategic" value of Heidegger's invocation of the Pre-Socratics rather than its nostalgic overtones, present especially in Heidegger's early writings. For the turn to the pre-Socratic thought means diagnosing the limit of philosophy and an attempt to think its other. Heidegger himself became increasingly skeptical about the "presence" or the trace of what he was after—another thinking—in the pre-Socratic texts or about placing so much emphasis on one historical moment in the history of thinking. Especially in *Vier Seminare* (Frankfurt am Main: Vittorio Klostermann, 1977), Heidegger dissociates himself from his earlier statements about Parmenides, claiming that one cannot find in Parmenides what he, Heidegger, tried to elaborate for forty years. See Pöggeler's discussion in *Neue Wege mit Heidegger* (Freiburg and Munich: Verlag Karl Alber, 1992), 416.

5. Martin Heidegger, *Basic Writings*, ed. David Farrell Krell (New York: Harper and Row, 1977), 236. Hereafter referred to as *BW*.

6. The term *inflection* is introduced here, among other reasons, for the purpose of deflecting a common objection against Heidegger's thought, one that accuses him of secreting in what he calls the unsaid something primordial, originary, something forgotten, which a purified language could be capable of reinstating. Inflection indicates, therefore, that for Heidegger and, by extension, the other works discussed here, there is nothing under, beside, apart, or beyond language that could be identified in terms of a subject, substance, or even word. The title *Inflected Lan-*

guage suggests that language unfolds as always already inflected: it can detect the commitments that such inflections impose upon it without ever being able to recognize or bring into words what effects this inflection.

7. The quotation comes from Levinas's short piece "As if Consenting to Horror," trans. Paula Wissing, *Critical Inquiry* 15 (Winter 1989): 487. In spite of Levinas's interest in Heidegger's work and his professed admiration for *Being and Time*, already in "Is Ontology Fundamental?" (trans. Peter Atterton, *Philosophy Today*, Summer 1989: 121–129) Levinas announces the "first contestation of the primacy of ontology" (128) and, later in "Signature," declares a passionate need to "leave the climate of this philosophy." In other words, Levinas's whole work is motivated and structured by a polemic with Heidegger, specifically with what Levinas identifies as Heidegger's displacement of ethics in favor of the priority of ontological thinking. In the end, Levinas points to the absence of ethics and concern for the other as the probable source of Heidegger's engagement with National Socialism. The question of to what extent Heidegger's rectorship and involvement with the Nazi ideology is a sign or result of the failure in his thinking to engage the ethical dimension of the relation to the other remains still a largely unexplored issue. However, many publications and studies, from historical and biographical (Ott) to philosophical (Derrida, Lacoue-Labarthe, Zimmerman, Pöggeler), have demonstrated Heidegger's interest and investment in some ideas of National Socialism and the impact of this engagement upon his own thinking, in particular between 1929 and 1943. Mindful of the difficulty, gravity, and sensitivity of these issues, I offer a reading of Heidegger in the context of Levinas and Celan that is responsive to Levinas's critique and its insistence on the non-thematizable alterity of the other. My interpretation follows a strand of Heidegger's thinking on otherness, developing and radicalizing it in order to tease out of Heidegger's work on language and poetry what I call here a "hermeneutics of nearness," a layer of Heidegger's thinking that may, in the long run, provide an illuminating context for the problematic involvements of his work with the issues of politics, the state, the people. The issues of the Levinasian critique of Heidegger and a rereading of Heidegger in response to them, both from within Heidegger's work and in the context of Celan's poetry, are discussed in chapters 3 and 7.

8. Emmanuel Levinas, "Ethics as First Philosophy." The English translation of this text can be found in *The Levinas Reader*, ed. by Seán Hand (Oxford: Basil Blackwell, 1989), 84–85.

9. The often unacknowledged substratum of the polemics with and dismissals of Heidegger is the much broader and more significant question of the political implications of philosophical modernity and its possible complicity with fascism. Such critiques of Heidegger (see, for example, Wolin's discussion of the Heidegger debate in France: "French Heidegger Wars," in *The Heidegger Controversy*, ed. Richard Wolin [Cambridge, Mass.: MIT Press, 1993], 272–300) have in mind, often via the implication of Hei-

degger's thought in National Socialism, an undermining of the neo- or post-Heideggerian critiques of the philosophical tradition of modernity. What they want to dismiss in truth is not simply Heidegger (because of the proximity of his early work to National Socialism) but the way in which his thought and its widespread influence implicate philosophy as such in the problem of domination (it is important to remember here that such diverse thinkers as Benjamin and Adorno, notwithstanding their sharp differences with Heidegger, would agree with the Heideggerian diagnosis of the complicity of the Enlightenment project with domination, violence, and suppression of otherness). These critiques of Heideggerianism often aim to safeguard the project of Enlightenment and metaphysical humanism, with their cultural, social, and political manifestations, against the critique of domination. They reject the Heideggerian suggestion that modernity, through its adherence to the humanist paradigm of the subject and the instrumentalized, technologico-scientific view of reason, leaves the door open for, perhaps even prepares as its outcome, the rise of totalitarianism, Stalinism, and fascism. Thus the widely advertized "Heidegger wars" have at stake nothing less than the possible implication of modernity in patterns of exploitation and domination. Those who reject the insights of Heidegger and poststructuralism often claim as the only possible way of thinking the critique of modernity from within, the critique that, for example, sees fascism as an aberration, not a consequence, of philosophical modernity. One has to keep asking, however, if this view of totalitarianism as the "other" of reason is also not a refusal to examine how the democratic forms of rationality are not a pure and simple antithesis of totalitarian impulses but may in fact harbor tendencies toward domination and erasure of alterity.

10. See in particular Adorno's critique of the concept of Enlightenment as well as his polemics about the complicity of the culture industry with technological mentality and its practices of domination and standardization: Max Horkheimer and Theodor W. Adorno, *Dialectic of Enlightenment*, trans. John Cumming (New York: Continuum, 1993).

11. This fragment comes at the end of Levinas's brief essay on Derrida, "Tout autrement," translated into English as "Wholly Otherwise" and published in *Re-reading Levinas*, ed. Robert Bernasconi and Simon Critchley (Bloomington: Indiana University Press, 1991), 8.

12. Bruns's *Heidegger's Estrangements*, the most sustained elaboration on the link between poetry and truth in Heidegger's work, is one of the exceptions.

13. Martin Heidegger, *On the Way to Language*, trans. Peter D. Hertz (New York: Harper and Row, 1971), 29. Henceforth referred to as *OWL*. The German text, "Aus Einem Gespräch von der Sprache," appeared in *Unterwegs zur Sprache* (Pfullingen: Neske, 1959), 88–155. The fragment in question can be found on page 121. This German edition is henceforth referred to as *UZS*.

14. Derrida's oeuvre has continued to readdress the problematic of difference in the context of Heidegger's work, often moving beyond the early assessment I have quoted here. Never losing sight of the moments when Heidegger's thought comes close to the rhetoric of origin, purity, or oneness, or involves itself with the terms it itself apparently disqualifies (for example, *Geist*, which Derrida discusses in *Of Spirit*), Derrida has elaborated on the relation between (the ontological) difference and various other aspects of Heidegger's work: politics, history, sexual difference, animality. My choice of Derrida's early work is strategic insofar as those are predominantly the texts that have structured the subsequent debates on Heidegger, as well as on Levinas.

15. I am indebted here to Véronique Fóti's recent study *Heidegger and the Poets: Poiēsis/Sophia/Technē* (Atlantic Highlands, N.J. and London: Humanities Press, 1992) and John Llewelyn's *The Middle Voice of Ecological Conscience: A Chiasmic Reading of Responsibility in the Neighborhood of Levinas, Heidegger, and Others* (New York: St. Martin's Press, 1991). Both works approach the issues of responsibility and otherness in Celan, Levinas, and Heidegger in terms of a chiasmic crossing between ontological and ethical significations.

16. An interesting corollary of this way of thinking would lead to the question of how Derrida's work itself can be seen as "inflecting" difference. I have in mind here not only the "neologism" *différance* but, primarily, the fact that Derrida makes clear that it is only one in a sheaf of terms that describe the workings of language: supplement, *pharmakon*, iterability, arche-writing, trace, etc. Furthermore, the problem of the "difference" between difference and proximity continues to resurface indirectly in Derrida's texts as they appear more and more preoccupied with Levinas's notion of alterity in political, historical, and institutional contexts (notwithstanding Derrida's criticisms in both of his essays on Levinas). Clearly, though, this is a task beyond the scope of my present study.

17. The need to highlight this peculiar modality in which alterity is figured in the texts I discuss came as a result of several discussions I had with Rodolphe Gasché. In this context, see Gasché's essay on Heidegger entitled "Perhaps," in *Graduate Faculty Philosophy Journal* 16 (1993): 467–484. In addition, the issue of the non-assertive mode of describing alterity in Levinas's work is discussed by Derrida in "At this very moment in this work here I am," published in *Re-reading Levinas*, ed. Robert Bernasconi and Simon Critchley (Bloomington: Indiana University Press, 1991).

18. Luce Irigaray, *This Sex Which Is Not One*, trans. Catherine Porter (Ithaca: Cornell University Press, 1985), 31. In another place, Irigaray articulates this halt perhaps even more forcefully and ironically, linking it explicitly to the problematic of sexual difference: "Neither one nor two. I've never known how to count. Up to you. In their calculations, we make

two. Really, two? Doesn't that make you laugh? An odd sort of two. And yet not one. Especially not one" (207). In a way, it is the work of Luce Irigaray that, through its multiple contexts—feminism, psychoanalysis, Heidegger, Levinasian ethics, deconstruction—may provide a most interesting and stimulating setting for discussing and critiquing Heidegger's work, especially his engagement with the notion of nearness (*Nähe*).

Chapter 1

1. Although *Heidegger and the Poets* by Fóti (Atlantic Heights, N.J. and London: Humanities Press, 1992) and *The Middle Voice of Ecological Conscience* by Llewelyn (New York: St. Martin's Press, 1991) differently evaluate the significance and the scope of the concern for ethics in Heidegger's work, they nevertheless concur in emphasizing the critical importance of Heidegger's encounter with the poets for this line of questioning.

2. The English translations of these texts appear in *Early Greek Thinking*; *Poetry, Language, Thought*; and *On the Way to Language*.

3. This "releasing bind" is discussed in *Unterwegs zur Sprache* (Pfullingen: Neske, 1959) as specifically the very way in which the event of manifestation (*Ereignis*) occurs, that is, as the mode of *ereignen* (262), which, as I argue, indicates a proximity—not quite or otherwise than identity and yet almost too close or near to speak of difference: "*Die Be-wëgung der Sage zur Sprache ist das entbindende Band, das verbindet, indem es er-eignet.*"

4. Martin Heidegger, *Sein und Zeit* (Tübingen: Max Niemeyer Verlag, 1986), 148–154/*Being and Time*, trans. John Macquarrie and Edward Robinson (New York: Harper and Row, 1962), 188–195. All subsequent references to this editions are marked parenthetically in the text, preceded respectively by *SZ*, and *BT*.

5. See "Das Ursprung des Kunstwerkes," *Holzwege* (Frankfurt am Main: Vittorio Klostermann, 1980, 6th ed.), 58. Cited in the text as *H*. Translation of "The Origin of the Work of Art" can be found in *Poetry, Language, Thought*, trans. Albert Hofstadter (New York: Harper and Row, 1971), 72. Henceforth referred to as *PLT*.

6. The latter term comes from Joseph J. Kockelmans, *Heidegger on Art and Art Works* (Dordrecht: Martinus Nijhoff, 1985), 194.

7. Martin Heidegger, *An Introduction to Metaphysics*, trans. Ralph Manheim (New Haven: Yale University Press, 1959), 144. All subsequent references to this translation are indicated in the text as *IM*.

8. Martin Heidegger, *What Is Called Thinking?*, trans. J. Glenn Gray (New York: Harper and Row, 1968), 233. Subsequently cited as *WCT*.

9. See, for example, Martin Heidegger, "Andenken," in *Erläuterungen zu Hölderlins Dichtung* in *Gesamtausgabe*, vol. 4 (Frankfurt am Main: Vit-

torio Klostermann, 1981), 100/"Remembrance of the Poet" in *Existence and Being*, ed. Werner Brock (Chicago: Henry Regnery Company, 1949), 279.

10. Christopher Fynsk, *Heidegger, Thought and Historicity* (Ithaca: Cornell University Press, 1986).

11. The translations of both essays, published in German in *Unterwegs zur Sprache* (Pfullingen: Neske, 1959), appear in Martin Heidegger, *On the Way to Language*, trans. Peter D. Hertz (New York: Harper and Row, 1971). These editions are referred to as *UZS* and *OWL*.

12. See Jacques Derrida, *De l'esprit: Heidegger et la question* (Paris: Galilée, 1987), 147–154.

13. Derrida finally argues that it is impossible to recommence the Heideggerian enterprise from the point of view of *Unterwegs zur Sprache*, to posit the *Zuspruch* "before" the ontological difference. Yet it seems that Heidegger does not intend it as a recommencing but rather as a consequence of the initial question. Throughout *Being and Time*, he repeatedly stresses the preliminary character of his analysis, the necessity of restating it immediately after it has been elaborated. Subsequent writings mark a gradual distancing not only from the analytic of *Dasein* but also from the ontological difference itself. In "Time and Being," Heidegger emphasizes the inevitability of thinking Being, however difficult and self-concealing it may be, not only apart but also without beings (see *On Time and Being*, trans. Joan Stambaugh [New York: Harper and Row, 1972], 2).

14. The alternative translation, which can be found in the new edition of Heidegger's *Basic Writings*, reads as follows: "Such way-making brings language (the essence of language) as language (the saying) to language (to the resounding word)" (*Basic Writings*, revised and expanded edition, David Farrell Krell, ed. (New York: HarperCollins Publishers, 1993), 418.

15. John Llewelyn, *The Middle Voice of Ecological Conscience: A Chiasmic Reading of Responsibility in the Neighborhood of Levinas, Heidegger, and Others* (New York: St. Martin's Press, 1991), 94.

16. In "The Origin of the Work of Art," Heidegger mentioned several ways in which "truth occus": the art-work, the thinker's questioning, the nearness to "the being that is most of all" (*"das Seiendste des Seienden"*), but also "the essential sacrifice" (*"das wesentliche Opfer"*) and the founding of a political state (*H*, 48/*PLT*, 62). The later disappearance of explicit references to founding a political state or to sacrifice would have to be carefully considered in the context of Heidegger's engagement with the Nazi state and his later apparent disillusionment with politics, and his political statements from the 1930s.

17. For Heidegger's discussion of the notion of "another beginning" see, among others, *Beiträge zur Philosophie: Vom Ereignis, Gesamtausgabe*, vol. 65 (Frankfurt am Main: Vittorio Klostermann, 1989), 171–206.

18. In *The Other Side of Language: A Philosophy of Listening*, Gemma Corradi Fiumara eloquently argues for a need to reinterpret *logos* in light of Heidegger's thought and shows how rationality and logocentrism were grounded in fact on a truncated notion of *logos*—the one stressing speaking and saying at the expense of listening and attentiveness. She makes it manifest that Heidegger's rereading of the pre-Socratic writings allows one to gain a better understanding of *logos* by restoring to it its propensity of listening and indicating that the function of speaking celebrated by the Western tradition is bound to and dependent upon listening. See in particular chapter 1, "Towards a Fuller Understanding of *Logos*," *The Other Side of Language* (London: Routledge, 1990), 1–17.

19. The adjective *stimmlich* means "vocal" and derives from the noun *Stimme* (voice). The verb *stimmen*, however, brings in the connotation of both tuning (a musical instrument) and inclining, disposing in favor of or against something. Most important, it refers to a derivative of *stimmen*, *übereinstimmen*: "to agree, concur, accord, harmonize, correspond to." *Stimmliche*, then, indicates not only voicing (or writing), the putting into words of *Dichtung-Denken*, but the necessary accord or harmony between the saying of Being and the human response to it (that is, *logos* as Heidegger employs it); it also indicates the primordial disposition of human beings, their mood (*Stimmung*), which directs thinking toward Being.

20. Martin Heidegger, *Early Greek Thinking*, trans. David Farrell Krell and Frank A. Capuzzi (New York: Harper and Row, 1975), 63. Subsequent references to this translation are marked as *EGT*.

21. Martin Heidegger, *Vorträge und Aufsätze* (Pfullingen: Neske, 1954), 215. Referred to as *VA*.

22. Martin Heidegger, *Identity and Difference*, trans. Joan Stambaugh (New York: Harper and Row, 1969), 38 and 103. Cited as ID.

23. Gianni Vattimo, *Les aventures de la différence*, trans. from Italian by Pascal Gabellone, Ricardo Pineri, and Jacques Rolland (Paris: Éditions de Minuit, 1985), 184.

24. "*[L]'être comme sens, . . . sens comme être*," Jean-Luc Marion, "L'étant et le phénomène" in Jean-Luc Marion and Guy Planty-Bonjour, ed., *Phénoménologie et métaphysique* (Paris: Presses Universitaires de France, 1984), 199.

25. See both "The Nature of Language" and "The Way to Language" in *On the Way to Language*.

Chapter 2

1. Martin Heidegger, *On Time and Being*, trans. Joan Stambaugh (New York: Harper and Row, 1972), 2 (translation slightly modified). This

edition is subsequently referred to as *TB*. The German text, which can be found on page 2 of Martin Heidegger, *Zur Sache des Denkens* (Tübingen: Max Niemeyer Verlag, 1976), reads as follows:

> Es gilt, einiges von dem Versuch zu sagen, der das Sein ohne die Rücksicht auf eine Begründung des Seins aus dem Seienden denkt. Der Versuch, Sein ohne das Seiende zu denken, wird notwendig, weil anders sonst, wie mir scheint, keine Möglichkeit mehr besteht, das Sein dessen, was heute rund um den Erdball *ist*, eigens in den Blick zu bringen, geschweige denn das Verhältnis des Menschen zu dem, was bislang "Sein" hiess, hinreichend zu bestimmen.

The German edition is henceforth cited as *ZSD*.

2. See, for example, "*Ousia* and *Gramme*: Note on a Note from *Being and Time*," in *Margins of Philosophy*, trans. Alan Bass (Chicago: University of Chicago Press, 1982), 29–67.

3. Kettering's interesting and methodical study has not yet received much response from the phenomenological circles. I have not seen its thesis discussed or appraised by other critics, especially not in the English-language literature. The value of Kettering's book lies in its systematic exploration of the manner in which nearness traces upon Heidegger's key terms, from early fundamental ontology to *Ereignis*, in other words, in its argument for a consistent undercurrent in Heidegger's thinking, an undercurrent that, I claim, eventually forces his departure from the ontological difference. See Kettering, *Nähe: Das Denken Martin Heideggers* (Neske: Pfullingen, 1987).

4. The German text reads: "*Ein Geben, das nur seine Gabe gibt, sich selbst jedoch dabei zurückhält und entzieht, ein solches Geben nennen wir das Schicken*" (*ZSD*, 8).

5. Beda Alleman, *Hölderlin und Heidegger* (Freiburg im Breisgau: Atlantis Verlag, 1954), 81–82.

6. See Albert Hofstadter, "Enownment," in *Martin Heidegger and the Question of Literature* (Bloomington: Indiana University Press, 1979), 31.

7. *Hölderlin und Heidegger*, 81.

8. Heidegger makes it clear that nearness should not be understood exclusively in temporal terms; rather, nearness nears, that is, reaches as it gives, in such a manner that it reaches what is ordinarily understood as time-space:

> Sie [Nähe] gewährt das Offene des Zeit-Raumes und verwahrt, was im Gewesen verweigert, was in der Ankunft vorenthalten bleibt (*ZSD*, 16).

> It [nearness] grants the openness of time-space and preserves what remains denied in what has-been, what is withheld in approach (*TB*, 16).

The giving in *es gibt Zeit* is, then, spatio-temporal in the sense that it reaches and gives time-space. Therefore one has to be careful not to limit nearness to merely its temporal scope and to keep in mind that space is at play in *Ereignis* just as primordially as time.

9. See "L'autre différant" and "La quatrième dimension," in *L'idole et la distance* (Paris: Fayard, 1975), 274–320.

10. Perhaps the most interesting example is Heidegger's use of phrases like "time times" or "space spaces" in an attempt not only to query the grammatical and syntactical differences but to circumvent the parametrical and calculative thinking of the world. See *OWL*, 104–108.

11. I remain here clearly indebted to John Llewelyn's provocative and thoughtful elaboration of the possible proximity between Levinas and Heidegger in *The Middle Voice*, particularly with respect to the ethical implications of this encounter. Beyond the business of quoting and referencing, I would like to acknowledge here my proximity to the intention of Llewelyn's project.

12. Martin Heidegger, *Basic Writings*, ed. and intro. David Farrell Krell (New York: Harper and Row, 1979), 232. Cited in the text as *BW*.

13. "Letter on Humanism" makes clear that what has been called here the thinking of nearness cannot be satisfactorily described in either ethical or ontological terms: "The thinking that inquires into the truth of Being and so defines man's essential abode [Heidegger's translation of the Greek *ēthos*] from Being and toward Being is neither ethics nor ontology" (*BW*, 235–236). The German text reads: "*Das Denken, das nach der Wahrheit des Seins fragt und dabei den Wesensaufenthalt des Menschen vom Sein her und auf dieses hin bestimmt, ist weder Ethik noch Ontologie*" (Martin Heidegger, *Wegmarken* [Frankfurt am Main: Vittorio Klostermann, 1978, 2d ed.], 354). Henceforth cited as *W*.

Chapter 3

1. Emmanuel Levinas, *Totalité et Infini: Essai sur l'extériorité* (The Hague: Martinus Nijhoff, 1961), 5–10/Emmanuel Levinas, *Totality and Infinity: An Essay on Exteriority*, trans. Alphonso Lingis (Pittsburgh: Duquesne University Press, 1969), 35–39. All subsequent references to these editions are cited parenthetically in the text, preceded respectively by *TeI* and *TI*.

2. Jacques Derrida, "Violence et métaphysique: essai sur la pensée d'Emmanuel Levinas," in *L'écriture et la différence* (Paris: Éditions du Seuil, 1967), 164/"Violence and Metaphysics: An Essay on the Thought of Emmanuel Levinas," in *Writing and Difference*, trans. Alan Bass (Chicago: Chicago University Press, 1978), 111. Henceforth cited as *ÉD* and *WD*.

3. Emmanuel Levinas, "La trace de l'autre," in *En découvrant l'existence avec Husserl et Heidegger* (Paris: Vrin, 1967), 194–197/"The Trace of the

Other," trans. Alphonso Lingis, in *Deconstruction in Context*, ed. Mark C. Taylor (Chicago: University of Chicago Press, 1986), 352–354. Referred to as respectively *DEHH* and *DC*.

4. See Emmanuel Levinas, *Autrement qu'être ou au-delà de l'essence* (The Hague: Martinus Nijhoff, 1974), 232–233/*Otherwise than Being or Beyond Essence*, trans. Alphonso Lingis (The Hague: Martinus Nijhoff, 1981), 184–185. All subsequent references to these editions are marked parenthetically in the text, preceded respectively by *AEAE* and *OBBE*; see also Emmanuel Levinas, "De l'être à l'autre," in *Noms propres* (Montpellier: Fata Morgana, 1976), 64–66.

5. See, for example, G.W.F. Hegel, Preface to *Phenomenology of Spirit*, trans. A. V. Miller (Oxford: Clarendon Press, 1977), 10–15.

6. Emmanuel Levinas, "La philosophie et l'idée de l'Infini," in *En découvrant l'existence avec Husserl et Heidegger* (Vrin: Paris, 1967), 165–178/ "Philosophy and the Idea of Infinity" in Emmanuel Levinas, *Collected Philosophical Papers*, trans. and ed. Alphonso Lingis (The Hague: Martinus Nijhoff, 1987), 47–59. The English translation in cited as *CPP*.

7. The seemingly paradoxical use of Descartes, one of the most totalizing and systematic thinkers, in the context of rupturing and transcending totality can be better understood in view of an excellent study of Descartes by Jean-Luc Marion, *Sur le prism métaphysique de Descartes* (Paris: Presses Universitaires de France, 1986). Adopting a Heideggerian interpretation of metaphysics as onto-theo-logy, Marion identifies two separate onto-theological figures in Descartes: one interprets reality according to thought (*cogitare*), equates being with thinking (*esse = cogitare*), and makes human beings (*res cogitans*) the center of the universe; the other sees being as creating/causing (*causare*), places God (*causa sui*) as the center, and interprets human being as *ens creatum* (130–131). This double metaphysical figure makes clear the twofold role of *ego* in Descartes: as the first principle (*cogitatio*) and as *ens creatum*, with God as the supreme cause. However, Marion points out that infinity in Descartes transcends both figures of onto-theology and marks the limits of metaphysics (288): "*la raison humaine, en se heurtant à l'incompréhensibilité divine, se surpasse véritablement elle-même et transcende le fini qu'elle est vers l'infini qui est*" (243–244). This rift through the totalizing figures of metaphysics indicates a breach of thought, a possibility of surplus and departure from the totalizing *cogitatio* of the *ego*. Such an insightful reading of Descartes confirms the legitimacy of Levinas's reference to the Cartesian conception of infinity as the moment of breaching and transcending the totalizing structures of philosophy.

8. See *TeI*, 87–89/*TI*, 114–115, and "La trace de l'autre," 192–194/"The Trace of the Other," 350–352.

9. These long and fascinating descriptions seem to be parallel to Heidegger's analysis of the modes of Being of *Dasein*. Though Levinas dis-

agrees that the overall structure of the human mode of Being is care (he prefers to talk about "enjoyment" [*jouissance*]), the way he describes how the ego enjoys the world, the "false" alterity, is reminiscent of the Heideggerian *existenzialen*. Unfortunately, there is no place here for even an introductory analysis of enjoyment, the modes of sensibility, its relation to representation, bathing in the elements, and *il y a*—the rustling of Being. For a "closest" parallel between the Heideggerian analysis of Being and Levinas's *il y a*, see Emmanuel Levinas, *De l'existence à l'existant* (Paris: Vrin, 1947, 1981)/Emmanuel Levinas, *Existence and Existents*, trans. Alphonso Lingis (The Hague: Martinus Nijhoff, 1978).

10. An interesting discussion of enjoyment as the ipseity of "myself" can be found in Bernard Forthomme's comprehensive work on Levinas, *Une philosophie de la transcendence: la métaphysique d'Emmanuel Lévinas* (Paris: Vrin, 1979), 140–151.

11. For this discussion see Emmanuel Levinas, "La philosophie et l'idée de l'Infini," *DEHH*, 172/"Philosophy and the Idea of Infinity," *CPP*, 54.

12. See Plato, Book VI of *The Republic*, trans. Paul Shorey, in *The Collected Dialogues of Plato*, ed. Edith Hamilton and Huntington Cairns (Princeton: Princeton University Press, 1961), 740–747.

13. For the discussion of Levinas in the context of Judaism and for his preoccupation with the Judaic as an inflection of the always already "Greek" language see, for example, Jill Robbins, *Prodigal Son/Elder Brother: Alterity and Interpretation in Augustine, Petrarch, Kafka, Levinas* (Chicago: University of Chicago Press, 1991), 100–132, and Susan Handelman, *Fragments of Redemption: Jewish Thought and Literary Theory in Benjamin, Scholem, and Levinas* (Bloomington and Indianapolis: University of Indiana Press, 1991), 177–345.

14. Jill Robbins articulates this Levinasian strategy very well when she points out how his writings destabilize the already hierarchical oppositions Greek/Hebrew, Christian/Hebrew, and radicalize the privative and negative characterizations of the Judaic (absence, blindness) beyond the oppositional scheme itself. Rereading the Judaic, Levinas proposes "to take a negative and privative description within a hierarchical opposition, radicalize a possibility inherent in it, and reinscribe it as no longer privative but anterior to the opposition" (*Prodigial Son/Elder Brother*, 115).

15. An excellent elaboration of the relationship between Hebrew and Greek, their literal and figural functions in Levinas's discourse, can be found in Robbins's *Prodigal Son/Elder Brother*, 124–128. As an example of the complexity of this issue, I quote a couple of concluding sentences from page 128: "To the extent that it dissimulates Greek *under* Hebrew, it is not a Greek we can get to except *as* a Hebrew that is dissimulated *as* a Greek that dissimulates the Hebrew. This double dissimulation is originary."

16. As several critics have noted, it is possible to approach Derrida's essay as enacting a double deconstructive reading of Levinas, repeating the intentions of his texts and, on the other hand, foregrounding and opening to debate their lacunae and blind spots. See, for example, Robert Bernasconi, "The Trace of Levinas in Derrida," in *Derrida and Différance*, ed. David Wood and Robert Bernasconi (Chicago: Northwestern University Press, 1988), 13–29.

17. See Emmanuel Levinas, *Quatre lectures talmudiques* (Paris: Éditions de Minuit, 1968), 68–69. In the second lecture, Levinas explains the essence of Judaism as the prescription *"faire avant entendre"* (doing before hearing, understanding). This prescription does not favor praxis over theory but implies the direction toward the other, the ethical order, in which the "temptation of knowledge" is inscribed. For the English translation see Levinas, *Nine Talmudic Lectures*, trans. and intro. Annette Aronowicz (Bloomington and Indianapolis: Indiana University Press, 1990), 30–31.

18. Theodore de Boer, "An Ethical Transcendental Philosophy," in *Face to Face with Levinas*, ed. Richard A. Cohen (Albany: State University of New York Press, 1986), 93–95.

19. Emmanuel Levinas, "Signature" in *Difficile liberté* (Paris: Albin Michel, 2d enlarged and revised ed., 1976), 379/ "Signature," trans. M. E. Petrisko, ed. A. Peperzak, *Research in Phenomenology* 8 (1978): 188–189. Quoted from Lyotard, "Levinas' Logic," in *Face to Face with Levinas*.

20. Levinas, *Existence and Existents*, 19.

21. *Prodigal Son/Elder Brother*, 123. See Robbins's instructive discussion of Levinas's relation to Heidegger and his claim that the ethical "may be" otherwise than Being (120–124).

22. See the analysis in *Sein und Zeit* (Tübingen: Niemeyer, 1986), especially page 152.

23. This is one of the most important moments in Heidegger's analysis of *Mitsein*, which, if not juxtaposed with Heidegger's later work, appears to harbor in it the possibility of reading "Being-with" in quasi-generic terms. See *Sein und Zeit*, 158.

24. Martin Heidegger, *Basic Writings*, ed. David Farrell Krell (New York: Harper and Row, 1977), 235. The original passage can be found in *Wegmarken* (Frankfurt am Main: Vittorio Klostermann, 1978), 353.

25. Emmanuel Levinas, "La signification et le sens," in *L'humanisme de l'autre homme* (Montpellier: Fata Morgana, 1972), 50 (henceforth cited as *HAH*); translated as "Meaning and Sense" in *Collected Philosophical Papers*, 95.

26. Emmanuel Levinas, "La Signifiance du sens," in *Hors sujet* (Montpellier: Fata Morgana, 1987), 141. Hereafter referred to in the text as *HS*.

27. The phrase appears in "La Signifiance du sens," 141.

28. Levinas's conception of the face has left its mark on Jean-Luc Marion's opposition between the icon and the idol (see *Dieu sans l'être* [Paris: Fayard, 1982]). For Marion, the idol, created by the gaze (*le regarde*), becomes a mirror that arrests seeing and enables consciousness to reflect upon itself and think. The icon, on the other hand, awakens an infinite gaze (*un regard infini*) and, escaping the gaze of the subject, opens it to the other. By signaling its alterity through the face (*envisager*), the other, through its own eyes, summons the subject toward the other's infinity: "*l'icône s'ouvre en un visage, qui regarde nos regards pour les convoquer à sa profondeur*" (31).

29. Emmanuel Levinas, *Humanisme de l'autre homme*, 17–63/"Meaning and Sense," in *CPP*, 75–107; and Emmanuel Levinas, "Dieu et la philosophie," in *De Dieu qui vient a l'idée* (Paris: Vrin, 1982), 93–127, henceforth cited as *DVI*/"God and Philosophy," in *CPP*, 153–173.

30. Levinas, "Dieu et la philosophie," 97/"God and Philosophy," 155.

31. The plurality of voices in Levinasian texts is lucidly explained by David E. Klemm in his essay "Levinas' Phenomenology of the Other and Language as the Other of Phenomenology," *Man and World* 22 (1989): 406–417.

32. See Heidegger's translation of the saying in *Identity and Difference*, trans. Joan Stambaugh (New York: Harper and Row, 1969), 38 and 103.

33. Martin Heidegger, *On the Way to Language*, trans. Peter D. Hertz (New York: Harper and Row, 1971), 129. The German text reads: "*Die Vereignung der Sterblichen in die Sage entlässt das Menschenwesen in den Brauch, aus dem der Mensch gebraucht ist, die lautlose Sage in das Verlauten der Sprache zu bringen*"; in Martin Heidegger, *Unterwegs zur Sprache* (Pfullingen: Neske, 1959), 260.

34. "*Das Denken legt mit seinem Sagen unscheinbare Furchen in die Sprache*"; Martin Heidegger, "Brief über den Humanismus," in *Wegmarken*, 360/Martin Heidegger, "Letter on Humanism," in *Basic Writings*, ed. David Farrell Krell (New York: Harper and Row, 1977), 242.

35. Jacques Derrida, "En ce moment même dans cet ouvrage me voici" in *Textes pour Emmanuel Levinas*, ed. François Laruelle (Paris: Jean-Michel Place, 1980), 30 (cited as EM). A recent translation of this essay as "At this very moment in this work here I am" appeared in *Re-reading Levinas*, ed. Robert Bernasconi and Simon Critchley (Bloomington: Indiana University Press, 1991) (hereafter abbreviated *RL*). For Derrida's reference to agrammaticality see page 19.

36. The discussion of *symplokè* is one of the key "threads" of Derrida's argument. See EM, 29/*RL*, 18.

37. Gianni Vattimo, *Les aventures de la différence* (Paris: Éditions de Minuit, 1985), 189.

38. Jacques Derrida, *Spurs: Nietzsche's Styles/Éperons: Les Styles de Nietzsche*, trans. Barbara Harlow (Chicago: University of Chicago Press, 1979), 116.

39. In his essay "Philosophie et violence," Guy Petitdemange discusses the Levinasian subject as *"denuclée,"* exposed into responsibility and unique in it; *Autrement que savoir—Emmanuel Lévinas* (Paris: Éditions Osiris, 1988), 21.

40. For Derrida's complex and engaging discussion of "work" of giving in Levinas, see EM, 25/*RL*, 13–15.

41. Emmanuel Levinas, "Sans identité," in *Humanisme de l'autre homme*, 105/"No Identity," in *Collected Philosophical Papers*, 147.

42. See also Forthomme, *Une philosophie de la transcendance*, 12.

43. The discussion of this paradoxical nature of the signifyingness of the trace, suggesting perhaps the "uniqueness" of tracing in the Levinasian sense, can be found in "La trace de l'autre," *DEHH*, 98/"The Trace of the Other," *DC*, 355.

44. In this context, see also Robbins's discussion of the Levinasian metalepsis with respect to the "firstness" of Heidegger's questioning of Being; *Prodigal Son/Elder Brother*, 120.

45. Derrida's reading of the two instances of "at this moment" focuses on the "difference" between them and its inauguration of a series: EM, 35/*RL*, 24.

46. EM, 48. The English translation opts here for the word *seriasure* to indicate the relation between series and erasure: a stringed series of enlaced erasures (*RL*, 36).

47. EM, 49. "To say 'il aura obligé'—in *this* work, taking into account what sets things to work within *this* seriasure—is not to designate, describe, define, show, etc., but, let us say, to *entrace* (*entracer*), otherwise said to perform within the intr(el)acement (*entr(el)acement*) of a seriasure that obligation whose 'he' will not have been the present subject for which 'I' hereby respond: Here I am, (I) come" (*RL*, 37).

48. It would be interesting, but the scope of the chapter forbids it, to look at seriasure in relation to Lyotard's description of Levinas's writings in terms of prescriptives and denotatives. For Lyotard, denotative language erases the prescriptivity of the ethical operative in Levinas (see Jean-François Lyotard, "Levinas' Logic," in *Face to Face with Levinas*, 144–153).

In the context of the laterality of the trace, seriasure seems to be the feature of writing, of language as it unfolds itself already in the trace of the other. Can one then say that seriasure, the series beyond or out of the series, breaks from the denotative to hear the ethical prescription of responsibility? Does it read in the trace of the other, or does it read the trace of the other?

49. Levinas, "Dieu et la philosophie," *DVI*, 124/"God and Philosophy," *CPP*, 141.

50. For Levinas's discussion of the "pre-subjective" exposition into the accusative, see *DVI*, 123/*CPP*, 170.

51. Emmanuel Levinas, "Énigme et phénomène" in *DEHH*, 212/"Phenomenon and Enigma," in *CPP*, 69.

52. *"Il n'y aurait pas de langage sans cette responsabilité (étique) mais il n'est jamais sûr que le langage se rende à la responsabilité qui le rend possible (à son essence simplement probable)"* (EM, 34).

53. Emmanuel Levinas, "Langage quotidien et rhetorique sans eloquence" in *Hors sujet*, 203–211.

54. Levinas's remarks on the relation between the trace and the phenomenal encounter with the other can be found in *DVI*, 116/*CPP*, 166.

55. Levinas's problematic use of the masculine pronoun to designate the ethical other as well as his figuration of femininity has received critical attention from various quarters. See, among others, Tina Chanter, "Feminism and the Other," and Alison Ainley, "Amorous Discourses: 'The Phenomenology of Eros' and Love Stories"; both essays are included in *The Provocation of Levinas*, ed. Robert Bernasconi and David Wood (London and New York: Routledge, 1988). Also Luce Irigaray, "Questions to Emmanuel Levinas: On the Divinity of Love," Catherine Chalier, "Ethics and the Feminine," and Tina Chanter, "Antigone's Dilemma," all in *Re-reading Levinas*. See also an earlier essay by Irigaray, "Fecundity of the Caress," in *Face to Face with Levinas*, and Ewa Ziarek's "Kristeva and Levinas: Mourning, Ethics, and the Feminine," in *Ethics, Politics, and Difference in Julia Kristeva's Writing*, ed. Kelly Oliver (New York: Routledge, 1993).

Chapter 4

1. Wallace Stevens, *The Collected Poems of Wallace Stevens* (New York: Alfred A. Knopf, 1954). Subsequently cited as *CP*.

2. See Helen Vendler, *On Extended Wings: Wallace Stevens's Longer Poems* (Cambridge: Harvard University Press, 1969), 168–205, and Harold Bloom, *Wallace Stevens: The Poems of Our Climate* (Ithaca: Cornell University Press, 1977), 167–218.

3. Marjorie Perloff, *The Poetics of Indeterminacy: Rimbaud to Cage* (Evanston, Ill.: Northwestern University Press, 1983), 20.

4. Perloff, *Poetics of Indeterminacy*, 22.

5. J. Hillis Miller, *The Poets of Reality: Six Twentieth-century Writers* (Cambridge: Harvard University Press, 1965), 262.

6. Joseph N. Riddel, *The Clairvoyant Eye: The Poetry and Poetics of Wallace Stevens* (Baton Rouge: Louisiana State University Press, 1965), 176.

7. In his more recent criticism on Stevens, Bruns moves away from the epistemological reading of Stevens, which stresses "the problem of how the mind links up with reality," and even from his own reading of Stevens in the context of the linguistic turn in *Modern Poetry and the Idea of Language*. Instead, he focuses on the otherness of the other human being and on the question of the appropriation of the other's voice into the song of the self in Stevens: "Stevens without Epistemology," in *Wallace Stevens: The Poetics of Modernism*, ed. Albert Gelpi (Cambridge: Cambridge University Press, 1985), 24–40.

8. Gerald L. Bruns, *Modern Poetry and the Idea of Language: A Critical and Historical Study* (New Haven: Yale University Press, 1974), 222.

9. Thomas J. Hines, *The Later Poetry of Wallace Stevens: Phenomenological Parallels with Husserl and Heidegger* (Cranbury, N.J.: Associated University Presses, 1976), 132 and 128.

10. Perloff, *Poetics of Indeterminacy*, 20.

11. As Eleanor Cook indicates, playing on the guitar becomes the figure for writing poetry and simultaneously for playing on words. This play also emphasizes the complex relationship between imagination and reality in the poetic language. See chapter 7: "Concerning the Nature of Things: 'The Man with the Blue Guitar'," in *Poetry, Word-Play, and Word-War in Wallace Stevens* (Princeton: Princeton University Press, 1988), 135–151.

12. J. Hillis Miller, *The Linguistic Moment: From Wordsworth to Stevens* (Princeton: Princeton University Press, 1985), 4–10.

13. Miller, *The Linguistic Moment*, 10.

14. See, for example, Jacqueline Brogan's discussion of the "interdependence of the imagination and reality" in Stevens's poetry in terms of the "unitive and disjunctive tendencies in language"; *Stevens and Simile: A Theory of Language* (Princeton: Princeton University Press, 1986), 3–26.

15. See especially J. Hillis Miller, "Theoretical and Atheoretical in Stevens" and Joseph Riddel, "Metaphoric Staging: Stevens's Beginning Again of the 'End of the Book'," both in *Wallace Stevens: A Celebration*, ed. Frank Doggett and Robert Buttel (Princeton: Princeton University Press, 1980).

16. J. Hillis Miller, "Theoretical and Atheoretical in Stevens," in *Wallace Stevens: A Celebration*, 284–285.

17. Joseph N. Riddel, "Metaphoric Staging: Stevens's Beginning Again of the 'End of the Book,'" in *Wallace Stevens: A Celebration*, 327.

18. In "Dwelling Poetically in Connecticut," Frank Kermode, using Hölderlin's poetry as the frame of reference, points to the essential similarities, and important distinctions, between the poetic sensibilities of Stevens and Heidegger. He calls attention to the question of death, the absence of god(s), and the role of the poet in time of destitution; in *Wallace Stevens: A Celebration*, 256–273.

19. As Stevens himself often remarks, his poetry continuously addresses the problem of "the nature of poetry"; see "The Noble Rider and the Sound of Words," in *The Necessary Angel: Essays on Reality and Imagination* (New York: Alfred A. Knopf, 1951), 27.

20. Wallace Stevens, *Opus Posthumous* (New York: Alfred A. Knopf, 1957), 206.

21. Beda Alleman, *Hölderlin und Heidegger* (Freiburg im Breisgau: Atlantis Verlag, 1954), 154.

22. Alleman, *Hölderlin und Heidegger*, 159.

23. Alleman, *Hölderlin und Heidegger*, 167.

24. Riddel suggests that the source of difference in Stevens's language is "the more than rational distortion," a place beyond the opposition between the rational and the irrational; "Metaphoric Staging," 324.

25. "Essence" has to appear here in quotation marks in order to indicate that the way Stevens describes the "grand" poem breaks with the traditional philosophical determinations of essence, either in its Platonic, eidetic sense or in the sense it is given in the Scholastic opposition of *essentia* and *existentia*.

26. Riddel, "Metaphoric Staging," 321.

27. Hines, *The Later Poetry of Wallace Stevens*, 91–93.

28. See Miller's emphasis on the disruptive, unnameable element in Stevens's poetry in "Theoretical and Atheoretical in Stevens," and Riddel's argument about the impossibility of closing the book in "Metaphoric Staging."

29. Riddel, "Metaphoric Staging," 318.

30. Also Joseph Kronick points out that Stevens dissociates the first idea from "natural or supernatural origins" and indicates through it the impossibility of naming the origin of language, which continuously slips

into the metaphorical transfer; see "Large White Man Reading: Stevens's Genealogy of the Giant," in *The Wallace Stevens Journal* 7 (1983): 93.

31. Riddel, "Metaphoric Staging," 318.

32. Hines, *The Late Poetry of Wallace Stevens*, 238–258.

33. Jacques Derrida, *Psyché: inventions de l'autre* (Paris: Galilée, 1987), 83.

34. See also Patricia Parker's discussion of Stevens and Derrida in "The Motive for Metaphor: Stevens and Derrida," in *The Wallace Stevens Journal* 7 (1983): 76–88.

35. Michael Beehler presents the metaphorical transfer as the fore-structuring of language, which determines Stevens's poetics of the fiction of the simple, direct, unstructured truth; see "Stevens's Boundaries," in *The Wallace Stevens Journal* 7 (1983): 106.

36. Kronick suggests that such displacement of the genetic link between the proper and the figural, the continuous transfer of one into the other, also moves Stevens's poetry "beyond romanticism and phenomenology"; "Large White Man Reading," 95.

37. Riddel makes clear that this "venerable myth" is not a substantial origin but rather an uncertain light, already a myth itself, an erasure of origin; "Metaphoric Staging," 320.

38. Hines, *The Late Poetry of Wallace Stevens*, 152–154.

39. *Embrace* is the term used by Stevens in "Notes toward a Supreme Fiction" to describe the unfolding of time:

> This is the origin of change.
> Winter and spring, cold copulars, embrace
> And forth the particulars of rapture come. (*CP*, 392)

40. Riddel suggests that Stevens's notion of pleasure replaces the poetics of representation, the possibility of achieving an ideal, "chief image," with the poetics of repetition and thus implies a displacement of the perfect image: "Metaphoric Staging," 323.

41. Perloff, *The Dance of the Intellect: Studies in the Poetry of the Pound Tradition* (Cambridge: Cambridge University Press, 1985), 9.

42. See Wallace Stevens, *The Necessary Angel* (New York: Vintage, 1942), 54.

43. In "Metaphoric Staging," Riddel describes Stevens's poetics in terms of notes: "In the beginning was 'notes toward'" (318). However, it seems that notes refer to the impossibility of creating the final poem, in the sense of a dispersion and displacement of this poem into a series or collec-

tion of poems/notes: "The figural origin of 'lesser poems,' the 'central poem' is a figure produced by /in what it authors" (335). Riddel reads those notes in the context of de Man's writings on Nietzsche and Rousseau, as notes that, instead of pointing to the grand poem, point to other notes, already inscribed in one another—an endless chain of displacing and deferring.

44. I have in mind here "Final Soliloquy of the Interior Paramour," which describes as the "intensest rendezvous" an encounter with the other (*CP*, 524).

Chapter 5

1. Paul Celan, *Gesammelte Werke*, vol. 1 (Frankfurt am Main: Suhrkamp Verlag, 1975), 19. All subsequent references to this edition are quoted parenthetically in the text, preceded by *GW* and followed by the volume number.

2. Paul Celan, *Poems of Paul Celan*, trans. Michael Hamburger (New York: Persea, 1988), 39. Hereafter referred to as *PPC*.

3. Paul Celan, *Speech-Grille and Other Poems*, trans. Joachim Neu-groschel (New York: E. P. Dutton, 1971), 29; abbreviated as *SG*. The German text reads as follows: "*wir trinken sie mittags und morgens wir trinken sie nachts / wir trinken und trinken / wir schaufeln ein Grab in den Lüften*"; "Todesfuge" (*GW* I, 41).

4. *Atemwende* is perhaps the single most important phrase used by Celan in "The Meridian" to characterize his poetics and also the title of his best volume of poetry. I will take up Celan's notion of *Atemwende* later on in this chapter and discuss it in detail in chapter 7.

5. Paul Celan, "Speech on the Occasion of Receiving the Literary Prize of the Free City of Bremen." The text of the Bremen speech is included in the volume *Collected Prose*, trans. Rosmarie Waldrop (Riverdale-on-Hudson, N.Y.: Sheep Meadow Press, 1986), 34.

6. See Theo Buck, "Zu Paul Celans 'Todesfuge'," in *Datum und Zitat bei Paul Celan. Akten des Internationalen Paul Celan-Colloquiums, Haifa 1986*, ed. Chaim Shoham and Bernd Witte (Bern: Peter Lang, 1987), 34.

7. Amy Colin, *Paul Celan: Holograms of Darkness* (Bloomington and Indianapolis: Indiana University Press, 1991), xix.

8. Colin, *Holograms of Darkness*, 78.

9. Christopher Fynsk's essay "Poetic Relation: Celan's Bremen Address" presents an excellent discussion of the question of the historicity of the poetic text as it unfolds itself in Celan's response to Heidegger's work. See *The Poetry of Paul Celan*, ed. Haskell M. Block (New York: Peter Lang, 1991), 22–29.

10. See Levinas's discussion of "my" death versus the death of the other in "Ethics as First Philosophy," *The Levinas Reader* (Oxford: Basil Blackwell, 1989), 82–86.

11. A brief and incisive summary of the various trends in Celan criticism can be found in the introduction to Amy Colin's recent *Paul Celan: Holograms of Darkness*, xvii–xxviii.

12. These terms have been proposed by Véronique Fóti in the context of her discussion of Celan's encounter with Heidegger's thought in *Heidegger and the Poets* (Atlantic Heights, N.J.: Humanities Press, 1992), 78–110.

13. This text was delivered in French at a conference on Paul Celan held at the University of Washington, Seattle, October 1984. It was subsequently revised and published in France as *Schibboleth: Pour Paul Celan* (Paris: Galilée, 1986). The English translation of the presentation Derrida gave at the Celan symposium appeared in *Midrash and Literature*, ed. Geoffrey H. Hartman and Sanford Budick (New Haven and London: Yale University Press, 1986), 307–347.

14. *Schibboleth*, 108/*Schibboleth*, 344–345.

15. *Schibboleth*, 346. The French text reads: "*le mot circoncis nous rappelle aussi le* double tranchant *d'un* schibboleth. *Marque d'alliance, il intervient aussi, il interdit, il signifie la sentence d'exclusion, la discrimination, voire l'extermination*" (*Schibboleth*, 111).

16. This overall framework manifests itself at the points where Derrida alludes to Heidegger's work on *datum* and giving (*es gibt*) (for example, an extended note to page 33, in which Derrida mentions Greisch's work on Celan and Heidegger and quotes Heidegger on the structure of datability), and to the extent to which Heidegger's thought figures in Celan's work, especially the terms *being* and *nothing* (*Nichts*) (see *Schibboleth*, 73–76).

17. *Schibboleth*, 316. The version published in French differs slightly, underscoring precisely the non-conventional, non-calendaric character of the dating in question: "*une datation de forme non conventionnelle, non calendaire, qui se confondrait, sans reste, avec l'organisation générale du texte poétique*" [*Schibboleth*, 34]).

18. Even though Levinas addresses Celan's work explicitly only in the short piece from *Noms propres*, one could argue that Celan's language informs Levinas's most important work, *Otherwise than Being or Beyond Essence*, surfacing in particular in the sections and phrases describing the impact of alterity in terms of interrupted or arrested respiration. What is more, the pivotal fourth chapter of Levinas's book, "Substitution," bears an epigraph from Celan, his famous line "*Ich bin du, wenn ich ich bin*, discussed already in the context of Hamacher's text on inversion. Both the epigraph and the title of the chapter suggest that the governing trope of

Levinas's book, in fact of his entire later work, that of substitution, of the-one-for-the-other, might be inspired by Celan's poetry and its figuration of the other's trace (*du*) in the I. It is indeed Levinas's language that indicates the extent to which his work becomes involved with Celan, turning the image of interrupted or involuted breath into the figure of openness to the other. See also my discussion of Celan's *Atemwende* and Levinas's use of the tropology of breathing in the Coda.

19. Paul Celan, *Gesammelte Werke*, vol. 3, 192–193. The English translation can be found in Paul Celan, *Collected Prose*, trans. Rosmarie Waldrop (Riverdale-on-Hudson, N.Y.: Sheep Meadow Press, 1990), 43. The English volume will be referred to as *P*.

20. Paul Celan, *Collected Prose*, 15. The German text reads: "*Ihre Sprache ist nüchterner, faktischer geworden, sie misstraut dem 'Schönen,' sie versucht, wahr zu sein*" (*GW* III, 167).

21. The original text from the third volume of Celan's *Gesammelte Werke* reads: "*mit dem* hier *und* solcherart *freigesetzten befremdeten Ich,— vielleicht wird hier noch ein Anderes frei?*" (*GW* III, 196).

22. In *Schibboleth*, Derrida elaborates through the notion of the date the structure that opens the poem to the other: "*Au lieu de l'emmurer et de le réduire au silence de la singularité, une date lui donne sa chance, et de parler à l'autre!*" (22). What in effect takes place in the experience of the date is an encounter with the wholly other ("*tout autre*"), which Celan discusses in "The Meridian" (see *Schibboleth*, 23–24).

23. Werner Hamacher, "The Second of Inversion: The Movement of a Figure through Celan's Poetry," in *Yale French Studies* (The Lesson of Paul de Man) 69 (1985): 276–311. Hereafter cited as SI.

24. Winfried Menninghaus, *Paul Celan: Magie der Form* (Frankfurt am Main: Suhrkamp, 1980). Hereafter cited as MF.

25. "You here, you: infused with life / by the breath of those names / caught in the / branchings of lungs laid / open // to-be-deciphered you" [translation mine]. I would like to thank here my colleagues Vera Profit and Randy Klawiter for their generous help and advice with rendering into English those of Celan's text that are unavailable, at least to my knowledge, in the English translation (see also note # 28). Any remaining mistakes or mistranslations are entirely my responsibility.

26. Emmanuel Levinas, *Noms propres* (Montpellier: Fata Morgana, 1976), 61. Hereafter referred to as *NP*.

27. Paul Celan, *Last Poems*, trans. Katharine Washburn and Margret Guillemin (San Francisco: North Point Press, 1986), 135. Hereafter referred to as *LP*.

28. "From its crumb(s) / you knead anew our names // . . . // (for) a

spot through which I / can awaken toward you, / the bright / candle of hunger in my mouth" [trans. mine].

29. Hans-Georg Gadamer reads the poem as the description of the writing of poetry; see *Wer bin Ich und wer bist Du?: Ein Kommentar zu Paul Celans Gedichtfolge "Atemkristall"* (Frankfurt am Main: Suhrkamp, 1986), 21–25.

30. Stéphane Mosés has illustrated Celan's deliberate recourse in "Gespräch im Gebirg" to Jewish German (ellision, idiomatic expressions) and to terms charged with negative connotations, used often to stereotype German Jews (see "'Wege auf denen die Sprache stimmhaft wird'. Paul Celans 'Gespräch im Gebirg'," *Argumentum e Silentio*, ed. Amy D. Colin [Berlin, New York: de Gruyter, 1987], 49). Mosés argues that Celan, taking a stance against Adorno, attempts to give value and importance back to poetry and German language. This is possible, however, only by taking upon and carrying to the extreme the guilt for the Holocaust, implied also in the corruption and abuse of language. Celan therefore deliberately employs pejorative forms, for example *Jud* instead of *Jude*, bringing language close to self-deprecation (50).

31. The original passage can be found in the third volume of *Gesammelte Werke*: "*eine Sprache . . . nicht für dich, sag ich, ist sie gedacht, und nicht für mich—, eine Sprache, je nun, ohne Ich und ohne Du, lauter Er, lauter Es, verstehst du, lauter Sie, und nichts als das*" (170–171).

32. See Hamburger's translation in Paul Celan, *Poems of Paul Celan*, 189.

33. Derrida's *Schibboleth* provides the best illustration of the full range and the complex interplay of the numerous connotations of otherness in Celan's work by assembling a sheaf of related notions—date, shibboleth, circumcision, cinders, etc.—that describe the organization of Celan's texts.

34. Lacoue-Labarthe, *La poésie comme expérience* (Paris: Christian Bourgois Editeur, 1986), 50. Hereafter cited as *PE*.

35. "*Le tout autre est le don de l'autre comme possibilité du même, c'est-à-dire comme la possibilité, pour le même, de se constituer en différance*" (*PE*, 91).

36. "*Cette addresse au toi est addresse à l'alterité du toi—de cet autre—, c'est l'addresse, obscurément surgie de l'intimité (de la différence intime), à l'être de l'autre, qui 'est' toujours et ne peut 'être' que l'être*" (*PE*, 97).

37. "*Le 'dire-toi', le nommer de la poésie est un autre mode de 'dire-être' que celui qui appartient proprement à la pensée, mais c'est encore un mode du 'dire-l'être'*" (*PE*, 98).

38. Mosés's essay "'Wege, auf denen'" seems to confirm this insight, as it highlights the tension between being and the other, opting in the end for a Levinasian reading of "The Conversation in the Mountains." Placing

Celan's piece in the context of Levinas's critique of Heidegger, Mosés discusses Celan's approach to language as mediation between impersonal and personal conceptions of language (see *Argumentum e Silentio*, 46), making it part of a chain of oppositions that run through "Gespräch im Gebirg": nature/the Judaic; the natural/the human; impersonal/personal; being/the other (in particular, pages 46 and 53).

Chapter 6

1. See Peter Szondi, *Celan-Studien* (Frankfurt am Main: Suhrkamp, 1972), 47–111.

2. One has to mention in this context Derrida's meditation on the place of date and dating in Celan in *Schibboleth: Pour Paul Celan* (Paris: Galilée, 1986). Although Derrida devotes most of the analysis to date and its structure of self-erasure, he makes clear that dating becomes possible only within the direction toward the other. He argues that in Celan words become "circumcised"; they are "wounded" and marked with a turn toward the other (102). The very opening of language, the moment of it becoming poetic (*devenir-poétique*, 105), already directs itself toward the other. Therefore the circumcision of language is not dated in history, but it itself makes place for a date and time: "*la circoncision d'une parole n'est pas datée dans l'histoire. En ce sens, elle n'a pas d'âge mais elle donne lieu à la date. Elle ouvre la parole à l'autre, et la porte, elle ouvre l'histoire, le poème, et la philosophie, et l'herméneutique, et la religion*" (112). The other's trace, then, marks language "beyond" or "otherwise than" in time, since his/her alterity opens the direction for time.

3. See Szondi, *Celan-Studien*, 77. Further on, referring to the strophe "*Sprach, sprach. / War, war*," Szondi postulates an equivalency between word and Being: "*Gleichzeitig stellt diese Strophe von zwei Versen, die allein aus zwei wiederholten Verben besteht, die Idenitität von Wort und Sein fest und weist auf die Übereinstimmung von poetischer Realität und poetischer Text*" (83). Indeed, the poetic text in Celan, especially in its "*Wordschatten*," becomes identical with Being. However, it also immediately departs into another direction—the ethical.

4. Szondi, *Celan-Studien*, 51.

5. For example, Thomas Sparr writes about *Textlandschaften* in Celan's poetry; see "Zeichenreflexion in Celan's Lyrik" in *Datun und Zitat bei Paul Celan* (Bern: Peter Lang, 1987), 69.

6. Menninghaus, *Magie der Form*, 80–129.

7. See Levinas, *Noms propres*, 59.

8. See Gerhard Buhr, "Über Paul Celans Gedicht 'Weggebeizt',"
Celan-Jahrbuch 1 (1987): 38.

9. Buhr, "Über Paul Celans Gedicht 'Weggebeizt'," 42.

10. Buhr, "Über Paul Celans Gedicht 'Weggebeizt'," 55–56.

11. See Neugroschel's translation in Celan, *Speech-Grille*, 232.

12. See Hamburger's translation in Celan, *Poems of Paul Celan*, 279.

13. See again Derrida's discussion of circumcision and wounding of language in *Schibboleth*, 100–113.

14. The German text reads: *"Ich finde das Verbindende und wie das Gedicht zur Begegnung Führende. Ich finde etwas—wie die Sprache—Immaterielles, aber Irdisches, Terrestrisches, etwas Kreisförmiges, über die beiden Pole in sich selbst Zurückkehrendes und dabei—heitererweise—sogar die Tropen Durchkreuzendes—: ich finde . . . einen* Meridian" (*GW* III, 202).

Coda

1. "Only image preserves the face / But the face rests in the poem," a couplet Heidegger used as one of the texts for a two-day seminar on the topic of "Wort und Bild" he held in Bremen in the summer of 1960. Quoted after Heinrich Wiegand Petzet, *Encounters and Dialogues with Martin Heidegger: 1929–1976*, trans. Parvis Emad and Kenneth Maly (Chicago and London: University of Chicago Press, 1993), 59.

2. See Otto Pöggeler, *Spur des Wortes: Zur Lyrik Paul Celans* (Freiburg and Munich: Alber, 1986), and *Neue Wege mit Heidegger* (Freiburg and Munich: Alber, 1992). Schmidt's and Fynsk's essays have appeared in the proceedings from the 1988 conference on Celan at the State University of New York in Binghampton, entitled *The Poetry of Paul Celan*.

3. In her two chapters from *Heidegger and the Poets* devoted to "a missed interlocution" between Heidegger and Celan, Fóti opposes Celan's "explicit negation of any unified source of poetic inspiration" to "a Heideggerian *essen*tializing retrieval" (82–83). It is to this different approach to the source of poetry that Fóti attributes Heidegger's failure to respond to the Holocaust and, by extension, to Celan. By contrast, Celan's poetry seeks to extend itself to the otherness of the other, while "repudiating 'all oracles' and any *essential* unification" (97–98). Thus the encounter of Heidegger and Celan is a missed interlocution, for, though Celan does not dismiss Heidegger's emphasis on the enigma and the structure of manifestation, he modifies it through the emphasis on the here and now, on the historical, which Heidegger refuses. It is this refusal that, in Fóti's reading, frustrates interlocution (106).

4. See Pöggeler's discussion of Celan's interest in Heidegger's work from the 1950s and 1960s in *Spur des Wortes*, 248.

5. *The Poetry of Paul Celan*, 35.

6. I am deeply grateful to John Llewelyn, who, responding to an earlier version of this chapter, reminded me of the extent to which the tropology of breathing describes, structures, and expands Levinas's figure of substitution and suggested its link to Celan's work.

7. *"Exposition à l'ouverture du visage, qui est le 'plus loin encore' de la dé-claustration du 'soi-même', de la dé-claustration qui n'est pas l'être-au-monde. Un plus loin—une respiration profonde jusqu'au souffle coupé par le vent de l'altérité"* (*AEAE*, 227). Levinas then continues to explore the connection between the interrupted breath and the difference between the saying and the said (181/228), making clear that language pivots on the "in-spiration" of the other, the involuted breath that figures the pre-original exposition to the other, the pre-original saying of language: "[i]n human breathing, in its everyday equality, perhaps we have to already hear the breathlessness of an inspiration that paralyzes essence, that transpierces it with an inspiration by the other, an inspiration that is already expiration, that 'rends the soul'!" (*OBBE*, 181–182/*AEAE*, 229). This "rending of the soul" signifies substitution of the-one-for-the-other, "expiration without return," responsibility.

8. Martin Heidegger, *Unterwegs zur Sprache* (Pfullingen: Neske, 1956), 13.

9. Paul Celan, *Gesammelte Werke*, vol. 2 (Frankfurt am Main: Suhrkamp Verlag, 1983), 275. The translation is taken from *Poems of Paul Celan*, trans. Michael Hamburger (New York: Persea Books, 1988), 299.

10. An excellent discussion of the proximity between Celan's speech and Heidegger's thought is offered by Fynsk in his essay "Poetic Relation: Celan's Bremen Address": "Celan begins his acceptance speech in terms that immediately evoke Heidegger." See *The Poetry of Paul Celan*, 22.

11. Emmanuel Levinas, *Noms propres* (Montpellier: Fata Morgana, 1976); Philippe Lacoue-Labarthe, *La poésie comme expérience* (Paris: Christian Bourgois, 1986).

12. *Noms propres*, 55. All translations from this text are mine. The French original reads: *"Le poème absolue ne dit pas le sens de l'être, il n'est pas une variation sur le dichterisch wohnet der Mensch auf dieser Erde de Hölderlin."*

13. *"Ne suggère-t-il pas la poésie elle-même comme une modalité inouïe de l'autrement qu'être?"* in *Noms propres*, 56.

14. Martin Heidegger, *Unterwegs zur Sprache* (Pfullingen: Neske, 1956). The English translation: *On the Way to Language*, trans. Peter D. Hertz (New York: Harper and Row, 1971), 57–59.

15. Martin Heidegger, *Wegmarken* (Frankfurt am Main: Vittorio Klostermann, 1967), 187.

16. Such understanding of ethics comes to the fore in particular in Levinas's two most important works: *Totalité et Infini: Essai sur l'exteriorité* (The Hague: Martinus Nijhoff, 1961) and *Autrement qu'être ou au-delà de l'essence* (The Hague: Martinus Nijhoff, 1974); both translated into English by Alphonso Lingis as *Totality and Infinity: An Essay on Exteriority* (Pittsburgh: Duquesne University Press, 1969) and *Otherwise than Being or Beyond Essence* (The Hague: Martinus Nijhoff, 1981).

17. John Llewelyn, *The Middle Voice of Ecological Conscience* (New York: St. Martin's Press, 1991).

18. "*Weil das In-der-Welt-sein wesenhaft Sorge ist, deshalb konnte in den voranstehenden Analysen das Sein bei dem Zuhandenen als* Besorgen, *das Sein mit dem innerweltlich begegnenden Mitdasein Anderer als* Fürsorge *gefasst werden*"; Martin Heidegger, *Sein und Zeit* (Tübingen: Max Niemeyer Verlag, 1976), 193.

19. See chapter 4 of *Sein und Zeit*, 113–130.

20. Within the space of this chapter, I can only make a gesture toward thinking Heidegger in this particular way. It is clear from all of Heidegger's writings how special a status *Dasein* holds among different modalities of being. By that token, *Dasein* both belongs among other modes of being—thingness, animality—and simultaneously excepts itself from this context. Likewise, the others (other entities with the modality of being designated as *Dasein*) both constitute part of *Dasein's* world, its *Mitsein*, and yet excuse themselves or overflow it; that is, they hold an additional significance than just as being within the horizon of intelligibility. This additional significance manifests itself in the fact that *Dasein* and its thinking already listen to the other, that the "world-with" (*Mitwelt*) in which others exist unfolds itself already marked by listening, already inflected by/toward the other. It is here that such thinking of the ethical folds and doubles itself, inflecting its economy of nearness and perhaps leaving open the possibility of an otherwise. It also shows how and why such otherwise remains so near "Being" that its signification is possible only as a "maybe", a perhaps to a second degree, marked only in its already erased difference from Being, or better yet, in its demand for listening to which thinking should not remain indifferent.

21. "*Hören der Stimme des Freundes, den jedes Dasein bei sich trägt*" in *Sein und Zeit*, 163/*Being and Time*, trans. Macquarrie and Robinson (New York: Harper and Row, 1962), 206.

22. "*Das Hören auf . . . ist das existenziale Offensein des Daseins als Mitsein für den Anderen*" (*Sein und Zeit*, 163/*Being and Time*, 206).

23. It is at this point that Levinas's critique is perhaps most forceful, denouncing what he sees as the neutrality and impersonality of the "call of Being."

24. Martin Heidegger, "Logos," in *Vorträge und Aufsätze* (Pfullingen: Neske, 1954), 215.

25. Martin Heidegger, *Erläuterungen zu Hölderlins Dichtung, Gesamtausgabe*, vol. 4 (Frankfurt am Main: Vittorio Klostermann, 1981).

26. See Krzysztof Ziarek, "Reception of Heidegger's Thought in American Literary Criticism," *Diacritics* 19 (1989): 124–126.

27. Heidegger, *Erläuterungen zu Hölderlins Dichtung*, 33.

28. Martin Heidegger, *Existence and Being*, ed. Werner Brock (Washington, D.C.: Regnery Gateway, 1988), 270.

29. The evocation of Levinas's distinction between the saying and the said is deliberate here, suggesting, Levinas's vehement criticism notwithstanding, a degree of proximity between Heidegger's texts on poetry and Levinas's essays on literature. See in particular "The Servant and Her Master": "Poetry can be said to transform words, the tokens of a whole, the moments of a totality, into unfettered signs, breaching the walls of immanence, disrupting order," in *The Levinas Reader*, ed. Séan Hand (Oxford: Basil Blackwell, 1989), 156.

30. Heidegger, *Vorträge und Aufsätze*, 203.

31. Heidegger, *Poetry, Language, Thought*, trans. Albert Hofstadter (New York: Harper and Row, 1971), 228.

32. "*dann dichtet der Mensch aus dem Wesen des Dichterischen*" (*Vorträge und Aufsätze*, 204/*Poetry, Language, Thought*, 229).

33. Martin Heidegger, *Hölderlins Hymne "Andenken"*, *Gesamtausgabe*, vol. 52 (Frankfurt am Main: Vittorio Klostermann, 1982), 156–194.

34. Heidegger, *Hölderlins Hymne "Andenken"*, 165.

35. Heidegger, *Hölderlins Hymne "Andenken"*, 165.

36. Llewelyn's *The Middle Voice of Ecological Conscience* articulates a broader approach to the question of ethics than the scope of my discussion allows me to address here. His interest lies primarily in elaborating an ecological ethics that, vis-à-vis Heidegger and Levinas, would take into account relations with non-human others. This exciting project has contributed significantly to our sense of the "relations" between Levinas and Heidegger through the optics of poetry, underscoring the tension between the ethics of the human others and the ecological conscience of non-human others. My study limits itself to the exploration of how the sense of the ethical traces itself in language, within the perspective opened by Levinas's work. However, the chapters on Heidegger, as well as the ones on Celan, underscore repeatedly the twofold otherness at stake in their work. The distinction between the ontological (otherness of Being) and the ethi-

cal, which my study highlights, cuts also across the division between the human and the non-human. In other words, Heideggerian *Gelassenheit* claims both sides of the issue: not only the ontological and the ethical but also the human and the non-human. In this context, my notion of the ontological already carries with it the ethical sense of responsibility that extends beyond the realm of the human. Not only in this respect, *Inflected Language* remains indebted to Llewelyn's revealing work.

37. *"Jedes Ding, jeder Mensch ist dem Gedicht, das auf das Andere zuhält, eine Gestalt dieses Anderen"* (*GW* III, 198).

38. To the extent that Derrida's reading diagnoses the tympanum (listening) as the regulatory force of philosophical discourse that establishes, defines, and maintains its margins, I see in it an opening onto the possibility of an other view of listening, which in the end may require the abandonment or revision of the term itself. See Derrida, *Margins of Philosophy*, trans. Alan Bass (Chicago: University of Chicago Press, 1982), xii–xiii.

৩ INDEX ৶

Abraham, 67, 71–72, 75. *See also* Abrahamic
Abrahamic
  departure, 90
  direction, 97
  journey, 71–72, 75, 79
accusativity, 98
Adorno, Theodor W., 7, 147, 209, 228
aesthetics, 124–125, 195
  of high modernism, 130
Ainley, Alison, 221
Alleman, Beda, 48–49, 110
alterity (otherness), 4, 7, 10, 12, 18, 34, 42, 45, 56–59, 63, 65–67, 77–79, 85–86, 89, 92, 95, 99, 132–134, 144, 147, 149, 153–154, 156, 165, 169–170, 173, 176, 178–179, 186–187, 195–196, 199, 204, 217, 222, 227, 229–230
  ethical, 5–6, 82, 93, 101, 135, 160, 200
  erasure of, 2, 83, 209
  Hebraic, 94
Aristotle, 108
Atemwende, 8, 11, 134, 153–154, 173–175, 177–179, 182–183, 194–195, 201, 225, 227
Aufhebung, 110

Beaufret, Jean, 60
Beehler, Michael, 224
Benjamin, Walter, 143, 147, 209
Bernasconi, Robert, 218
Bloom, Harold, 106
Brogan, Jacqueline V., 222
Bruns, Gerald L., 107, 207, 209, 222
Buber, Martin, 146
Büchner, Georg, 137–138, 188
Buck, Theo, 134

Buhr, Gerhard, 176

Celan, Paul, 1, 5, 7–8, 10–12, 15–18, 57, 63–64, 103, 133–190, 192, 194–195, 199–203, 226–231, 234
  on language, 137, 141–144, 153, 155, 166, 169, 172, 179, 195
Chalier, Catherine, 221
Chanter, Tina, 221
chiasm of the ontological and the ethical, 7, 12–13, 16–18, 22–23, 62, 64, 102, 136, 140, 151, 153–154, 156, 160, 182–183, 188, 192, 195, 200–201, 210, 234
Colin, Amy, 225, 226
Cook, Eleanor, 222

das andere Denken (other thinking), 3–4, 6–7, 13, 18, 25, 47, 57, 61–62, 129, 191, 199. *See also* poetic thinking
de Boer, Theodore, 75
de Man, Paul, 225
Denken, 23, 26–27, 30, 35, 38, 92, 203
Derrida, Jacques, 3, 11, 13, 16, 27, 31, 39, 45, 61, 65, 72–74, 76–77, 87–90, 94–100, 104, 118, 135–136, 139, 204, 208, 210, 212, 218, 220, 226, 228–230, 234
Descartes, René, 68, 121, 216
Dichten-Denken, 26–29, 32, 34, 213. *See also* the poetic and the philosophical
Dichtung (the poetic), 3–4, 8, 18, 23–28, 30, 32, 35, 38, 42, 119, 124, 137–139, 153, 161, 174, 181, 188–189, 199

différance, 11, 151
difference, 11–16, 18, 24, 28–30,
    33, 36–37, 39–47, 52, 54–55,
    58, 61, 65, 72, 75, 77, 97,
    101, 104–105, 110–114, 123,
    131–132, 135–137, 147, 155,
    157, 204, 210
  inflection of, 18, 21, 23, 37,
    39–40, 42–43, 49–51, 72, 210
dire, (saying), 66, 85–89, 91–92,
    95, 98–99, 188–189, 195,
    201, 231, 233
direction
  in Levinas, 70, 75–76, 79,
    83–84, 91, 93, 99–100, 102,
    218. *See also* sens
  in Celan (*Richtung*), 146, 148,
    153, 155, 159–161, 170–171,
    173, 201, 229

Enlightenment, 147, 209
Entsprechung, 9, 30, 32, 38–40, 49,
    55, 160, 189, 198, 202–203
Ereignis, 27, 30, 36–37, 43–55, 58,
    79, 85–86, 89, 91, 93, 97,
    102, 109, 128, 202, 214, 215
ethical, the, 1–2, 5, 13–15, 23, 70,
    78–79, 83–84, 88, 135, 140,
    148, 159–162, 170, 174, 180,
    200, 229, 234. *See also* onto-
    logical
  dimensions of language, 12, 135
  in Heidegger, 7, 10, 21, 60–62,
    79, 100, 102, 191, 197, 203,
    232
  in Levinas, 83, 218, 221
  significance, 10, 17, 88–89, 150,
    177, 179
  stakes, 158
  thematic, 3
ethicity, 62, 140, 174, 176, 179,
    203
ethics, 60–62, 65, 80–81, 89,
    100–101, 181, 190–192, 204,
    233–234
ēthos, 80–81, 191, 215

face, 74–75, 78–79, 81–83, 91, 96,
    98, 100, 154, 156, 219
first idea, 112, 115–117, 119–121,
    124, 224
Fiumara, Gemma Corradi, 213
Forthomme, Bernard, 217
Fóti, Véronique, 21, 63, 181,
    210–211, 226, 230
Fynsk, Christopher, 29, 181, 226,
    230, 231

Gadamer, Hans-Georg, 3, 181, 228
Gasché, Rodolphe, 210
Gegenwort, 10, 135, 168–170, 175,
    177, 179, 200
Gelassenheit, 6, 45, 55, 61–63, 193,
    234
German idealism, 110
Greek
  conceptuality, 71–73
  language, 74–75, 77, 94, 217–218
  source of philosophy, 72–73
  style, 76
Greisch, Jean, 226

Habermas, Jürgen, 3
Hamacher, Werner, 135, 141–142,
    144, 147, 227
Hamburger, Michael, 163, 228, 230
Handelman, Susan A., 217
hearing, 35, 40. *See also* listening
Hebrew, 72–73
Hebrew Bible, 68
Hegel, G. W. F., 67, 73–74, 216
  on art, 125
Hegelian tradition, 140
Heidegger, Martin, 1–18, 21–66,
    73, 78–81, 83–85, 89, 98,
    100, 107–110, 114, 118–120,
    123–125, 128–130, 135, 138,
    140, 151–153, 159, 161, 174,
    181–187, 207–212, 215, 217,
    220, 223, 226, 230–234
  on ethics, 13–14, 17, 55, 60–62,
    80–81
  on language, 22, 25, 33, 35–36,
    38–40, 42, 51, 53–54, 86,

101–104, 118, 122, 154,
184–185, 196–200, 202
on difference, 21–25, 28–30, 33,
36–47, 52–55, 58, 61
otherness, 31, 34, 42, 45, 56–59,
63, 89, 102–103, 208
Heraclitus, 25, 33, 51, 80, 194
hermeneutics, 8–9
hermeneutics of nearness, 2, 6, 10,
16, 18–19, 31, 56, 64, 129,
198, 203, 208. *See also*
hermeneutics of otherness
hermeneutics of otherness, 3, 8,
11, 17, 21, 39, 46, 54, 63
Hines, Thomas, 107, 111, 114, 117,
119–121
Hofstadter, Albert, 214
Holocaust (Shoah), 5, 7, 133–135,
147, 181–182, 202, 204, 228,
230
Horkheimer, Max, 209
Hölderlin, Friedrich, 21, 25, 63,
109–110, 151, 186–187, 189,
191–192, 196–197, 200, 203
humanism
critique of, 6
Husserl, Edmund, 73

inflection, 4, 12–17, 37, 39–41, 44,
47–48, 55, 59, 62–63, 85,
109, 130, 135, 137, 148, 155,
160–161, 173–174, 179, 207.
See also ethical; ontological
ethical, 61, 66, 76, 83, 95,
101–102, 134, 140, 162, 173
Hebraic, 75–76, 217
infold, 22, 37–38, 40–44, 47–49,
51, 53–55, 86, 97, 104, 109,
113–114, 117–118, 161
Irigaray, Luce, 16, 210, 221

Kermode, Frank, 223
Kettering, Emil, 46, 214
Klemm, David E., 219
Kockelmans, Joseph, 211
Kronick, Joseph, 224

Lacoue-Labarthe, Philippe, 135,
151–153, 157, 159, 181,
186–187, 208
Levinas, Emmanuel, 1, 3, 7–8,
10–12, 15–18, 47, 56, 60,
63–102, 121, 130, 134, 146,
151–153, 155–157, 159, 168,
173, 181–182, 192–193, 202,
204, 210, 216–221, 226, 227,
231–234
on alterity, 65–67, 77–79, 85–86,
89, 92, 95, 99, 186, 200
ethics, 5, 13, 65, 189, 232
femininity in, 221
critique of Heidegger, 5–7, 208,
217, 229, 233
on language, 66, 72, 74, 77–78,
82–84, 87–88, 91, 94,
99–102, 195
listening, 8, 17, 39, 79, 155,
183–186, 188, 191, 193–194,
196–205, 213, 232, 234
Llewelyn, John, 21, 32, 63, 191,
193, 210–211, 215, 231,
233–234
logocentrism, 34, 37, 184
logos, 33–34, 36–38, 73, 213
Lyotard, Jean-François, 220–221

Marion, Jean-Luc, 38, 52, 216, 219
maybe, 76, 94, 96, 98–101, 125,
127, 130, 232. *See also* perhaps; *peut-être*
McCarthy, Thomas, 207
Menninghaus, Winfried, 135,
142–144, 165, 167, 171–173
metaphysics, 6, 13, 43, 45–47, 50,
78, 106, 110, 114, 126, 189
overcoming of, 4–5, 45
Miller, Hillis J., 106, 108–109, 223
modernity
critique of, 17, 209
Moisés, Stéphane, 228–229

National Socialism
Heidegger and, 5–7, 181, 185,
203–204, 209, 212

nativeness, 104, 111, 113, 127–128, 130–132, 152
nearness, 9–12, 14, 16–17, 23, 29, 46–63, 91–93, 152, 188–189, 211, 214, 232. *See also* proximity
neighborhood of poetry and thinking. *See* the poetic and the philosophical
Neugroschel, Joachim, 230
Nietzsche, Friedrich, 17, 21, 28, 225
non-indifference, 12, 14, 65–66, 75–77, 84, 97, 101–102, 157, 159–160

Odyssean journey, 71. *See also* Odyssey; Ulysses
Odyssey, 72, 75. *See also* Odyssean journey; Ulysses
Oliver, Kelly, 221
ontico-ontological difference. *See* ontological difference
ontological, the, 5, 13–15, 22, 48, 61–62, 78, 100, 140, 187, 234
dimensions of language, 1, 12
inflections, 15
significance, 10, 17, 150, 196
stakes, 30, 158
thematic, 3
ontological difference (ontico-ontological difference), 33, 41–46, 50, 52, 214
ontology, 60–62, 69, 78, 80, 191
onto-theology, 73, 216
other thinking. *See das andere Denken*
otherness. *See* alterity
Ott, Hugo, 208

Parker, Patricia, 224
Parmenides, 21, 25, 33, 36–37, 41, 85, 207
perhaps, 15–16, 99, 101, 125, 130, 201, 210, 232. *See also* maybe; *peut–être*
Perloff, Marjorie, 106–107, 126
Petitdemange, Guy, 220

Petzet, Heinrich Wiegand, 230
peut–être, 43, 94, 96, 99, 153, 201. *See also* maybe; perhaps
phonocentrism, 34, 183–184
Plato, 68, 70, 73, 115
poetic, the. *See Dichtung*
the poetic and the philosophical (neighborhood of poetry and thinking), 8, 17, 19, 22, 24, 27, 28–30, 32–33, 47, 52, 55, 61, 63, 103, 128–129, 186, 189, 202
poetic language, 145–146, 197–198, 200, 202
poetic thinking, 5, 42–43, 60. *See also das andere Denken*
poetics (poetry) of notes, 104–105, 117, 126–131, 225
postmodern thought, 2, 6
poststructuralism
debates, 1, 43
theories, 12
Pöggeler, Otto, 181, 207, 230, 231
Pre-Socratics, 4, 8, 22, 25, 33–34, 37, 73, 182, 207, 213
proximity, 4, 9, 11–12, 16–17, 23, 39, 47, 50–51, 53, 56, 60, 66, 70, 84, 91–93, 104, 112, 127–130, 152, 189, 198. *See also* nearness

Richtung. See direction
Riddel, Joseph, 106, 109, 113, 117, 223–225
Robbins, Jill, 79, 217–218, 220
Romanticism, 105–107, 224
conceptions of art, 137
poetry, 109
poetics, 110
rhetoric, 113
Rousseau, Jean-Jacques, 225

Sage (saying), 22, 27, 29–38, 40–41, 47–49, 52–55, 84–88, 91, 101–102, 104, 117–119, 122, 128–129, 157, 161, 184, 198, 202, 213

saying. *See dire; Sage*
Schmidt, Dennis J., 181–182, 230
sens, 75–76, 79, 83, 99, 102, 160.
　See also direction
Shoah. *See* Holocaust
Sparr, Thomas, 171, 229
Steiner, George, 134
Stevens, Wallace, 1, 8, 11–12,
　15–17, 103–132, 222–225
　on otherness, 105–109,
　　111–112, 115–116, 119,
　　129–132
　on poetic language, 104–105,
　　107–113, 116, 119, 121–122,
　　124, 129, 222
　poetics, 102–104, 110–113, 117,
　　125–126
supreme fiction, 105, 109, 115,
　121, 125–130, 132

Symbolism, 106–107, 110
Szondi, Peter, 167, 170–171, 229

the-one-for-the-other, 70, 90–91,
　231
trace, 75–79, 85, 87–88, 92–100,
　125, 130, 134–135, 146, 154,
　156–157, 161, 168, 176–179,
　185, 187, 191, 220–221, 227
Trakl, Georg, 182

Ulysses, 67, 71–72, 75. *See also*
　Odyssean journey; Odyssey

Vattimo, Giorgio, 36, 89
Vendler, Helen, 106

Ziarek, Ewa, 221
Zimmerman, Michael, 208